LIBRARY BOOKS - WITHDRAWN FOR SALE

ITALY
ON
BACKROADS

ITALY
ON
BACKROADS

Peter Greene and Richard Dixon

DUNCAN PETERSEN

First published 1993 by Duncan Petersen Publishing Ltd,
54, Milson Road, London, W14 0LB

Copyright © Text Peter Greene and Richard Dixon 1993
© Text Duncan Petersen Publishing Ltd 1993
© Maps Instituto Geografico De Agostini 1993

All rights reserved. No part of this publication may be reproduced, stored in a retrieval system or transmitted in any form, or by any means, electronic, mechanical, photocopying, recording or otherwise without the prior consent of the publishers and copyright owners.

Conceived, edited and designed by Duncan Petersen Publishing Ltd,
54, Milson Road, London, W14 0LB

Distributed in the UK and Ireland by World Leisure Marketing,
117, The Hollow, Littleover, Derby, DE3 7BS

Typeset by Duncan Petersen Publishing; output by BTG, Bourne End, Bucks
Originated in Italy by Reprocolor International, Milan
Printed in Italy by G. Canale & C. SpA, Turin

A CIP catalogue record for this book is available from the British Library

All routes in this book are undertaken at the individual's own risk. The publisher and copyright owners accept no responsibility for any consequence arising out of use of this book, including misinterpretation of the maps and directions.

Editorial director Andrew Duncan
Editor Rosanne Hooper
Assistant editor Joshua Dubin

Art director Mel Petersen
Design Chris Foley, Beverley Stewart

Picture Credits
All photography: Peter Greene and Richard Dixon.

ISBN 1 872576 26 5

The authors

Every kilometre of Italy on Backroads was not only planned and written, but personally driven by the authors, both Italophile writers who live and work together in a rural corner of Italy's Marche region.

Peter Greene, one-time press officer for London's Royal Festival Hall, is a freelance journalist and travel writer who has written for many magazines and newspapers, including The Independent.

Richard Dixon, a former London barrister, is a playwright whose work has been performed by the BBC. When not writing, he tends his vineyard and assorted animals.

The authors would like to thank Glyn Russ for his invaluable help with the southern Italian tours. Ringraziamenti, also, to Aldo Tavianucci, Carla Mensali, Marco Moscardi, Ketty Pompili, Bruno Marcucci and la comitiva di Cagli. We are also indebted to Andrew Duncan for putting his faith in us.

- Information on opening and closing times, and telephone numbers, was correct at time of publication, but those who run hotels, restaurants and tourist attractions are sometimes obliged to change times at short notice. If your enjoyment of a day out is going to depend on seeing, or eating at a certain place, it makes sense to check beforehand that you will gain admission.

- Many of the roads used for tours in this book are country lanes in the true sense: they have zero visibility at corners, they are too narrow for oncoming cars to pass, and they include hairpin bends and precarious mountain roads with sheer drops. Please drive with due care and attention, and at suitable speeds.

Contents

The tours are arranged in a north-south sequence, beginning in the Dolomites in the north of Italy, and ending in the south, at Sicily. Where several tours fall within the same region, for example Piemonte or Tuscany, these are grouped together, even if it means deviating temporarily from the north-south sequence.

NUMBER ON MAP		PAGE NUMBER
	Touring with *Italy on Backroads*	8
1	Alto Adige: THE DOLOMITES	14
2	Friuli: ITALY'S EASTERN FRONTIER	24
3	Veneto: THE COLLI EUGANEI AND THE MONTI BERICI	34
4	Northern Piemonte: LAKE ORTA AND THE VALSESIA	42
5	Southern Piemonte: THE WINE LANDS OF ALBA	52
6	Val d'Aosta: THE VALLEY OF THE DORA BALTEA	62
7	Liguria: INLAND FROM THE WESTERN RIVIERA	70
8	Emilia: FROM THE PADANA TO THE PIACENTINE HILLS	80
9	Northern Tuscany: THE THRESHOLD OF THE GARFAGNANA	88
10	Western Tuscany: VOLTERRA AND THE METAL HILLS	96
11	The Northern Marche: THE LANDS OF MONTEFELTRO	106
12	The Flaminian Way: FROM ROME TO ASSISI	116
13	Northern Lazio: ROME'S VOLCANIC LAKELAND	124
14	Abruzzo: THE PEAKS OF THE GRAN SASSO	134
15	Southern Lazio: THE CIOCIARIA	144
16	Campania: THE CILENTO PENINSULA	156
17	Northern Puglia: THE GARGANO PENINSULA	168
18	Southern Puglia: VALLE D'ITRIA	180
19	Calabria: LA SILA GRANDE	190
20	Sicily: VAL DI NOTO	196
	Index	206

Touring with *ITALY ON BACKROADS*

Italy's great cities remind us of elderly relatives: although we may see them rarely, or never, they remain familiar in the mind's eye.

By contrast, the delights of rural Italy remain strangers to hundreds of thousands of visitors every year. This book is their letter of introduction.

Driving from lonely Roman ruins to tottery medieval hill towns, stopping for a picnic in the shade of an olive tree with only crickets to serenade you, sipping a chill *aperitivo* in a perfect Renaissance piazza; for many, this is *la dolce vita* and this book is dedicated to them. It is also written for those who want to break free from the usual tourist circuit and see some of the many faces of this contrasting and contrary peninsula, even if for just a day or two.

The routes

The 20 locations from the Alps to Sicily have been chosen to give a taste of Italy's strikingly diverse countryside and little-recognized historic towns. Mostly figures-of-eight, the tours can be driven in one or two days. But you will get more pleasure if you drive them in two or more – there is so much to enjoy that it would be a shame to treat them as rally driving courses.

Even taking them slowly, you do not have to stop at every attraction. Look on the routes as guides to help you find what interests you, not as military orders to be carried out to the letter. There are no prizes if you complete them in a given time – take them at the pace you enjoy and modify them to suit yourself.

Sometimes, however, time may be short. With an average length of around 170 km, the tours can be driven inside a day; you will not be able to make many stops but you will get the overall feeling of an area.

The itineraries have been carefully chosen to give a rounded mixture of pleasures: interesting backroads; beautiful countryside; arresting towns and villages; strong local identities; fine food and wine; and, just occasionally, an unmissable major tourist attraction. Italy is a crowded country invaded each year by millions of tourists – several of the tours visit important sights where you will be forced to leave tranquil backwaters. Do not

Touring with *Italy on Backroads*

worry, though, as the routes soon return you to quieter reaches. In contrast, some tours take pains to avoid full-blown tourist haunts that are best seen on a special visit.

The roads This book is about country roads; in Italy you must expect the worst. Many tours explore upland areas where roads wind tortuously through the hills. Others chart courses through country where motorists are few – always be ready for speedy Italian driving. (Italian drivers pride themselves on having faster reflexes than most other Europeans and drive accordingly.) Signposting, too, can be a nightmare; directions in the book are as exhaustive as possible, but a degree of stoicism is useful on any driving holiday in Italy. Both driving habits and signposting degenerate markedly the further south you head, reaching a nadir in Sicily.

The maps The routes are drawn on the general-purpose motoring maps at a scale of 1:250,000 produced by the Istituto Geografico de Agostini.

Touring with *Italy on Backroads*

De Agostini's cartography carries plenty of helpful information for the tourist and road user. The scale allows road bends as close as 250 metres apart to show up; and the 'white' roads, with no coloured infill, are a faithful representation of the network of country lanes. However, in common with all mapping on this scale, not every single minor road is featured – some tours, indeed, use short stretches of unmarked road – and the names of a few small settlements are omitted. Main roads in Italy are designated as *strada statale*, SS for short; although the maps give only the number for these roads, SS has been added in the text to help with signpost-reading. In a country that prides itself on its linguistic diversity, the spelling of some place names differs on the map and on the ground; the text follows the version on the map.

Hints on map-reading

When on the road, mapread actively, rather than passively. This comes down to knowing where you are on the map all the time. It is essential to understand the implications of scale. On 1:250,000 mapping, one centimetre on the map represents 2.5 km on the ground. So for every kilometre you travel, you need to tick off the appropriate portion of map. To do this, you need a point of reference from which to start – obvious landmarks present themselves continuously in the shape of villages and road junctions.

The route directions

Printed in italics, these are an aid to trouble-free navigation, not join-up-the-dots instructions for getting round the routes. They are most detailed on tricky stretches, especially when signposting is absent or when the occasional road not marked on the map is used. In a country that welcomes strangers, do not be afraid to ask directions if you get lost; even if your Italian is not up to much, vigorous miming with a gracious smile will get you a long way.

Road signs and parking

Road junctions in Italy are often festooned with direction signs like Christmas trees, yet lack the name of the place you want to get to. In the text the first or most obvious signs are given. Town centres are almost always well signposted with either *centro*, *centro storico*, or a sign with three concentric circles around a dot. Parking in town centres is often for a limited period. You should

Touring with *Italy on Backroads*

set your *disco orario* (the parking disc obtainable from most newsagents and tobacconists) on your windscreen at the time you arrived. Drivers of foreign-registered cars are unlikely to be fined for outstaying their welcome, but you can never be certain...

Food There are two myths about Italian food: first, that it exists and, secondly, that it is cheap. The diet changes from region to region as much as the scenery, and Italian cookery only exists as the sum total of widely diverse regional traditions. The days, however, when a handful of lire would buy you a slap-up banquet for two are long over. Italy is now one of the most expensive countries in Europe and the cost of eating out is no exception. The authors, fired with a passion for Italian regional cookery, have searched out some of the best-value restaurants on the routes.

In each of these you will eat well. But remember that Italian restaurants allow you to eat as much or as little as you want, and the bill will vary accordingly. If you are not too hungry, just have a pasta for a *primo* followed by a salad, cheese or fruit; you will save a lot of money and be doing what most Italians do. You will also have to be prepared for the absence of menus in more humble establishments. Some areas are not as well endowed with restaurants as others, and this is reflected in the varying numbers of recommendations. Although the restaurant information was accurate at the time of going to press, remember that opening hours can change. While some establishments close on national holidays, it is by no means the rule. In some places, where visitors are rare out of season, restaurants and hotels often close in the quieter months. The text points these areas out.

Hotels Like the restaurant recommendations, these are not exhaustive. They are a selection of sound value places, with a touch more charm than most of Italy's often dowdy *alberghi*.

Fuel In some parts of Italy, particularly in rural backwaters, petrol stations are scarce and the text draws your attention to these stretches. Major cities apart, they also close for a long lunchbreak – often from 12 to 4pm – and on Sundays. Fill up when possible in the morning. Unfortunately, gasoline or petrol coupons that, in the past, dramatically lowered the price for foreign tourists, have now been stopped.

National holidays New Year's Day; 6 Jan (La Befana); Easter Monday; 25 Apr (Liberation Day); 1 May; 15 Aug (Assumption); 1 Nov (All Saints'); 8 Dec (Immaculate Conception); Christmas Day; 26 Dec (Santo Stefano).

Opening hours Italy grinds to a halt for lunch. Shops, opening early in the morning, close at around 1 to re-open at around 4 until 7. Further south, afternoon opening tends to be later. They all close on Sunday; in addition, each town has its own early closing day. Museums often open only in the morning, or, if also open in the afternoon, close between 1 and 3. Open air sights, such as gardens or archaeological ruins, tend to be open until sunset, closing for the usual lunch-break. Monday is the most common closing day every week for both museums and outdoor attractions. Although the text points out unusual opening hours, they can be rather haphazard, particularly in the south.

Time Italy is one hour ahead of Greenwich Mean Time in winter and two hours ahead in summer. From the United States, Italy is six hours ahead of Eastern Standard Time.

THE PRICE BANDS

To give an indication of cost, four restaurant price bands are quoted. They represent approximate prices for lunch, typically a *primo, secondo*, fruit and coffee with a modest quarter litre of local wine.

Price band A	under 25,000 lire
Price band B	25-35,000 lire
Price band C	35-50,000 lire
Price Band D	over 50,000 lire

Price band D covers the large price differential found in Italy's famed establishments – the highest, a temple to gastronomy in Piemonte, charges 100,000 lire for a set menu without wine.

Prices quoted were correct at the time of going to press, but, of course, are liable to increase. In most cases, however, increases will remain in proportion so that the price banding system is likely to remain useful. Note that the price banding does not apply to accommodation, even when rooms are available at the same establishment.

Alto Adige
THE DOLOMITES

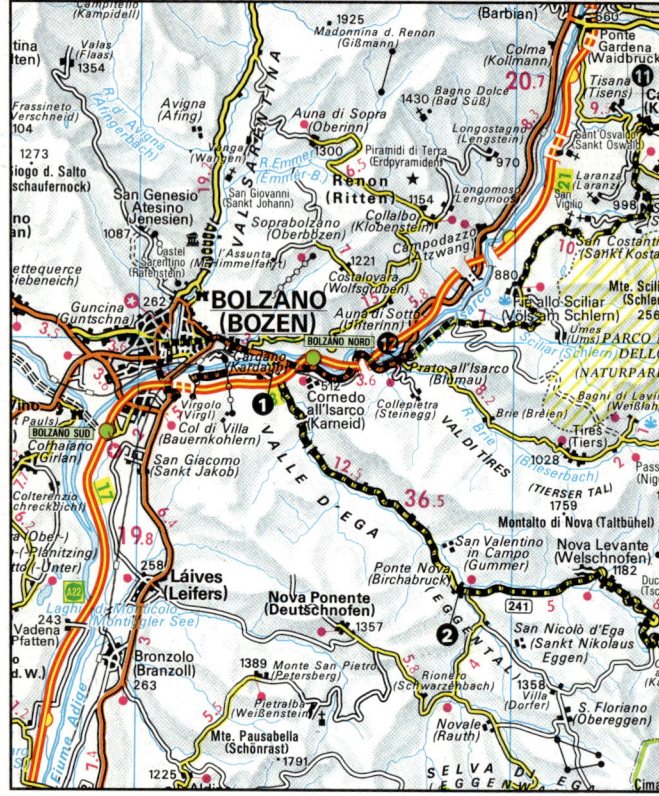

Superlatives are apt to take over when describing these limestone giants. The Dolomites, after all, provide some of the most awe-inspiring mountain scenery in Europe. This circular roller-coaster tour takes in the most breathtaking views. Although well-trodden by tourists, it would be a sin of omission to leave this area out of a book on rural Italy. Moreover, outside the winter sports season and the high summer, it is relatively quiet. Alto Adige, the northernmost region of the peninsular, has only been part of Italy since 1918 and remains doggedly un-Italian. Its people, its architecture and its food owe more to Austria than to its modern parent, and the bilingual signposting is a constant reminder that you are barely in Italy. German place names are given alongside the Italian names in the headings to the text.

Alto Adige

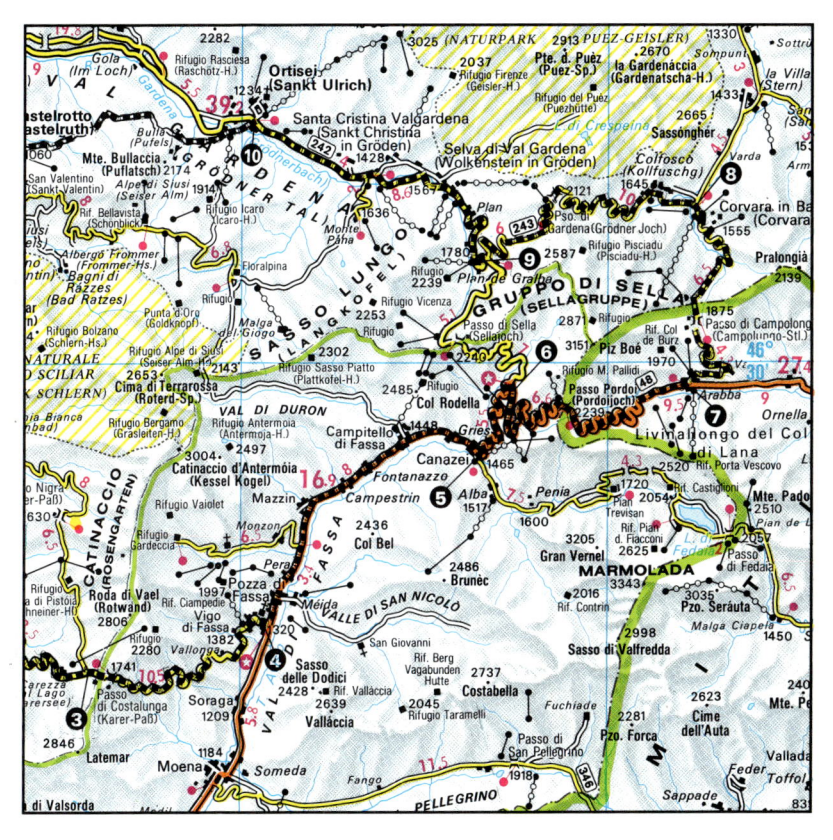

The route, starting at the well ordered regional capital of Bolzano, can be driven in one day. You may prefer, however, to stay overnight at Nova Levante or in the Val di Fassa to let this enchanting landscape work its spell. Hotels and restaurants abound and even the smallest villages have an *azienda di soggiorno* (helpful tourist offices with information on accommodation). Picnickers can stock up at Bolzano with *schlagbrot* (the excellent local bread), delectable *vezzena* and *graukäse* cheeses and *speck* (cured meat), while drivers should fill up their tanks there are few petrol stations on the route.

ROUTE: 158 KM

**Bolzano/
Bozen**

Park in the large underground car park under the Piazza Walther, the

Alto Adige The Dolomites:

town's main square; parking spots outside the pedestrianized centre are hard to find. Set in a deep valley hemmed in by mountains, it is a city whose architecture and colourful daily food market bear witness to its mercantile past. In Renaissance times Bolzano was already an important staging-post for merchants travelling to Northern Europe on the historic Brenner road. As well as being an ideal base for exploring the Dolomites, its old, car-free centre is a pleasant place to pass an hour or two. Start with an Austrian lager at one of the smart bars on the Piazza Walther, named after Walther von der Vogelweide. The great 12thC German lyric poet, whose statue presides over the square, was born in this valley. Admire the colourful chequerboard roof of the Gothic cathedral which lightens an otherwise coolly Germanic building. Then stroll through the warren of streets to the north, lined with richly decorated stuccoed houses and distinctive Tyrolean arcades, to arrive at the market in Piazza delle Erbe.

Croce Bianca This cosy *gasthof* in Piazza del Grano, just off the main square, makes a
(hotel, central base for the tour and has congenial, inexpensive rooms. *Tel*
Bolzano) *0471-977552.*

Cavallino Tucked away in Via Bottai, a few minutes' walk north from Piazza
Bianco Walther, this is the right place to try South Tyrolean cooking – perhaps
(restaurant, *canederli*, small bread dumplings dressed with cheese and herbs, as a
Bolzano) starter, and a selection of boiled meats with *sauerkraut* for a main
course. *Tel 0471-973267; closed Sat eve and Sun; price band B.*

Leave following the signs for Brennero and carry on for 3 km until the road descends alongside the railway line.

① *Turn right at the sign for Val d'Ega and cross over the level crossing into the hamlet of Cardano. After 200 metres continue straight ahead at the main road under the flyover. (You can also reach the road from the main SS12.)*

Val d'Ega/ The road now edges between the cliffs of the gorge that forms the
Eggental gateway to the Ega Valley. The grandeur, though, is a pale shadow of what is to come. After a few kilometres the valley opens out and you have your first taste of the gothic forms of the Dolomites, with a view of the ragged peaks of the Latemar Massif ahead of you. Continue on to the village of Ponte Nova.

Ponte Nova A less manicured spot than the touristy resorts further along the route, this collection of unvarnished Alpine chalets has little to detain you unless you want a room or a meal.

② *Bear left at the fork heading for Nova Levante. The road now climbs*

Chapel of San Sebastiano, Nova Levante.

up through pine plantations. After a short tunnel, you enter Nova Levante.

Nova Levante/ Welschnofen
Spread out across the velvet turf of the valley, this popular ski resort in the shadow of the Latemar Massif makes a good place to break the journey. The tourist office on the main road will help you to find accommodation in one of the many attractive chalet-style hotels that dot the surrounding meadows. There is also a score of houses on the roadside offering *affitarsi camere* (rooms to let). The Central Hotel *(tel 0471-613164)* has comfortable rooms - if you can put up with the tasteless furnishings - and a restaurant that remains open when many others are closed. Head on to Carezza al Lago, climbing ever more steeply up through a forest of sturdy conifers.

Lago di Carezza/ Karersee
Stop to peer into the emerald green depths of this mysterious tarn, or scramble round its rocky, tree-lined shore. You are unlikely to be alone, though, as it is a favourite halt for coach parties - the gift stalls in the car park will appeal to collectors of kitsch.

Catinaccio/ Rosengarten
A little further on, the great bulk of the Rosengarten Massif looms up to your left. The violet-rose light that bathes these mountains at sunset is one of the wonders of the Dolomites. A certain dwarf king, so the leg

Alto Adige The Dolomites:

Peaks of the Sella Group.

end goes, laid a curse on the rose garden that once flourished on this magic mountain, vowing that it should never flower again, "neither by day or night". Luckily for us, he forgot to mention dusk, when the roses still bloom on the barren slopes.

③ *At the next junction, bear right towards Vigo di Fassa.*

Passo di Costalunga/ Karerpass

Barely a kilometre after the junction, you arrive at this pass into the Fassa Valley. At 1,752 metres it is small beer compared to the passes ahead, but, as the road drops down, the views are just as intoxicating. The valley is dwarfed by the triple crags of Sasso Lungo and the rocky fortress of the Sella Massif to your left, while ahead of you rises Marmolada, the haughty Queen of the Dolomites.

Val di Fassa

This deep glacial valley is a come-down after the heady descent – somehow the views lose their majesty when seen from the valley bottom, and a string of rather anonymous ski resorts do not help. Still, the maintained, straight road is a relaxing change and there is no shortage of lodgings.

Alto Adige

Vigo di Fassa This is the first of this valley's resorts and, although set in open Alpine meadows worthy of *The Sound of Music*, affords little reason to pause. *Passing the small main square, bear left taking signs for Canazei and Passo Sella.*

④ Reaching the main road, turn left to pass through Pozzo di Fassa and Pera, where there is a chairlift up to the lower slopes of Rosengarten.

Campitello This is a useful spot for picnic fare - the supermarket opposite the tourist office will make up sandwiches fit for a trencherman. Another reason to stop is for an ear-popping ride up the cable car to the Col Rodella and grandstand views of the Dolomites.

⑤ At Gries continue along the main road following signs for Cortina. The climb now begins in earnest as the road zigzags up through a seemingly endless series of hairpin bends towards the towering walls of the Sella Group. Apart from the occasional pull-in, it is difficult to stop on this narrow road.

⑥ At the junction at the top of the first climb, bear right for Cortina and the Passo Pordoi. If time is short, the left-hand turn takes you over the Sella Pass to the Val Gardena ⑨, cutting off some 30 km of the route; it would be a shame, though, to miss the breathtaking scenery ahead.

Passo Pordoi As you climb up past the Hotel Pordoi (built in 1905 and the oldest hotel in these parts), the southern face of the Sella rises up with the distinctive three spires of the Sasso Lungo across to the left. Far below in the valley where this extraordinary ascent began, Canazei looks like a toy town. At 2,239 metres, the summit of the pass is literally the high spot on this tour. Stop here to give your engine a well earned rest and to take the four-minute ride up the cable car to see the Sella at close quarters.

The Sella Group/Sella gruppe This daunting citadel of a massif is topped by a circular tableland from which the name Sella (saddle) comes. It is magical walking territory for the hardy rambler; the rest of us will be content to just stand and take in the heart-wrenchingly beautiful views. Instead of the cable car, you may prefer the easy 15-minute walk up from the pass station to the Col del Cuc for regal views of Marmolada.

Leaving the pass, the road descends into open grassland as sharply as it rose. Look out for families of polecats frolicking by the roadside.

Arabba This Heidi village of Alpine chalets with neat front gardens is one of the most agreeable spots to break the journey. Although there are hotels and rooms to let, the place still looks much as it must have done before

Alto Adige The Dolomites::

Wooden carving of St Peter, Val Gardena.

tourism made inroads.

⑦ *At the centre, turn left following signs for Brunico and Corvara. After another quick ascent through the hamlet of Varda and back up into the silent mountains, the Sella turns another cheek.*

Passo di Campolongo
This is the only one of the four passes around the Sella that stands at a height of under 2,000 metres. The chairlift here trundles up to Crep de Mont in the Sella from where a cable car runs down to Corvara - there is also a well marked downhill footpath. Passengers with a self-sacrificing chauffeur might like to make this mountain journey to meet up later at Corvara.

Leaving the pass, the road meanders down to Corvara. The distant finger of a mountain that juts up behind the hillside in front of you is Sassongher. Further on, the whole of this towering monolith appears in all its majesty, dwarfing Corvara in its shadow.

Alto Adige

Painted shop façade, Santa Cristina.

Corvara in Badia/ Corvera

One of the larger villages in the area, this is a typical Alpine resort, packed with pretty hotels, restaurants and souvenir shops but no ancient memories. Its main attraction is a restaurant.

La Perla
(restaurant/ hotel, Corvara)

Although some may find the Tyrolean tweeness overpowering, this luxury hotel has a restaurant where you can try some of the finest cooking in the region. It also has a wine cellar rivalled by few others in Italy with the rarest bottles costing millions of lire. Whether you stay or just eat here, this is an experience for those with a well lined wallet. *Tel 0471-836132; closed late spring and autumn; price band D.*

⑧ *At the very foot of Sassongher turn left towards the Passo di Gardena. After Colfosco another handful of hairpin bends takes you up to the Sella's north face and the next pass.*

Passo di Gardena/ Grödner Joch

Arriving at these Dolomite passes will be a familiar experience by now – the cable car, the restaurants and the souvenir shops. But once again the views are unforgettable, this time of the bristling triple peaks of Sasso Lungo.

⑨ *At the junction with the road from the Passo di Sella bear right to continue down to the Val Gardena.*

Val Gardena/ Grödner Tal

This gentle, open valley is a populous place with a clutch of interesting villages noted for their traditional woodcarving and folk painting. Passing through the village of Selva, stay on the main road following signs for Bolzano.

Alto Adige The Dolomites:

SantaCristina Valgardena/ St Christina in Gröden
This large and fashionable resort has particularly impressive views of the peaks of Sasso Lungo. There are also several enticing woodcarving shops. *Leave turning right at the sign for Ortisei to arrive there by the backroad (not marked on map).*

Ortisei/ St Ulrich
An attractive town, if rather touristy, Ortisei is the centre for Gardenese woodcarving and folk painting. The Museum de Gherdëina houses a collection of some of the best work, while the souvenir stalls offer the worst. The church of St Ulrich, just by the main square, magnificently combines the two crafts – the pastel and gilt interior decked with lively woodcarving is entirely the work of local craftsmen. As if Italian and German were not enough, this town is also the stronghold of a third language, Ladin, a Latin-based dialect that has evolved quite apart from those of surrounding regions. Test your linguistic aptitude with the trilingual museum leaflet.

Ramoser
(restaurant, Ortisëi)
Imaginative cooking and sublime puddings are the marks of this excellent restaurant just off the main square in via Purger. Like most of the restaurants hereabouts, it is not cheap. *Tel 0471-796460; closed Thur and June; price band C.*

⑩ *Returning to the main SS242, continue on for Bolzano and pass through the short tunnel just outside the town. Then turn left, following signs for Altipiano dello Sciliar and Castelrotto.*

Passo di Pinei/ Panider Sattel
This is the last and the least of the passes on the tour. From here a new, softer landscape unfolds as the road enters the Parco Naturale dello Sciliar. To the right, in the valley far below, runs the Brenner-Verona motorway hidden from view. The wooded slopes of the Corno di Renon rise further to the west. As you approach Castelrotto look out for the wooden-tiled roofs that are fast disappearing from the region.

Castelrotto/ Kastelruth
This picture postcard Tyrolean village is one of the prettiest on the tour and has yet to sell its soul to tourism. Leave your car in the car park at the bottom and amble up through the passageways to the tower that overshadows the small piazza.

⑪ *Keep on the main road as it edges towards the face of Monte Sciliar before dropping down into the villages of Siusi and Fiè allo Sciliar.*

Tschafon
(restaurant, Fiè allo Sciliar)
Mme Bidard, the French cook and patronne of this superb restaurant, adds a strong Gallic ingredient to the *cucina locale*. There is no written menu for the fixed price meal and the best course is to follow the recommendations of her genial husband. Sadly it is only open in the evening and for Sunday lunch. Housed in a typical rustic Tyrolean

Alto Adige

A painted house in Ortisei.

building, it stands on the main road a few metres after the turn off for the village. *Tel 0471-725024; closed Mon; booking essential; price band C/D.*

From here on, the road steadily descends to Bolzano.

⑫ *Arriving at the main SS12, turn left to return to Bolzano (use the mirror ahead of you to check for oncoming traffic).*

Friuli
ITALY'S EASTERN FRONTIER

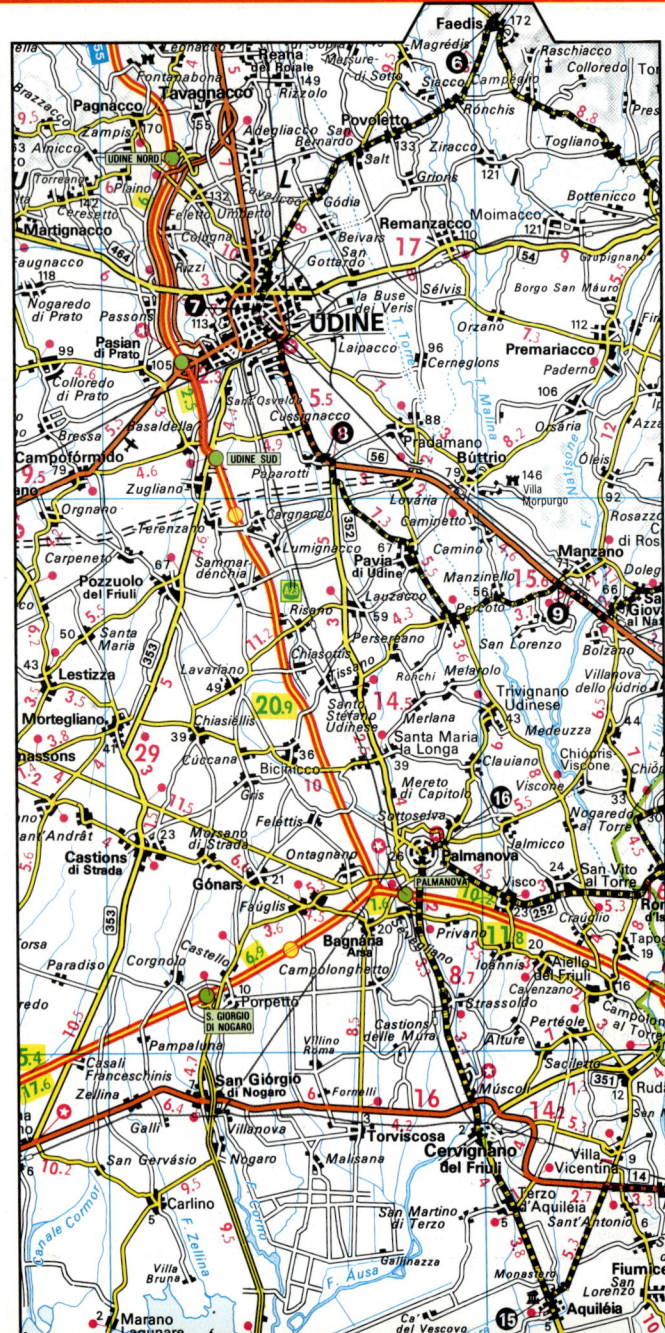

24

Friuli

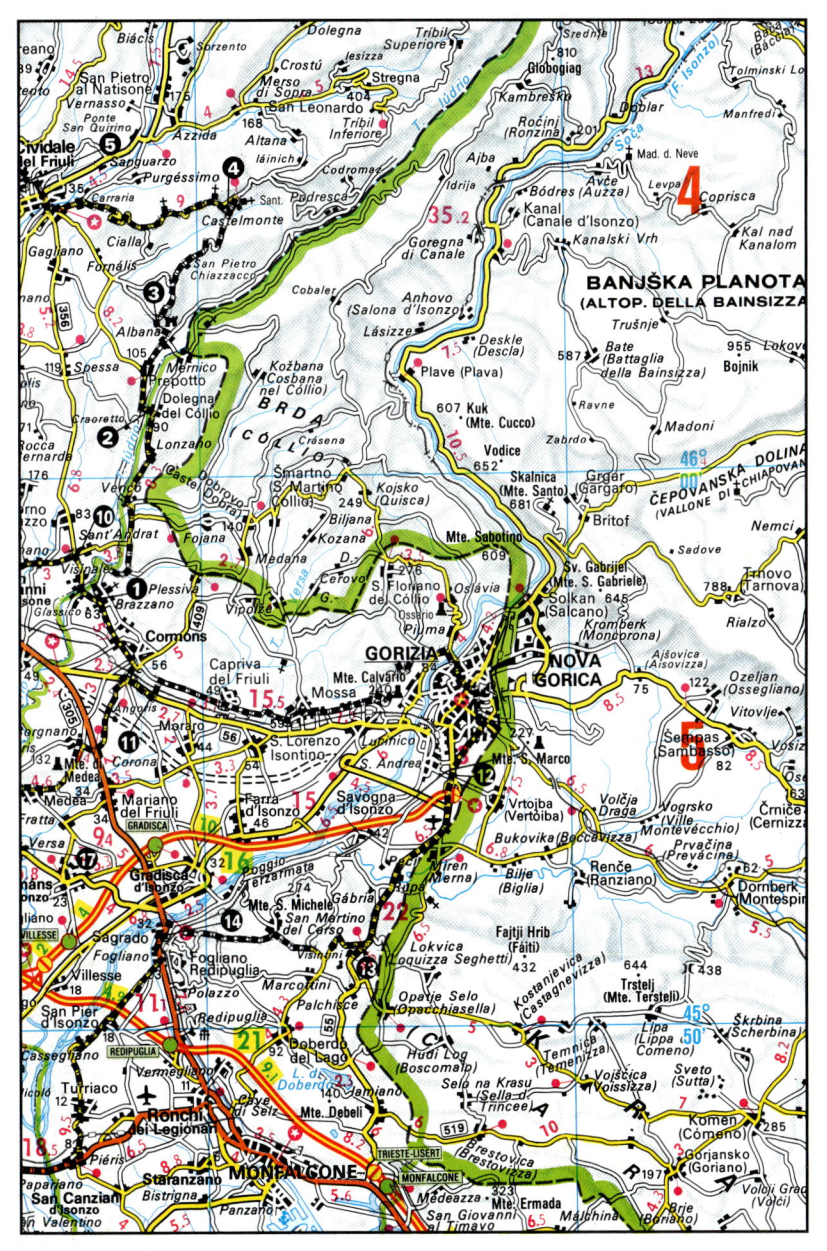

25

Friuli: Italy's eastern frontier

This contrasting landscape of Alpine foothills and sweet plains spangled with ancient towns sees few visitors these days, but in the past it was a different story. First on the guest list were the Celts, who arrived sometime around the 5thC BC. Inevitably the Romans made themselves at home, only to be thrown out by the Germanic Lombard tribes. Later, Venice made its stately entrance, while the Austro-Hungarian Empire stayed put in the eastern part of the region, only briefly interrupted by Napoleon in 1797. Today, even some 120 years after the Unification of Italy, the southern bureaucrats seem unwelcome guests and the nationalistic Movimento per Friuli remains a powerful force. It comes as some surprise, then, that the Friulani are amongst Italy's friendliest people.

History's comings and goings have left a cosmopolitan legacy. In many of the eastern towns you can hear three languages spoken: Italian, Slovenian and the area's own linguistic hotchpotch, Friulano. The food, too, is similarly jumbled in its origins, the use of cream and spices coming more from Austria and the Orient than *cucina italiana*. Other dishes, such as the heavyweight spaghetti known as *bigoli,* have a Venetian pedigree, while such things as the humble turnip speak volumes for Slovenia's contribution.

ROUTE ONE: 84

Cormons

An unhurried market town with a restrained elegance, Cormons makes an appealing centre for this tour. The statue of Maximilian I that holds court in the neat, stucco-fronted square is a reminder that until 1918 this was part of the Austrian Empire. Memories still linger of the cherry harvest being sent by the night train to Vienna markets and of journeys across the border to Italy to buy cheaper clothing and shoes. "One day God will make you part of Italy", the Italians would say. And He did, if only in name.

Felcaro
(hotel, Cormons)

In the outskirts just above the town, this three star hotel in an indifferently modernized 18thC hunting lodge is an inexpensive choice as a base. 45, *Via San Giovanni; tel 0481-60214.*

Al Giardinetto
(restaurant, Cormons)

Just off the main square in via Matteotti, the Zoppolatti family run this elegant restaurant with charm and efficiency. Their menu takes regional dishes and transforms them into altogether more sophisticated offerings, without being extravagant with the prices. *Tel 0481-60257; closed Mon eve and Tue; price band C.*

Leave following signs for Cividale. Note that there are no petrol stations until Cividale.

Friuli

① *At Brazzano bear right at the signpost for Prepotto and Dolegna and keep on this road through Venco to Dolegna.*

② *At Dolegna del Collio turn left over the river towards Cividale; then bear right, passing Prepotto. After 2 km turn left at Albana, signposted Cividale. Here the road winds up into dense deciduous woodland.*

③ *After 2 km turn right towards Castelmonte, your next destination. The next 3 km of road require careful navigation. A little further on, bear left at the handpainted sign for Castelmonte; then right at the signpost for Ristorante Il Bracconiere. At the next junction turn left at the sign to S Pietro di Chiazzacco, turning left again at the small shrine and pass under the village of San Pietro. The narrow road continues on through dappled woods, with plenty of picnic stops, before dropping down towards Castelmonte. At the junction with the main road, turn right and stop at the car park beneath the village.*

Castelmonte Although it claims to be one of the oldest shrines to the Madonna in Christendom, the 1950s refit of this pilgrimage centre has left little trace of its ancient origins – even the 15thC church itself has been rudely messed about with. But still the pilgrims flock to the feet of a magnificent statue of the Madonna. The village, despite the souvenir shops, still retains something of its medieval character and there are grandstand views to the foothills of the Giulian Alps in nearby Slovenia.

④ *Leave the village, retracing your steps, and continue along the main road, following the signposts for Cividale. The fine views stay with you as you descend. At the bottom of the hill, turn left, then right and cross the bridge into the centre of Cividale.*

Cividale del Friuli A noble town with an illustrious past, it was the site of a Celtic settlement centuries before Julius Caesar set up the Roman town of Forum Iulii (the origin of the name Friuli). The Ipogeo Celtico, a 5thC BC Celtic necropolis carved deep in the rock, is a haunting reminder of these ancient times (it is well signposted; ask for the key at the bar next door). But it is to the Lombard invasions that we owe the star attraction of the town – indeed of the tour. The Tempietto Longobardo is a tiny 8thC Lombard chapel whose timeless beauty will change your vision of the Dark Ages. The crowning glory is the group of stucco female figures, known as the 'Six Martyrs', that stand on either side of an archway delicately carved with vines. Hunt out other remarkable Lombard relics in the Museo Cristiano inside the 15thC Venetian Gothic Duomo by the square, and take a look at the medieval Piazza Paolo Diacono, a short walk from the square along via Mazzini.

Friuli: Italy's eastern frontier

Cividale, viewed from the Ponte del Diavolo.

Trattoria Longobarda
(restaurant, Cividale)

Turn into the last alleyway to the left before the bridge over which you arrived. Amelia Zorzettig, the charming *padrona* of this smart little trattoria, cooks with a strongly Slovenian touch. The speciality is *bollito misto*, a mixture of boiled meats served with *brovada* (turnip marinaded in wine) and *kren* (horseradish sauce). For pudding try *gubana*, Cividale's own version of fruit cake, sprinkled with *sliwovitch* (plum brandy). *Tel 0432-731655; closed Tue eve and Wed; price band B.*

Locanda Al Castello
(hotel/restaurant, Cividale)

This ivy-clad, converted 19thC convent overlooking the town has spacious, rustically furnished rooms at affordable prices. *Turn right just after the traffic lights to get there. Tel 0432-733242.*

⑤ *Continue on through the town. At the traffic lights, drive straight ahead following signs for Tarcento and Faedis. From here to Udine the route follows the quiet country road in the shadow of the wooded foothills of Monte Vogu. Turn right after about 3 km, signed for Faedis and pass through Togliano and Campeglio. This area was at the edge of the 1976 earthquake which killed almost 1,000 people.*

⑥ *Arriving at Faedis, follow the signs for Udine heading back south.*

Udine

Follow the signs for *centro*. The road takes you straight into the car

Friuli

parks in Piazza I Maggio. Udine was under the thumb of Venice for 400 years and the great republic has left its print on this patrician city. Pick up a street plan from the tourist office in the corner of the square and head for the Piazza della Libertà. Considered – and not just by the Udinese – as one of the most distinguished squares in Italy, it is flanked by exuberant examples of Venetian architecture that seem curiously familiar. The clock on the 16thC Loggia San Giovanni has been cribbed from the famous Torre dell'Orologio in Venice's Piazza San Marco and the town hall might remind you of a miniature Doge's Palace. With so much else to see, this historic city deserves at least a half-day to explore.

⑦ *Leave the city on the SS56, the main Trieste road, following the signs for Trieste and Grado.*

⑧ *After a mercifully fast 5 km dead straight drive through the city's industrial suburbs, there is a curve to the left. Just afterwards, turn right for Palmanova but after 50 metres turn left, signposted Pavia di Udine. The road now returns to open fields that stay with you to Cormons.* These lands have been in constant use since the days when Rome first colonized the area, parcelling out the land as pensions for its old legionaries.

Pavia di Udine

Passing through this placid village, pause to glance at the fine, faded frescos that decorate the façade of the church of San Giovanni Battista at the end of the main street, via Roma. *Leave the village, turning right at this church, following the signs to Percoto and on to Manzano.*

⑨ *At Manzano you arrive back at the main road from Udine to Trieste. Turn right along it for a brief 2.5 km stretch, turning left immediately after the bridge over the River Natisone.*

At San Giovanni al Natisone drive under the railway line and turn right at the fork in the main street. After the town, turn right and go through the village of Dolegnano.

⑩ *At the junction after Dolegnano, turn right, signed Cormons.*

Il Mulino
(restaurant, Visinale)

This much lauded restaurant in a tastefully restored old watermill stands off the road, along a track to the right immediately before the bridge over the River Judrio. Marcello Saturno uses entirely organic ingredients to create refined and imaginative dishes that provide a contrast to the more prosaic *cucina locale*. The duck breast accompanied by seasonal sauces is a reliable choice. *Tel 0432-759540; closed Wed; price band B/C.*

Continue on through Brazzano, passing the junction ① from which the tour departed, and return to Cormons.

Friuli: Italy's eastern frontier

ROUTE TWO: 95 KM

Leave Cormons on the quiet old road to Gorizia. The easiest way to find this road is to reach it from the modern highway to Gorizia, the SS56. Follow the signs to Gorizia, crossing under the railway line, and turn left at the traffic lights on to the SS56.

⑪ *After 1 km turn left again, back under the railway and immediately right. You are now on the old road running alongside the tracks.* It marks the boundary between the two great wine-growing areas of Cormons. The large vineyards to the left are on the clay of the Collio region. To the right, on the other side of the tracks, lie the gravel soils that produce the Isonzo wines. Compare the difference for yourself at the Enoteca at Cormons (in Piazza XXIV Maggio, above the main square).

Capriva del Friuli

Passing Castello Spessa in the trees to your left, you arrive at this small village with a pleasantly forgotten air about it. *Ignoring the signposts to Gorizia that would simply take you back onto the main road, turn left and then immediately right, at the road signposted Mossa, and carry straight on, still following the railway embankment.*

Mossa

Turn left towards the centre, then keep on the road bearing right, back to the railway embankment. This village, too, has the atmosphere of a backwater; nothing much seems to have changed here since the 1940s. To the left you see the hills of Slovenia. *After a kilometre or so, turn left at the sign to Monte Calvario, leaving the railway behind. After a short distance, bear right at the fork in the road. The road snakes up through acacia woods. Now follow the signposts for Gorizia. At the bottom of the hill, turn right following the signs for the centre.*

Gorizia

A fascinating place with a long and violent history, the city, like old Berlin, was one of the territorial casualties of World War II, split in two by the Slovenian border. From the central Piazza della Vittoria, walk through the elegant Viale D'Annunzio (this part still has the atmosphere of a Habsburg town with its *fin de siècle* architecture). Continue up to the citadel, once home to the pugnacious Counts of Gorizia, perennial thorns in the side of Venice. From here you can look over the drab blocks of flats which make up Eastern Gorizia (barbed wire divided the city until as recently as 1979).

Alla Luna
(restaurant, Gorizia)

You will find this low-priced trattoria with decidedly Slovenian fare in Via Oberdan, the street running off the Piazza della Vittoria by the Palazzo del Governo. Try one of the excellent soups, then sample the nutty local cheeses. *Tel 0481-530374; closed Sun eve and Mon; price band A.*

Leave following the blue signposts for Trieste and the SS55, ignoring the signs for the autostrada. ⑫ *At the large roundabout outside the city, continue to follow the Trieste signs on to the flyover. From here the road runs right up against the Slovenian border, entering an impressive avenue of cypress trees after a few kilometres, then gently rising into woodland.*

⑬ *About 6 km after the roundabout, turn right at the sign for Doberdo and after another kilometre right again, signposted S Michele and S Martino. The open woodland and grassy clearings here make ideal spots for a picnic or a snooze after a good Gorizian lunch.*

San Martino del Carso This peaceful corner saw one of the toughest Italian campaigns of World War I, the Battle of San Michele. On 6 August 1916 the Italians could claim victory over the Austro-Hungarians but at the cost of 111,000 lives. To see the museum and the impregnable Austro-Hungarian fortifications carved into the rocky hillside, *turn right into the village and follow the signposts. Otherwise turn left and continue down to the valley of the Isonzo.*

⑭ *At the bottom of the hill, drive under the railway bridge to the T-junction. Do not turn left, even though that is the direction in which you want to head - it is a one-way system. Instead, turn right, bearing left around the one-way system and leave it, following the signposts to Trieste and Fogliano Redipuglia. After a short distance, turn right at the traffic lights, following the signposts for S Pier d'Isonzo.*

S Pier d'Isonzo Don't stop here, unless you want to fraternize with the troops – this village in the middle of a rather dreary flat landscape is populated almost entirely by army personnel. *Carry straight on. At the main SS14, turn right, enticingly signed for Venezia, and cross the river Isonzo. After just under 3 km turn off left at the well-marked sign for Grado.* Shortly you see ahead of you the tall *campanile* of the Basilica of Aquileia soaring up from the plain.

Aquileia This little backwater was once the fourth most important city in Roman Italy. Founded in 181 BC, it boasted a population of 70,000. Later it became the seat of the great Patriarch of Aquileia and the site of an outstanding Basilica. But war and the anopheles mosquito gradually forced this proud city to bow out of history and today it is home to barely 3,500 people.

⑮ *Passing the ruins of the Roman forum, turn left and park by the Basilica.* Inside, see the vast 4thC mosaic floor which undulates across the enormous nave, happily mixing pagan and Christian motifs. Covered over when the church was rebuilt in the 11thC, this time-darkened masterpiece was only returned to the light earlier this century. If you

Friuli Italy's eastern frontier

Ruins of the Roman forum, Aquileia.

have time, visit the crypt to see more early mosaics. There is also ample testimony to Aquileia's great past in the archaeological museum opposite the Basilica and in the excavations that lie behind it.

Returning northwards along the course of the ancient via Giulia Augusta there are still as many chariots along this stretch as ever - pass through Cervignano heading for Palmanova.

Palmanova Even on the map it looks striking. From the moment you arrive, passing over the enormous grassy earthworks and through the solid tunnel of a gateway, there is a feeling of security. Who else could have built this singular, fortified, new town but the Venetians, rulers of this territory in the closing years of the 16thC and at daggers drawn with Austria. The architect was none other than Scamozzi, Palladio's famous pupil. At the centre stands the large but vacant round 'square' from which three main roads depart, carving the town into wedges so perfectly symmetrical that it is the easiest place for the stranger to get lost.

Trattoria San Marco
(restaurant, Palmanova)

This excellent fish restaurant is worth the 1 km detour on the road to Udine and is a reminder that you are near the sea. The delicious seafood *antipasti* are a filling *tour de force* but leave a little room for the fresh fish which Signor Maricchio grills in the fireplace in front of you. *Tel 0432-928433; closed Wed; price band B.*

From the square take the well signposted road to Gorizia and Jalmicco. ⑯ *Through the gate and over the earthworks, turn right and follow the signs for Trieste. Here the road zigzags for a while around the points of the star-shaped bastions before heading off eastwards. Continue on through Visco to Versa.*

⑰ *Turn left at Versa, at the road signposted Cormons. The scenery becomes rural here, passing through a patchwork of maize and corn fields and the occasional vineyard before crossing the river Judrio. Pausing to admire the cypress-ringed church at Medea, carry on through Borgnano and cross the main SS56 to return to Cormons.*

Veneto
THE COLLI EUGANEI AND THE MONTI BERICI

As the Po rolls seawards, its seemingly unending plain is suddenly broken by two small eruptions of volcanic hills. To the west of Padua stand the sugar-loaf shapes of the Colli Euganei, immortalized by Shelley in his 'Lines Written among the Euganean Hills'. To their north-west rise the Monti Berici. From prehistoric times people have been drawn to the rich earth and cool heights of these pastoral hills. Later, the Romans came here to bathe in the celebrated hot springs that still attract droves of health-conscious Italians. In the 16thC, Venetian nobles turned their gaze to the mainland, switching their investments from the sea to agriculture. As a legacy they have left behind grand villas in the style of the local architect, none other than the great Palladio, whose revival of Classicism was to have such a profound influence on the whole of European architecture.

From the tour's centre at Noventa Vicentina, set on the plain between the two ranges, the first loop of the tour meanders through the idyllic Colli Euganei taking in a handful of fine ancient towns, stately villas, an exquisite garden, and the tomb of Italy's greatest lyric poet. The second circuit explores the equally attractive countryside of the Monti Berici with a glimpse of a pair of Palladio's masterpieces, some great art of the Late Renaissance and an intriguing lakeside beauty spot.

ROUTE ONE: 72 KM

Noventa Vicentina

The urbanely Classical 16thC Villa Barbarigo that adorns the central square sets the tone for this spacious little market town. Built by a noble family that could boast two Venetian Doges among its ancestors, it now houses the municipal offices. In the adjacent baroque Chiesa Arcipretale, the rococo flourish of Giambattista Tiepolo is unmistakable in the ravishing painting of Saints Rocco and Sebastian which hangs over one of the side altars.

The town's one hotel, the modern Albergo Romagnolo *(tel 0444-887277)* is cheap, clean, and little else. You may do better at one of the many other hotels on the route.

Primon
(restaurant, Noventa Vicentina)

This serious restaurant, with uncluttered decoration and discreet service, has a reassuringly short menu based on Veneto cooking. *On the main street; tel 0444-887149; closed Thur; price band B/C.*

Leave following signs for Este.

① *After 1 km bear right on to the main road.* You now follow the course of one of the numerous drainage canals which mesh the region. Many date back to disastrous floods in 589 AD that swept

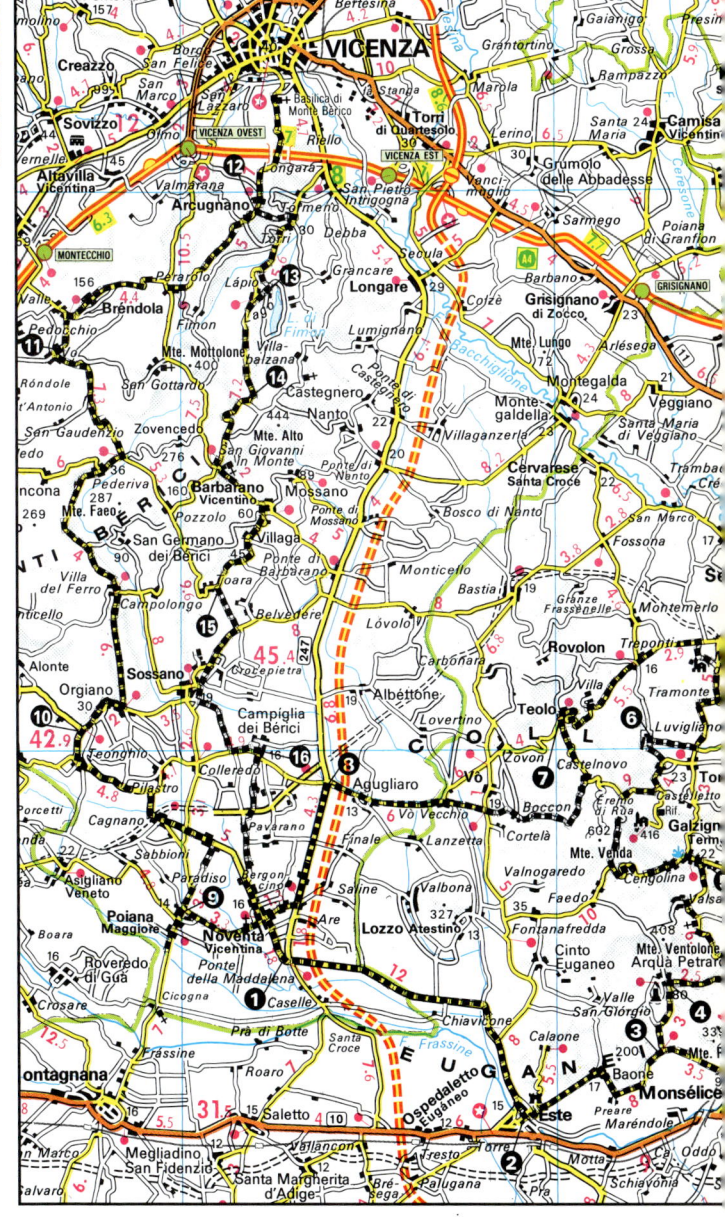

Veneto

Veneto: the Colli Euganei and the Monti Berici

A curious front garden on the road to Este.

away the villages of the Atestino peoples who populated the area. Ahead of you stand the outlying mounds of the Colli Euganei, looking almost man-made.

Este

A Renaissance town with a blousy touch of baroque, this genteel backwater started life as home to the Veneto's earliest prehistoric settlers. Search out the Museo Nazionale Atestino by the Castello to see one of Northern Italy's most outstanding collections of pre-Roman archaeological finds. Then visit the Duomo to see Tiepolo's stirring painting commemorating Este's miraculous deliverance from the plague, before wandering through the arcades of Via Cavour and a string of small squares to the Piazza Maggiore. Romantics may like to know that Shelley's paean to the Euganean hills was written in Villa Kunkler outside the castle walls.

Da Piero Ceschi
(restaurant, Este)

Signore Ceschi, gourmet and aspiring poet, is the jovial host of this simple osteria – a dining-room behind the bar where you can eat a decent plate of *baccalà alla Vicentina* (stockfish poached in milk), rabbit or, if you are lucky, snails. In the summer you can also eat outside under the colonnades. *At the far end of Piazza Trento, between the Duomo and the main square; tel 0429-2855; closed Thur; price band B.*

Albergo Centrale
(hotel, Este)

This small hotel in Piazza Beatrice, tucked away between the main square and the gardens of the Castello, has inexpensive rooms. *Tel 0429-601757.*

Leave bearing left around the castle walls.

② *Turn left at the end of the wall, following the sign to Baone. As the old road skirts the hills, look out for a glimpse of the stately Villa Caborini on your left. At Baone bear right for Monselice.*

Veneto

Monselice *your left. At Baone bear right for Monselice.*
Reaching the centre, turn right at the river and cross the bridge into the small main square, then continue straight ahead and park. You are now in the Via del Santuario, the monumental heart of this aristocratic town, graced with a succession of architectural set pieces ranging in style from gaunt medieval to refined Palladian. From the solid medieval Castello Ca'Marcello *(open daily; guided tours only)*, you pass a fine 17thC villa and the old Romanesque Duomo before arriving at the gates of the elegantly simple 16thC Villa Duodo, built by Scamozzi, Palladio's disciple and torchbearer. Walk on up to the top along the ceremonial approach flanked by seven small chapels.

Leave the town along the one-way Via Roma, turning left to cross back over the canal. Then turn left along the river's bank and right into Via Petrarca, the road on which you first arrived.

③ *Around 3 km outside the town turn right following signs for Arqua Petrarca.*

Arqua Petrarca Italy's – some would argue Europe's – greatest lyric poet spent the last years of his life among the cobbled streets and modest old cottages of this medieval village. The love songs and humanist thought of Francesco Petrarca, or Petrarch, profoundly influenced the whole of European literature, blowing away the courtly niceties of medieval poetry, and it is to him that we owe the sonnet form. First make a pilgrimage to his tomb. His red marble sarcophagus stands in front of the church – the broken corner is the work of a Dominican monk who broke open the tomb in 1630 to steal the poet's arm. The sober retreat in which Petrarch passed the last five years of his life until his death in 1374, stands above the village. Surrounded by vines and olives, it is a haunting place that has been lovingly preserved, though the surviving frescos have the patina of age and poor restoration.

Serena
(hotel, Arqua Petrarca) This small, mid-price hotel, 2 km outside the village and well-signposted, is set amidst vineyards and has views that have not changed much since Petrarch contemplated them. *Tel 0429-718044.*

④ *From the main crossroads by the church leave along the narrow cobbled street, following signs for Padova. After 2 km turn left again towards Valsanzibio, passing through the village to arrive at Villa Barbarigo. An ornate pavilion to Diana the Huntress to the left of the road heralds the entrance to the gardens.*

Villa Barbarigo The villa here plays second fiddle to one of the finest gardens in the Veneto, laid out for the Barbarigo family in 1669. Set in a natural amphitheatre, it looks out into the Euganean slopes. Along its shady

Veneto: the Colli Euganei and the Monti Berici

rabbit island and, best of all, an unfathomable maze *(closed Sun, Mon morning).*

Carry on to Galzignano Terme, one of the smaller of the popular Euganean spa towns.

⑤ At the T-junction, turn left and head away from the town. The road climbs once more away from the plain into the slopes of the Colli Euganei, past small vineyards clinging to the hillside. Follow the signs for Faedo until you arrive at the junction at the top and turn right into the Parco Naturale dei Colli Euganei. After 4 km, turn right at the junction and head towards Torreglia.

Shortly after the turn for the monastery of Monte Rua (open Sundays for men only), turn left to Luvigliano and Treponti along an avenue of young umbrella pines, then left again.

Luvigliano Their Lordships the Bishops of Padua had a good eye for worldly beauty judging from the site for their summer palace, built here in the 16thC. Turn left at the war memorial to visit this superb villa – you see it on the small hillock in front of you *(open Mon, Wed, Fri 10.30-12.30, 2.30-6).* At the adjacent Azienda Agricola you can taste the large selection of wines produced on the villa's estate and in the surrounding area, from the light, *frizzante* Serprino to full-bodied, red Cabernet and Merlot wines.

⑥ Returning to the war memorial, continue on ahead, bearing right after 50 metres towards Tramonte. After another 1.5 km, turn left at the sign for Tramonte.

Tramonte This is not so much a village as an ensemble of grand Euganean villas, each trying to outdo its neighbours. The first you see is also the finest – the 17thC Villa della Rosa stands directly ahead through a pair of delicate, wrought-iron gates.

Just outside Tramonte, turn left at the sign for Praglia. You shortly catch sight of the imposing Benedictine monastery rising up in the shadow of the hills, across the vineyards to the left. Turn left, then left again to reach the entrance.

Praglia The ancient abbey of Praglia is one of the world's most important centres for antique book restoration – many of the damaged manuscripts from the 1966 floods in Florence were put to rights here. Founded in medieval times, the major part of the building dates from the 15th and 16thC. Inside its solemn Venetian walls you can visit four beautiful cloisters, the library and the famous workshops. *Guided tours between 3.30 and 5.30; closed Mon.*

Veneto

From the gates of the monastery drive straight ahead; then, after several hundred metres, turn left towards Teolo, passing through Treponti. The scenery becomes more dramatic as the road winds back up into the hills, with rugged rocky outcrops breaking the soft curves of the hillside.

Teolo This little village in an idyllic setting is reputed to be the birthplace of Livy, the celebrated, if unreliable, chronicler of the history of Rome. Little evidence remains, however, of its illustrious past, apart from the Town Hall which was once the palace for the local Venetian governor.

⑦ From here, bear left to Castelnuovo, where you turn right at the junction towards Vo. The road begins to drop back to the plain. Keep following the signs for Vo.

Villa Sceriman Under the shady loggias of this handsome Palladian villa there is an *enoteca* with a comprehensive selection of local wines.

Turn left by the gate of the villa along Via Ca'Sceriman, then right and continue straight ahead at the next crossroads. Stay on this road, by-passing Agugliaro, to ⑧ the main SS247 where there is no choice but to turn left and join the traffic. After 3 km, turn right at the traffic lights to Noventa Vicentina.

ROUTE TWO: 96 KM

Leave Noventa Vicentina along the main street from the Villa Barbarigo, passing the Duomo on your right, and following signposts for Poiana Maggiore.

Poiana Maggiore *⑨ Arriving at the centre, turn left along Via Roma, taking a short detour to see Villa Poiana.* This sublime piece of architecture is one of only 20 villas built by Palladio that still survive. Dating back to the late 1540s, and recently restored, its perfectly proportioned façade is stately without being pompous. *Return to junction ⑨ and carry straight ahead along the main street for 2 km. Then turn left for Lonigo, passing through Cagnano.*

⑩ After 5 km, as the road reaches the slopes of the Monti Berici, turn right for Orgiano and Sossano.

Orgiano Slow down here to admire the extravagantly baroque Villa Fracanzan Piovene. Like many of the villas on the route, it is closed to the public. It matters little, however, as most were designed simply to impress from afar. Turn left just after the villa towards Brendola and Grancona, on to a stretch of quiet road which runs along the plain into a natural amphitheatre. At Villa del Ferro pause to peer through the gates of the

Veneto: the Colli Euganei and the Monti Berici

squirely Villa Custozza Lazzarini before heading on through Spiazzo to Pederiva.

Trattoria Isetta
(restaurant, Pederiva)

On the left just before the village, an undistinguished façade hides an excellent restaurant with a decidedly regional bent – polenta or bigoli (a giant spaghetti) for starters and authentic baccalà alla Vicentina to follow. It also has a few sound-value rooms. *Tel 0444-889548; closed Tues eve and Wed; price band B.*

After Pederiva the road begins to rise into the hills through vineyards before crossing over to the other side of the compact Monti Berici.

⑪ *Turn right at the junction just before the small village of Vo, following the signposts for Brendola and Vicenza.*

Brendola

Turn right at the junction in the modern town and drive up to the ruins of the vast church of San Michele. This folly, started earlier this century, was to have been the mausoleum for the town's obscure saint, Maria Bertilla Boscardin. When the building was almost complete, the nuns of the convent where she was buried decided not to release her body and the new shrine was left to decay. Head on up the hill opposite the ruin to visit the old part of Brendola and to enjoy the splendid views across the plain.

Back at the ruin, turn left, continuing along the road under the old village and heading up towards Perarolo. After a few kilometres bear right, continuing along the main road into Perarolo. Now follow the signposts to Arcugnano, bearing right, then left. Down the hill just outside Arcugnano, stop to eye up the stately Villa Franceschini Salasco.

Basilica of Monte Berico
(detour)

Vicenza's deliverance from the plague in the 15thC was said to have been signalled by two appearances of the Madonna on the summit of this hill, the spot now marked by a great domed church. Hidden in this jungle of high baroque are two great paintings, a *pietà* by Montagna near the altar and Veronese's *Supper of St Gregory* (follow the neon

---

Vicenza, the home of Palladio (1508-1580), is only a few kilometres away. Throughout its streets you can see works by the man who changed the course of European architecture. The star attractions are the Piazza dei Signori, flanked by Palladio's great Basilica (not a church but a meeting-place for Vicentine gentry), and the Teatro Olimpico, completed to Palladio's design in 1585, with its extraordinary *trompe l'oeil* perspective of the streets of a classical city.

Veneto

signs to confessionals, offertories, masses and souvenirs and you will find it in the small Sala del Quadro). Afterwards, peer out of the rear window to catch a glimpse of Palladio's famous Rotunda, one of the great landmarks in the history of architecture.

Retracing your steps towards Arcugnano, ⑫ turn left at the sign to Hotel Villa Michelangelo, along Via Sacco, passing the hotel on your right (a de luxe overnight stop for those with a fat wallet or an expense account) *and carry on along the narrow shady lane which winds down to Torri. At the junction at the bottom, turn right through the modern village, along an incongruous short stretch of dual carriageway. Immediately afterwards, bear left, on the road signposted for Lapio. After 2 km, turn left again at the green sign for Lago di Fimon.*

Lago di Fimon

Seeds of primitive vines dating back some 6,000 years – the earliest evidence of wine-making in Italy – were found on the slopes by this cool, hidden lake in the 1960s. Take a break from driving and walk the 4 km footpath which encircles the lake.

Retrace your steps for 300 metres and ⑬ take the second of the two left turns at the crossroads up Via Capitello towards Lapio. The narrow road climbs sharply with occasional glimpses of the still lake below. At the brow of the hill at Lapio, turn left past the church. ⑭ Bear right where the road divides, continuing to head upwards. At the next hamlet bear left, then go straight ahead at the next junction. At the T-junction after a couple of kilometres turn left, heading down to Barbarano.

Barbarano Vicentino

Pause by the church to look at the sad 15thC Venetian Gothic Palazzo dei Canonici discreetly decaying into oblivion, before taking the small road opposite, signposted to Villaga. It winds up out of the town, passing the sternly medieval Castello Vescovile, now housing a shop selling local farm produce – olive oil, honey and grappa, together with local Garganego and Tocai Rosso wines.

From Villaga carry on following signposts for Toara, bearing left then turning right. The road here runs along the very edge of the plain.

⑮ At the junction just before Toara, turn left, heading away from the hills. After another 1.5 km turn right for Sossano on to a main road. Remain on the road for 6 km and, by-passing Sossano, turn left at the first set of traffic lights, signposted for Poiana and Noventa.

Campiglia Dei Berici

Before the village, to the left, stands the once splendid 17thC Villa Repeta, now desperately in need of restoration. *⑯ At the next junction turn left for a closer look at the villa or turn right to pass through the village. Cross the main road and follow the signs back to Noventa.*

Northern Piemonte
LAKE ORTA AND THE VALSESIA

At the threshold of the Alps, ancient glaciers scoured deep valleys to form the famed Italian Lakes. This itinerary provides an alternative to the usual lakeland circuits and, instead, heads west to the luxuriant valley of the River Sesia and the least-visited of the lakes, Lago d'Orta. Reputed to be Italy's greenest river valley, the Valsesia runs northwards from the plain of the Po to the very foot of Europe's second highest mountain, Monte Rosa. This tour starts in its lower reaches and explores the tree-mantled hills to either side which bear the marks of startlingly different human activities over the last few centuries. The first loop stops off at Varallo - a holy mountain with one of Italy's most intriguing religious shrines - before heading eastwards through several unspoilt villages to Lake Orta. The second, more challenging circuit, goes west to wind through the contradictory landscape of the Val Sessera, where small mill towns of

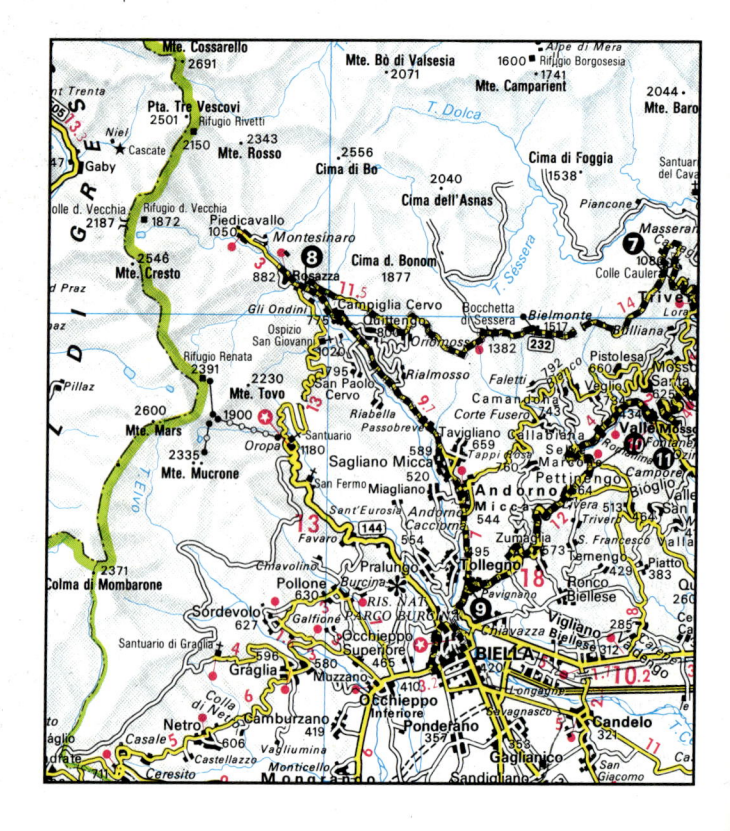

Northern Piemonte

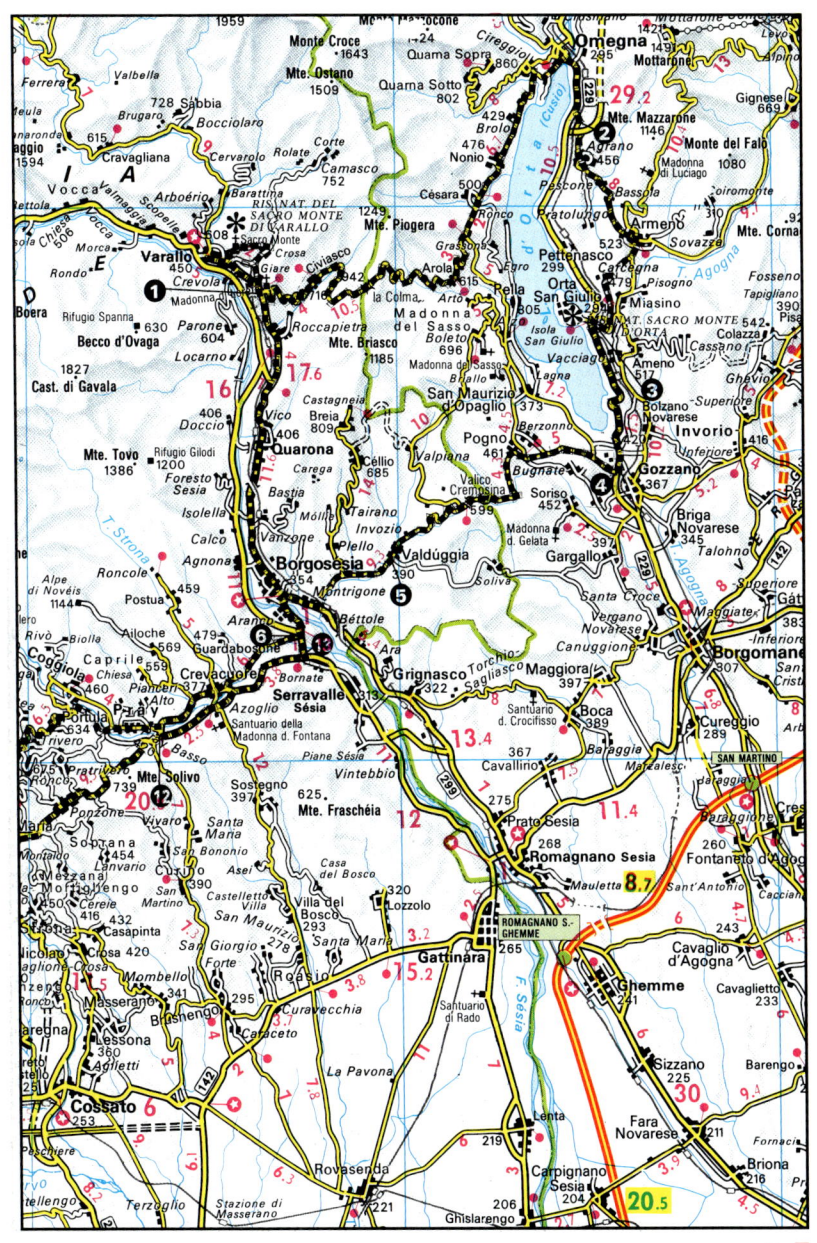

Northern Piemonte: Lake Orta and the Valsesia

ambiguous beauty squat in lush vales, then climbs up to breathtaking views of the peaks of the Italian Alps. This second loop, though not the orthodox Italian idyll, is an adventurous excursion for those who can appreciate the fascination of the relics of 19thC industry. While restaurants are few and far between, bon viveurs need have no worries; the restaurants that there are provide fine Piemontese cooking, some of the best in Italy.

ROUTE ONE: 84 KM

Borgosesia Like the curate's egg, this small wool town is 'good in parts'. Despite its splendid setting in the green valley of the Valsesia, there is little else to detain you here. There are hotels – La Campagnolo in the northern outskirts is inexpensive and pleasant enough – but it is probably better to stay in Varallo or one of the other interesting villages along the route.

Borgosesia - Varallo *Leave the centre, taking signs to Varallo. The road heads north, following the eastern bank of the River Sesia. 3 km after Quarona, bear right off the main road at the sign for Rocca Pietra and Varallo Centro. ① Arriving at Varallo, turn right following the signs up to the Sacro Monte.*

Sacro Monte, Varallo This Renaissance display of religious tableaux, begun in 1491, was one priest's idea for bringing religion alive. Fra Bernardino Caini planned the 52 chapels with lavish frescos and 800 life-sized figures to populate them, employing an army of artists and craftsmen. The most famous of them was Gaudenzio Ferrari, a native of these parts and rated in his day among Italy's top seven painters. The English writer Samuel Butler was a great admirer of the Sacro Monte. He visited it almost yearly from 1871 to his death in 1902 and his book, *Ex Voto*, is still the most comprehensive study of its art.

Vecchio Albergo Sacro Monte (hotel, Sacro Monte) Originally built in 1594 to house the artists working on the Sacro Monte, this recently restored hotel still keeps some of its ancient ambience; the comfortable rooms are simply furnished and reasonably priced. *Tel 0163-54254.*

Varallo Below the holy mountain, Varallo's intimate streets are worth exploring before heading on. Returning back the way you came, turn left at the bottom of the hill into the centre. Gaudenzio Ferrari worked here for a considerable part of his life and the town boasts fine examples of his work – his magnificent polyptych in the church of San Gaudenzio and an entire wall depicting the life of Christ in La Madonna delle Grazie are the best. *Leave, retracing your steps towards Borgosesia (be careful to avoid taking the new by-pass road). Back at the junction to the Sacro Monte ①, carry on for 300 metres and then turn left to Civiasco and*

Northern Piemonte

Valsesian village.

Omegna. Look out on the left here for the Cappella della Madonna di Loreto – only in Italy could you find a roadside chapel as beautiful as this. Gaudenzio Ferrari painted the lunette above the triple porch. The road now snakes up the wooded slopes of the valley.

Civiasco   This is an unexpectedly grand village, its houses adorned with loggias and frescoed stucco and its narrow streets with fountains. Further along the road, spot the houses with wooden balconies on each floor, following the style of the Alpine chalets of the German-speaking Walser people who live further north.

Keep on the same road to weave up through the hills to the Passo della Colma and your first distant glimpse of Lake Orta through the trees. Dropping down, you catch sight of the lake again, just before Arola, this time with its island of San Giulio. Pause here to admire another gem of a roadside chapel, the 17thC Chiesa della Madonna Assunta with a fresco over its porch.

La Zucca
(restaurant, Arola)

The small building directly opposite the church is one of the epicurean highspots on the route. It has a set price (and top price) gastronomic banquet of the finest Piemontese cuisine with a large selection of *antipasti*, three pasta dishes and a wide choice of second courses. There is also an excellent, simpler menu *(price band C)*. Booking preferred. *Tel 0323-821114; closed Tues; price band D.*

Northern Piemonte: Lake Orta and the Valsesia

Orta San Giulio, looking out to the island.

Reaching the junction at the bottom of the hill, turn left towards Omegna to pass several undistinguished modern villages before dropping down to the lake.

Omegna

Head down to the water's edge for a glorious view of the Isola San Giulio, like a jewel set in the glittering lake. It is worth parking by the bridge to stroll around the streets or to relax at one of the bars which overlooks the lake – there are not many other opportunities to admire the waters at close quarters.

Omegna - Orta San Giulio

Follow the road along the waterfront until it rejoins the main road, turning left for Orta San Giulio.

② *At Borca, just outside Omegna, turn left at the sign for Armeno (opposite the petrol station). Leaving the busy road, you now cross the railway and wind up a clutch of sharp bends, catching marvellous views across the seductive lake.* The road is little more than an asphalt cart track, threading its way clumsily through meadows and stony hamlets that sit in the folds of the hillside. *At Armeno, turn right at the centre of the village and head back down, following the signs for Lago d'Orta.* After the village of Carcegna, the lake reappears with the hilly spit of Orta San Giulio jutting out before you.

Northern Piemonte

③ *At the traffic lights keep straight on, passing the extravagant minaret-like tower of Villa Crespi, and park in one of the car parks.*

Orta San Giulio

A walk down to the central square and waterfront takes you through narrow passages, passing terraced gardens and stone-roofed houses. The town's two main hotels stand on the lakeside at either end of the serene Piazza Motta, half square, half promenade, looking for all the world like an opera set. The island of San Giulio lies alluringly in front of you.

Isola San Giulio *(boat trip)*

When San Giulio came here in 390 to found his sanctuary, the villagers, fearful of the monsters which lurked beneath its waters, refused to take him across the lake. So he crossed on foot, using his staff as a rudder and his cloak as a sail. Today a daily boat service from Piazza Motta makes the journey easier.

③ *Returning to the traffic lights, turn right for Novara, passing the genteel turn-of-the-century summer villas which line most of this side of the lake. At the head of the lake ignore the slight charms of Gozzano and ④ turn right, following the signs to Borgosesia. At Pogno the road bears sharply to the left and heads up into a dumpy landscape thick with trees. At the top, drive through the curious single track tunnel and carry on down to Valduggia.*

⑤ *Bear right from the bypass road into this romantically time-worn village.*

Valduggia

After seeing so many of his paintings, now is your chance to see Gaudenzio Ferrari face to face. The statue of Valduggia's most famous son (he was born here in 1484) stands in the middle of the intimate square, in front of another of his frescoed chapels. To the other side is the church of San Giorgio with a gloomy interior that remains refreshingly unrestored.

Back on the main road, Borgosesia is only 4 km away.

ROUTE TWO: 94 KM

Leave Borgosesia, following signs for Vercelli, passing through the modern suburb of Aranco.

⑥ *Just outside the town turn left on to the main road to Vercelli but turn off right after 400 metres towards Trivero. The road immediately plunges into the lush, jungly woodland that provides the backdrop for most of this route. Bear left at the hamlet of Guardella to Crevacuore, by-passing the village to the left; then take the second left turn at the traffic lights to Pray. At Pray, bear left across the bridge, following the signs for Trivero. After a few kilometres you pass Coggiola to your right.*

Northern Piemonte: Lake Orta and the Valsesia

The Castello, Rosazza.

Coggiola This frayed village stands in stark contrast to the beauty of the valley which surrounds it. Yet it provides a fascinating example of the industrial history of the area. This was one of the clutch of woollen mills which grew up in these hills during the 19thC. At the centre of each is a stream whose reliable flow provided the most valuable resource of all. These must have been well-kept places in the days when the *padrone* ruled from his nearby villa. But now many have been taken over by large conglomerates, while others have been abandoned to be reclaimed by the forest around. *From Coggiola, keep on up the main road towards Trivero.*

Northern Piemonte

Portula Just before Trivero, turn left to see the Museo Opere dei Bimbi. Around the old parish church, the children of the area have brightened the concrete retaining walls with several hundred metres of pictures painted on tiles – youngsters will love it, even if nobody else does. Returning to the main road, continue up to Trivero.

Trivero Pause in the square by the church to the left of the road to look up at the largest wool village in the area – its plain features redeemed by its verdant setting. Below you lies the hazy plain of the Po.

⑦ From Trivero follow signs to Bielmonte and the Strada Panoramica Zegna, turning right at the T-junction just outside. The road climbs through tight bends, past severe buildings endowed by the Zegna family, the local landlords who also built this spectacular road.

Strada Panoramica Zegna Reaching the other side of the ridge, you escape from morose relics of a once-thriving textile industry to enjoy the finest views on the tour, across the valleys of the Sesia to the majestic snow-capped mountains of the Alps and the bulky massif of Monte Rosa, Europe's second highest mountain. This area is rich in wildlife – roe deer, chamois and marmot wander among these slopes. Along the road there is a small car park where you can stop to take in the panorama. Further along, at Bocchetta Luvera, a `Last Chance Saloon'-style bar also serves meals. After two narrow cobbled tunnels, you reach Bielmonte, a tiny ski resort that is a ghost town for most of the year.

Bielmonte - Rosazza Passing the col of Bocchetta Sessera, the road now begins a descent through exposed moorland relieved by the odd stand of birch before the woodland returns. Pass down through the hamlet of Piaro and Forgnengo, a village of grey stone houses piled up the hillside. The roofs of the older houses are still covered with stone slabs.

⑧ At the junction at the bottom of the hill, turn right to Rosazza.

Rosazza From the moment you enter, past its over-the-top burial ground (modelled on Genoa's celebrated 19thC Staglieno Cemetery), this quirky village stands out from the rest. It displays an eclectic blending of styles – the church is reminiscent of English Arts and Crafts, while the villa of the Rosazza family and the colonnaded Municipio next to it seem almost Bavarian. This concoction was the brain-child of Federico Rosazza, a government senator at the turn of the century, whose monument stands by the church. He transformed the place with the labour of the villagers whom he trained to extraordinary perfection – in several nooks around the church you will see small carvings of some of them.

⑧ Go back over the bridge to the junction and turn right, following signs for

Northern Piemonte: Lake Orta and the Valsesia

Biella. The road passes under an unusual tiled roof which shelters a roadside chapel.

Le Betulle
(restaurant, Campiglia Cervo)

This refined restaurant in the centre of the village is one of the few in the area to serve a lunchtime *menu turistico (price band A)*, although you can, of course, go the whole hog, Piemontese style. *Tel 015-60079; closed Wed; price band C for hogs.*

Albergo Asmara
(hotel, San Paolo Cervo)

This hotel looks as if it has seen better days but has simple, clean rooms at very reasonable prices. The bonus is the lovely setting, overlooking the river Cervo with views down the valley. You will see it to the right just after Campiglia Cervo. *Tel 015-60021.*

Continue along the valley, passing a string of down-at-heel villages; you might marvel at how they can appear so drab in a valley as attractive as this. *At Sagliana Micca turn off, bearing right, to see this typical rough-cut village and drive along its long cobbled street to rejoin the main road.*

From now on the valley begins to widen out, becoming more populated. *Entering the Comune of Biella, continue on to Pavignano.*

⑨ At the traffic lights carry straight on towards Biella if you want to take the detour, or turn left for Valle Mossa and Mossa S Maria.

Borgo Piazzo, Biella
(detour)

Take this short detour to visit the medieval merchants' quarters of Biella. *Turn right at the bottom of the hill to centro città and cross the bridge. At the first traffic lights, continue straight ahead; at the second set turn right and right again at the third, following the road up to the top of the hill. Then turn left at the yellow sign to Borgo Piazzo.*

The august buildings of this 14thC mercantile fortress stand along a narrow ridge above Biella. The colonnaded pavements, often wider than the road itself, retain an atmosphere which the centuries have done little to alter. The city below, now linked by funicular railway, looks depressingly squalid until you reach its medieval core, where the streets are as elegant as only Italian shopping streets can be. Also see the beautiful 10thC baptistery to the side of the Duomo. Driving to the far end of the Borgo, rejoin the metalled road. *At the bottom of the hill, turn left and follow the signs for Andorno back over the bridge to ⑨, the start of the detour where you turn right.*

As the road climbs up, there are magnificent views back to the right of the peaks of Monte Mucrone and Monte Camino. *Continue on through Zumaglia, Biella's patrician retreat, to Pettinengo.* Like Trivero, it is a moth-eaten place, centred around its *lanificio* (the wool factory). Its only asset is the grandstand view of the plains.

Northern Piemonte

Under the colonnades of Borgo Piazzo, Biella.

⑩ *Just after Pettinengo bear left towards Mossa S Maria. The road returns to cool, lush woodland, winding through the folds of the valleys. Carry straight ahead at the crumbling mill.*

Just after Veglio, bear right towards Valle Mosso, passing the pretty, recently restored, frescoed façade of San Rocco ai Ponti.

Valle Mosso   This is another melancholy mixture of fading 19thC grandeur and the impatient architecture of our own age, already prematurely ageing.

⑪ *Just after its two small squares, bear left up the narrow street (sign posted Croce Mossa and Borgosesia) and turn left on to the main road at the top. Up at Croce Mossa take the second right turn, and keep following signs for Ponzone and Borgosesia.*

Ponzone   Among the undistinguished buildings of this town stand two architectural curiosities. Directly opposite the mill is an unusual example of ecclesiastical architecture of the Fascist 1930s, its stark rectangular interior inscribed puritanically with the ten commandments and hardly a religious symbol in sight. Further along the road, you pass the local mill owner's villa in fin de siècle stucco-work, its ceremonial steps circling up from a grotto.

From here follow the signs for Crevacuore.

⑫ *Passing the bridge to Pray, keep on the road following the signs to Borgosesia.*

⑬ *After 6 km turn left on to main road into Borgosesia.*

Southern Piemonte
THE WINE LANDS OF ALBA

A Busby Berkeley landscape of regimented rows of vines stretching as far as the eye can see provides the backdrop for this gourmand's paradise. The rolling green country of castle-topped hills not only yields up the king of Italian wines but also that most Epicurean of treasures, the truffle. Barolo, a worthy match for the finest Bordeaux, is produced just south of Alba. The secret of this garnet nectar lies in the dry soil, rich in calcium and minerals, with a microclimate that matures the nebbiolo grape to perfection. To the north lie the lands of Barbaresco, Barolo's queen, a wine with lighter, more feminine qualities. Keeping this regal couple company is a rather more common wine, Asti Spumante, perhaps the most famous - some might say notorious – of all Italian wines.

The proximity of France and the company of fine wines has given the region Italy's most refined cuisine. The Piemontese speciality is antipasti and restaurants will often serve as many as six or seven of these unforgettable taste bombs at the start of the meal. It is hard to eat badly here – and hard to eat cheaply. Meals on average tend to be well into price band C and the wine can easily double your bill - but anyone leaving without abandoning themselves at least once to these culinary indulgences will have missed one of the great wonders of Italy.

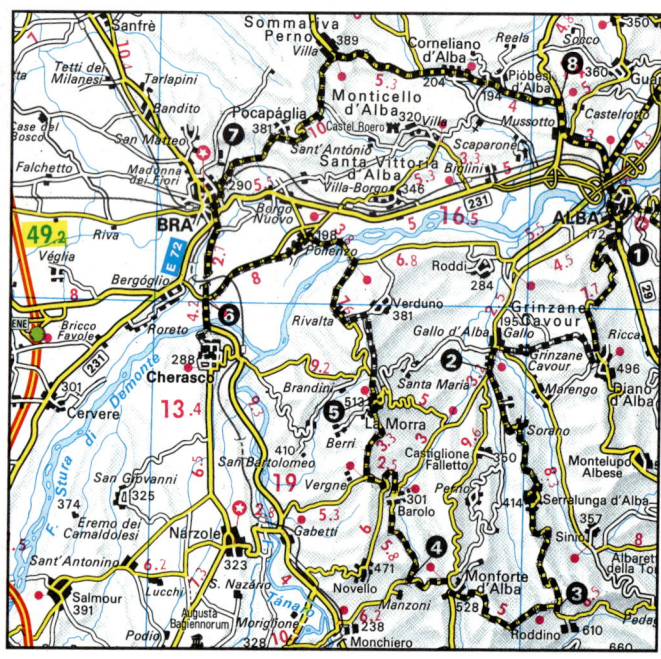

Southern Piemonte

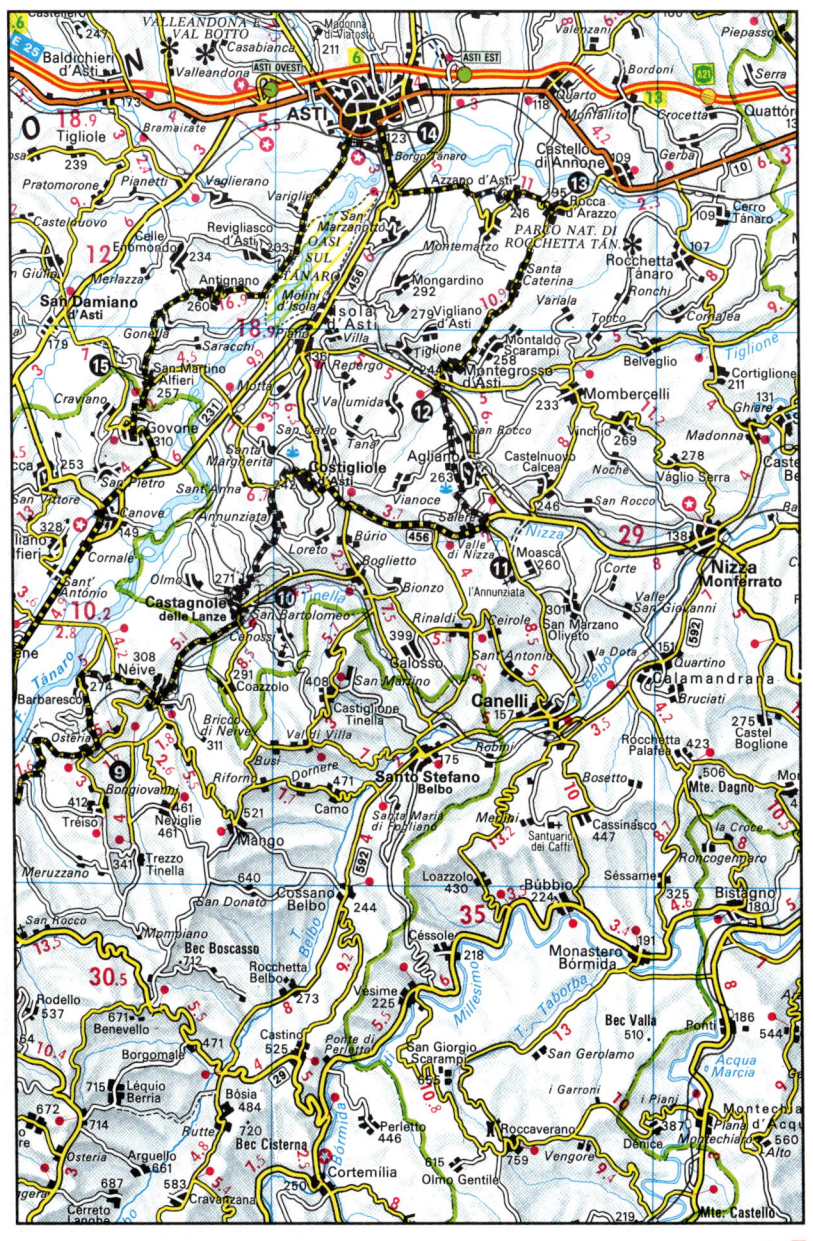

Southern Piedmont: The Wine Lands of Alba

ROUTE ONE: 88 KM

Alba

This medieval, red-brick city of narrow streets and alleyways was once known as La Città delle Cento Torre. Although only a few towers remain, it still bears the imprint of its worthy past and makes an ideal centre for the tour. Head for the central Via Vittorio Emanuele in the evening as the whole town descends for the *passeggiata*, browsing around its elegant shops or clutching ice-creams from one of the local *gelaterie* (the average Italian eats 6 kg of ice-cream per year).

Bar La Torre
(restaurant, Alba)

It is no surprise that Italy's truffle capital boasts several excellent restaurants; this small unfussy place at the foot of the Casa Riva tower in Via Cavour is a decent, moderately priced choice. For an *antipasto* try *toma d'Alba*, small round cheeses under oil. During the truffle season have *tajarin all'Albese* (truffles grated over tagliatelle), one of the simplest ways of tasting this sublime fungus. *Tel 0173-441647; closed Mon; price band B/C.*

Alba has a handful of passable hotels. At the top end of the price scale, the bland three star Hotel Savona in Piazza Savona (*tel 0173- 440440*) has all modern comforts, while at the other end the Albergo Piemonte (*tel 0173-441354*), just behind the Duomo, has pleasant rooms without the frills, leaving you with a few more lire for food.

From the fountained Piazza Savona, follow the signpost for Savona, heading out of town along the Corso Italia.

① *Turn right just before the church at the end of the straight stretch of road, signposted Diano D'Alba. The road immediately begins to twist upwards into the hills of the Langhe. After 5 km turn right just before the village of Diano D'Alba to Grinzane.* You are now in the Barolo wine zone. A patchwork of vineyards covers every acre as far as the eye can see, broken only by the castles or tiny villages that crown the hilltops and the occasional grove of hazelnut trees.

Grinzane Cavour

Camillo Cavour, the wily Piemontese Prime Minister who laid down the blueprint for the Unification of Italy, is remembered in the name of this attractive village. In the early 19thC he was the owner of its austere block of a castle which today houses an *enoteca*, agricultural museum and an expensive trattoria (*closed Tues*).

Carry on down to Gallo D'Alba and turn left at the T-junction towards Barolo.

② *Just outside the village turn left again, signposted Serralunga and Roddino, and bear left, continuing on to Serralunga.*

Southern Piemonte

The vintners' and trufflers' guild, Alba.

Serralunga d'Alba

Its tall compact castle, the best preserved in the area, is encircled by a striking row of estate cottages. Climb up to visit the evocatively medieval tower (*closed Mon*) and enjoy the magnificent views. At the delicatessen L'Infernot del Castel you can buy truffles under oil, locally-cured meats and cheeses, as well as wines and fiery grappa.

Keep on heading south.

③ *Turn right just before Roddino, signed Dogliani and Monforte.* Far off in the distance ahead of you lie the Maritime Alps and the French border.

Monforte

The ramshackle old hilltop village has been eclipsed by the modern town that has grown up around the anonymous square down below. Take a sharp hike up through its narrow main street to the church and castle at the top. The ancient Castello degli Scarampi was converted into a private villa in the 18thC and is firmly closed to the public, but a track takes you round the back to a hidden gravel square where you

Southern Piedmont: The Wine Lands of Alba

Looking out from the Belvedere at La Morra.

will find a delightful 17thC oratory and the medieval Torre Campanaria. *Leave along the main raod, following the signs for Barolo, bearing left just outside the village.*

④ *Turn right after about 2 km.*

Barolo

For a village immortalized in Italy's noblest wine, it is a surprise that its castle is such a dowdy affair. Little of the original medieval building is now visible, and the stucco which covers its brick walls is crumbling away. Inside, the state rooms and library of the Count of Barolo, together with an engrossing wine museum, are open to the public (*closed Thurs*). Around it are several shops offering you free tastings of Barolo – but beware, few things in life are really free.

Locanda del Borgo Antico
(restaurant, Barolo)

The elegant atmosphere of this small, welcoming restaurant is the ideal background for classic *cucina Albese* washed down with... what else but Barolo. *Tel 0173-56355; closed Wed; price band C/D, without wine.*

Returning to the road above the castle, continue on past Hotel Barolo,

Southern Piemonte

turning left outside the village and, after 2 km of tight bends, sharp right and right again to La Morra.

La Morra This is one of the most handsome of the Barolo villages. Park just off the main Via XX Settembre and walk up the hill, topped by the church of San Martino and a couple of wine *cantinas*. The nearby shady park of the Belvedere has the finest views of the tour, looking out over the gently undulating vineyards of the Langhe bathed in a hazy azure brilliance.

L'Angelo On the main road, just before the Piazza dei Martiri, this is among the
(restaurant, best-value restaurants on the route for a full Piemontese blow-out. The
La Morra) fabulous succession of *antipasti* is followed by two home-made pasta dishes (*agnelotti* – Piemontese ravioli – is the speciality of this area) and a *secondo*. Those with smaller appetites can capitulate at any time without losing face. *Tel 0173-50192; closed Fri; Price band B/C, without wine.*

⑤ *From the main street, turn left opposite the Piazza dei Martiri, signposted for Bra, and right after 1 km for Bra and Verduno. A little way on, turn right to Verduno.*

Verduno Go straight ahead at the crossroads into the village, following the signs to the castle. Park by the Castello and have a walk, or a siesta, in the shady park to the right of the church. The view, not as splendid as La Morra's, includes the Martini plant at Cinzano.

Real Once really the royal castle of King Carlo Alberto, this hotel is still full of
Castello the atmosphere of an aristocratic country villa. There are eight very
(hotel, reasonably priced bedrooms, some beautifully frescoed. The two
Verduno) Burlotto sisters run the hotel with a welcoming informality and also serve memorable, if expensive, meals (*price band D*). *It is essential to book well in advance. Tel 0172-459125.*

Returning to the crossroads, turn right towards Bra and right again just after the cemetery at Rivalta. Leaving Barolo country, the land is planted with hazelnut groves and poplar plantations. *Follow the signs for Bra and Pollenzo.*

Pollenzo Turn left just before the traffic lights to enter the village. Turn left again at the yellow sign for the archaeological area and drive to the open space at the centre of the village. The perfectly oval set of vegetable gardens that confront you may seem of minor interest until you realize that they mark the arena of the vast amphitheatre of Roman Pollentia, whose tiers are fossilized in the form of the houses around.

Drive straight on into the square, leaving by the arch to the right, then keep on until you meet the main road to Cherasco. Turn left here. Passing under

Southern Piedmont: The Wine Lands of Alba

the railway, you see Cherasco straight ahead.

Cherasco

⑥ *Turn left at the traffic lights and right after the bridge to drive up into the town.* This stage-set town is the architectural highlight of the tour – "Le plus beau coin d'Italie", enthused Napoleon when he came here in 1806. Its grid of wide streets lined with baroque *palazzi*, its ornamental archway and the vast domed Basilica seem like a small-scale model for the Ideal City. If all this were not enough, Cherasco's name has been immortalized in Helix Pomatia Cheraschensis, a prized breed of edible snail.

Retrace your steps to **⑥** *the traffic lights and carry on straight ahead towards Bra and up the hill into the town. Turn right at the junction at the top and straight ahead at the first traffic lights. Turn right at the second set of lights and park in the Piazza XX Settembre ahead of you.*

Bra

The town's dog-eared fringes are hardly uplifting, but its *centro storico* boasts some outstanding baroque flourishes. Make for the Piazza Caduti per la Libertà, dominated by the exuberant church of Sant'Andrea with its flamboyant gilt and marbled interior.

⑦ *To avoid the busy main road back to Alba, leave the Piazza XX Settembre, continuing along the road by which you arrived (the sign to Pocapaglia is barely visible), passing a depot to the right and then the hospital. Now follow the signs for Alba.*

Pocapaglia - Alba

There is little reason to leave the main road here, though the village has its requisite 12thC crumbling castle, baroque church and plenty of narrow lanes. From here the road meanders through quiet wooded vales before passing through the orchards of Corneliano d'Alba.

⑧ *After another 4 km, turn right on to the main road which takes you back to Alba.*

ROUTE TWO: 97 KM

Follow the road which encircles the town to the rough car park at Piazza Grassi behind the Duomo. Turn here along the road signed Treiso-Neive and Barbaresco. Across the railway line the road passes up into the hills with fine views over the towers of the city. Continue following the signs for Neive.

⑨ *After 7 km turn left just after Osteria at the sign for Barbaresco.*

Barbaresco
As you approach, the baroque church at its centre is upstaged by the

Southern Piemonte

tall, square medieval tower which stands behind it. Nearby, at the Enoteca Regionale, you can try the ruby wine which has made the village famous (*closed Mon and Tue*).

Retracing your steps for 500 metres, turn left, signposted Asti. At the bottom of the hill, turn right at the T-junction towards Neive. After another 2 km, a left turn takes you along an avenue of plane trees into Neive. Pause in the small piazza of this seductive village before heading on out through its gate; then bear right and drive down the hill. At the bottom, arriving at the modern part of the village, turn left on to the main road. After a short while the road passes into the Asti Spumante wine region.

Castagnole delle Lanze   This modern town, calling itself La Città del Vino, is one of the centres for the ubiquitous sparkler. Try the sweet, still Moscato d'Asti if your palate rebels at the *spumante*.

⑩ *Turn left at the centre of the town, signed Asti-Alba, and right at the top of the hill towards Costigliole. The road now climbs through the old town of Castagnole, passing on through vineyards of the perfumed moscato grapes that go to make Asti Spumante. Just before Costigliole, take the left-hand turn for the town and climb up under the castle walls to the Piazza Re Umberto I.*

Costigliole d'Asti   The town's *enoteca*, housed in a solid, turreted castle, sells a comprehensive selection of the *spumante* wines of the area – many decidedly a cut above the sickly sparklers that you will find at home. If you overindulge, the castle's gardens have plenty of quiet, sleepy corners.

Da Guido (*restaurant, Costigliole d'Asti*)   Behind an undistinguished exterior lies one of Italy's temples to gastronomy. The culinary creations of Signora Alciati, her husband's wine list and the family's impeccable service have been universally judged faultless. Booking – and a fat wallet – are essential for this once-in-a-lifetime experience. *Tel 0141-966012; closed Sun; price band D... and beyond!*

Drive from the square along the main street through the modern part of the town and turn right at the T-junction at the end, signed Nizza.

⑪ *After about 7 km, beyond the village of Salere, take the second left turn, signed Agliano. The road climbs up out of the valley on to a ridge bordered by vineyards and fine views.*

Agliano   Arriving at the village, turn left along Via Mazzini unless you want to visit the older part which lies directly ahead; of interest is the baroque church, rebuilt after the Spanish destroyed it in 1657. Along Via Mazzini, turn sharp left, down the hill towards Montegrosso and right at the junction at the bottom.

■ Southern Piedmont: The Wine Lands of Alba

Agliano - Rocca d'Arazzo
Continue on, following signs for Montegrosso.

⑫ *At the main road just before Montegrosso, turn left and then right and go straight ahead into the village. Pass the vestiges of the castle walls to the left and follow the signposts for Rocca D'Arazzo. The road runs along a hilly ridge past a string of hamlets and villas.*

Rocca d'Arazzo
This rustic village has little else but its standard church and private castle (few of Asti's 85 castles are open to the public).

⑬ *Turn left, following the signs for Asti. A drive through idyllic countryside takes you through Azzano d'Asti to arrive at the main highway for the busy but mercifully short stretch to Asti.*

Asti
Drive straight ahead and park at the large roundabout of the old Campo del Palio. Historic Asti hides its charms behind a welter of modern developments but its centre still bears the stamp of its medieval greatness. The central Piazza Vittorio Alfieri, named after Italy's great poetic dramatist born here in 1749, lies on the other side of the modern Intendenza di Finanza building. Just behind the square, look out for the city's finest church, dedicated to Asti's patron saint San Secondo – he was decapitated where the ancient crypt now stands. From the square, stroll along the elegant Corso Alfieri for some window shopping and a glance at two splendid medieval towers, before hunting out Piemonte's largest Gothic cathedral behind the Palazzo Alfieri. If you are around on the third Sunday of September, don't miss the annual *palio* (horse race), older even than the famous race in Siena.

Reale *(hotel, Asti)*
In Piazza Alfieri, this 200-year old hotel has recently been imaginatively restored. Its large bedrooms tricked out in the very best modern Italian style are well worth the highish price. *Tel 0141-50240.*

⑭ *Leave the Campo del Palio following the signs for Alba, cross the railway line and turn right at the first traffic lights. After 400 metres turn right again (unsignposted) and cross the railway. The road runs parallel with the railway for a short while before turning south.*

Asti - Govone
For several kilometres the road remains in the flat valley, bounded on either side by fields, before rising up to the village of Antignano. The older, though unremarkable, part is tucked away behind the church to the left as you arrive. Follow the signs from here to Govone.
⑮ *At San Martino Alfieri bear left, continuing towards Govone, then take the middle of three roads at the next junction. The road now goes from the province of Asti into Alba's wine region of Roero; vineyards once more dominate the landscape.*

■

Southern Piemonte

Telamones *on the Castello façade, Govone.*

Govone   Turn left off the main road to visit the castle and village, parking in the small square ahead of you. The 16thC *castello* houses the local government offices, though its grounds are open to the public. Walk up to admire the two magnificent pairs of *telamones* on the central façade. *Turn left back on to the road and left again, following the signs for Alba.*

Val d'Aosta
THE VALLEY OF THE DORA BALTEA

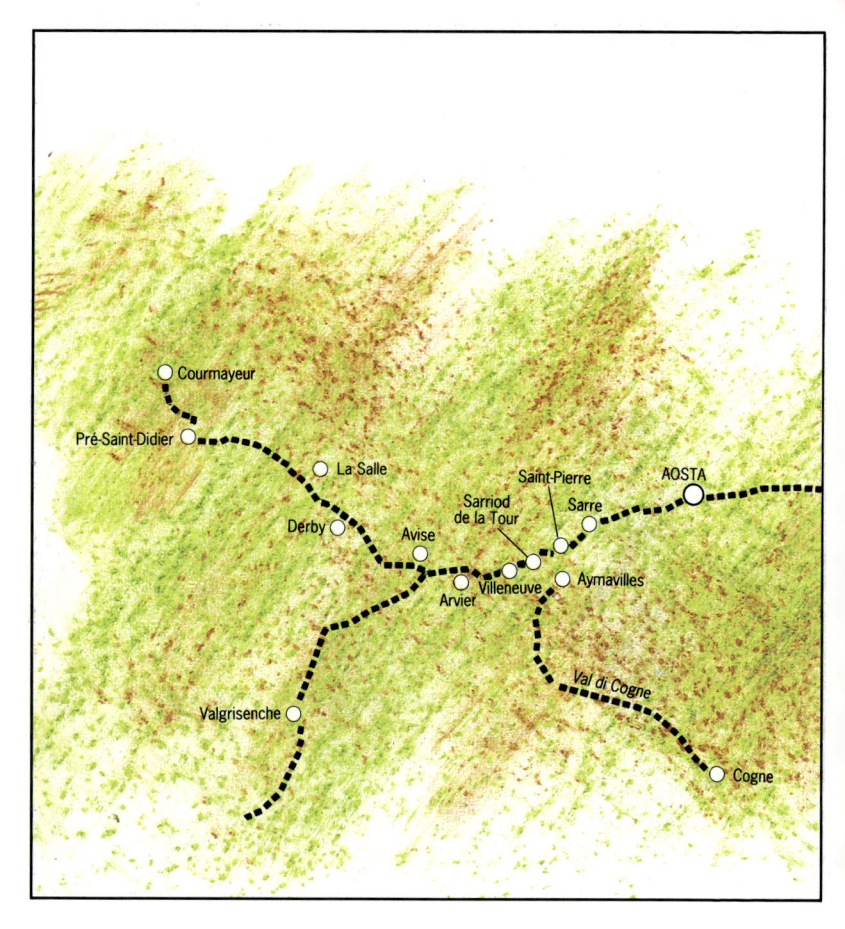

To the south of Mont Blanc lies the region of Val d'Aosta, cleft in two by the central valley of the Dora Baltea. From ancient times this Alpine corridor has been one of Italy's most important gateways to Europe, jealously guarded by a profusion of feudal fortresses strung out along its length. Napoleon, just one of the many military leaders to pass this way, described it as "a countryside of vineyards and misery". Today, it is the wealthiest region in Italy. Apart from the skiers who come here for some of the finest winter sports resorts on the sunny side of the Alps, too few stop to explore the polished villages and magnificent valleys of this mountain wonderland. Most foreigners speed past to the

Val d'Aosta

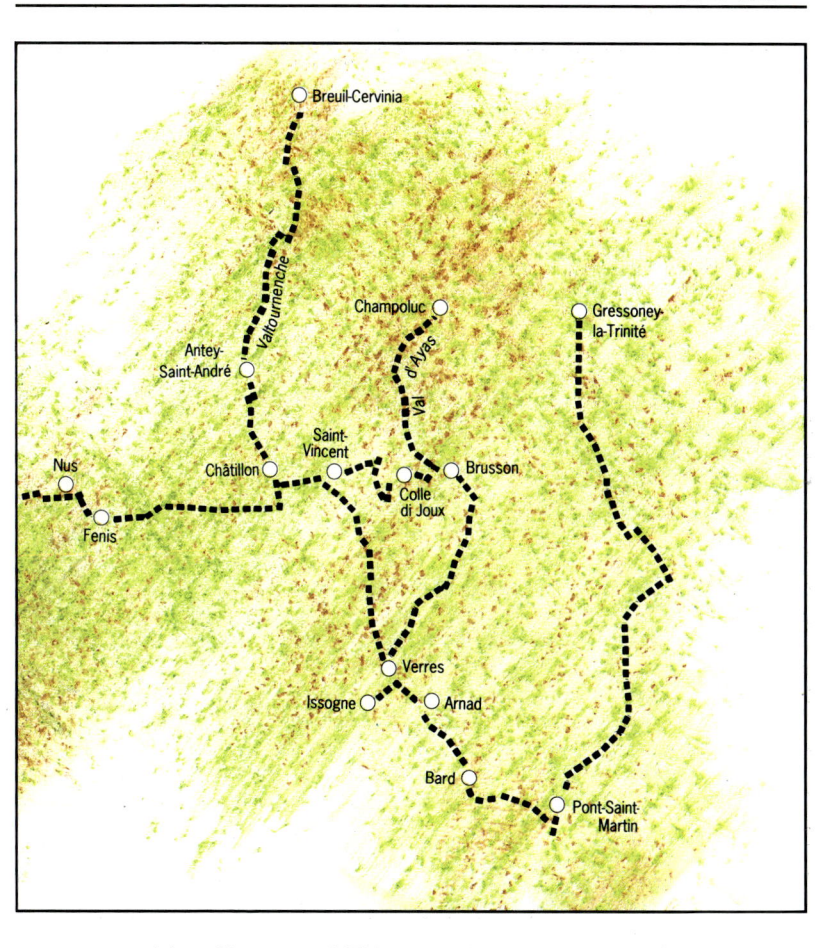

Mont Blanc tunnel. This route abandons the usual figure-of-eight and offers instead a guide for more discerning northbound travellers who would like to savour the area's many allures as they bid arrivederci to Italy. From Pont-Saint-Martin, where the valley of the Dora Baltea starts, to the regional capital of Aosta, the route follows the old SS26, a quiet alternative to the motorway. From Aosta to chic Courmayeur, the advanced construction work on the last stretch of motorway to the mouth of the Mont Blanc tunnel means that you may just have the old road to yourself. If not, there are still plenty of intriguing places to discover in peace just off the road.

Val d'Aosta: The Valley of the Dora Baltea

ROUTE: 90 KM

Pont-Saint-Martin

The historic bridge that arches high above the torrent by the main square was built by the devil in exchange for the first soul to cross it, but Saint Martin outflanked him by sending across a dog. Some may prefer to believe that it stands as one of the finest examples of Roman bridge building of the Augustan era. Either way, it carried the traffic of the main road until 1831 and makes an impressive centrepiece for this bustling town.

Valle di Gressoney (detour)

Leaving to the west of Pont-Saint-Martin, the first of the Valdostano valleys branching off the Dora Baltea ends at the foot of the majestic Monte Rosa, Europe's highest mountain after Mont Blanc. In this linguistic melting-pot, the usual Italian and French is ousted by the German Walser dialect imported by medieval Swiss immigrants.

From Pont-Saint-Martin, head along the straight road towards Bard, passing through Donnas. Ahead of you the valley is almost blocked by the rocky outcrop; behind it stands the massive fortress of Bard. Just after Donnas, stop in the layby to the right to see a notable stretch of the ancient paved Roman road, carved through solid rock.

Bard (detour through the village)

This short loop through the most spectacular village street on the tour is for drivers who know the width of their car. *Turn right for the castle. Then bear right past the Municipio-Mairie down the long narrow street, under the houses built out over the road, and pray that no one is coming the other way. At the end of the road you rejoin the main highway.* Napoleon, when he invaded Italy in 1797, chose to stay on the main road. He managed to tiptoe past the menacing ramparts using straw to muffle the noise of his army. Look back for a picture postcard view of this mighty castle, one of the oldest in the valley.

After Bard, the valley widens and the road passes boulder-strewn fields and small terraced vineyards. The vines are trained high over wooden pergolas to give them more sun and avoid damage from the winter frosts. On summer evenings you will see the *contadini* (tenant farmers) with their wives and a flask of wine tending their plots. The road crosses the valley here and for a moment you are conscious of the motorway as you pass under it.

Arnad

The old village, away from the road to the right, is celebrated for its *lardo*. This cut of fat bacon is a perfect partner for *mocetta* (lean, cured chamois meat). Search out the venerable Romanesque church of St Martin, the oldest in the region, with its boldly carved entrance.

Issogne

Turn left just before Verres, following the sign for Issogne to see one of

Val d'Aosta

The Castello at Bard.

the finest castles in the valley (*open 9-6.30; closed Mon*). More a Renaissance palace than a fortress, the vaulted ceilings around its fine interior courtyard are decorated with lively frescos depicting the daily grind of the 15thC.

Verres Returning to the main road, after a short distance you arrive at Verres. Its solid 14thC cube-shaped fortress is another outstanding example of military architecture (*open 9-6.30; closed Wed*). This, like many of the other hundred or so Valdostano castles, was built by the Challant family, feudal overlords of the valley for seven centuries.

Val d'Ayas (detour) Just north of Verres, the Val d'Ayas is one of the quieter side valleys. The road, flanked by pine and chestnut forests, meanders through a number of pristine villages. After 27 km along the valley, at Champoluc, a cable-car and chairlift take you up to Testa Grigia for one of the finest Alpine views on the tour. Back at Brusson you have a choice – either to head on to Saint-Vincent via the following, slower detour, or to arrive there by way of Verres.

Colle di Joux (detour) *From Brusson, turn left to climb through glorious hairpin bends to the high pass of Colle di Joux for grandstand views of the Gran Paradiso, before corkscrewing down to Saint-Vincent.*

Val d'Aosta: The Valley of the Dora Baltea

The Castello, Aymavilles.

Leave Verres to return to the majestic scenery of the Val D'Aosta. Passing Montjovet with its ruined 13thC castello above, the road nudges against the motorway before passing through the Montjovet Gorge up to Saint-Vincent, on the northern slope of the valley.

Saint-Vincent A haven for lounge lizards in this land made for outdoor types, Saint-Vincent is known as the 'Riviera of the Alps'. A fashionable spa resort since the 18thC with a mild climate, it also boasts one of the largest casinos in Europe. A funicular railway takes you up to the spa, Fons Salutis, with thermal cures for a whole gamut of stomach and intestinal complaints – helpful if you overindulge in the cheesy Valdostano diet.

Châtillon Drive through the narrow streets in the centre of Châtillon to see the Roman bridge. Then follow the signs to Valtournenche for a detour to the region's most impressive valley. The town's castle, destroyed first by the French and then by earthquake and twice restored, stands guard at the mouth of the valley.

Val d'Aosta

Valtour-   A fast 8 km of road takes you up to the small resort of Antey-Saint-
nenche   André for a magnificent view of Monte Cervino, Italy's name for The
(detour)   Matterhorn. If you have time, drive another 20 km to the ski resort of
Breuil-Cervinia for an unforgettable cable-car trip to within 1,000
metres of the Matterhorn's summit. Returning to Châtillon, you will see
Castello d'Ussel across the valley.

Fenis   At Chambave, where the valley widens out, take the left turn to Fenis.
Crossing the river, the small road passes through several unassuming
villages to arrive at Fenis. Built in 1340, this fairy-tale castle is a profusion
of small towers and turrets surrounded by a pentagonal wall, topped by
swallow-tail battlements. Its magnificent courtyard is ringed by wooden
balustraded galleries, decorated with frescoes of saints, sages and old
French proverbs *(open 9-6.30; closed Tue)*. *From Fenis, continue on for
another kilometre to get back to the road.*

Nus - Aosta   Passing Nus, the road is guarded to the right by its castle, while to the
left rise the peaks of Grand Roise and Monte Emilius. The motorway
ends shortly before Aosta, bringing a mass of traffic on to the old road.
The construction of a new stretch of motorway is well under way –
when it is finished you will have the last stretch to yourself.

Aosta   Follow the signs for *centro*. Once through the ugly industrial fringes that
spoil the approach, you find yourself in one of Italy's most stunningly-set
cities. This Rome of the Alps, at the crossroads to the passes of Mont
Blanc and the Great St Bernard, was founded in 25 BC as a Roman
bridgehead to Gaul. Much of its original street plan remains, as do its
walls strung with some 20 towers. Inside, see the ruins of the forum and
a 22-metre-high section of the Roman theatre. Passing through the
Porta Pretoria, you arrive in the main Via Sant'Anselmo, named after
the English Archbishop, born here in 1033. Aosta is a good place to
break the journey – the tourist office in Piazza E Chanou *(tel 0165-
35655)* has details of hotels.

Da Nando   This is an excellent place to try *cucina Valdostana*. As an *antipasto*, try
(restaurant,   perfumed *lardo di Arnad* with *mocetta* followed by crêpes or *polenta alla*
Aosta)   *valdostana*, both dishes rich in the *fontina* cheese of the area. In Via Tillier,
just past the main square. *Tel 0165-44455; closed Thur; price band B.*

The road outside Aosta splits as some of the traffic heads north up to
the Great St Bernard pass. Our route, however, carries on along the
Dora Baltea valley towards Courmayeur.

Aymavilles   At Sarre, turn left at the sign to Cogne and drive up to the eccentric
(detour)   building at Aymavilles which cannot decide whether it is a castle or a
villa. Between the towers of a 12thC castle, a member of the ruling

67

Val d'Aosta: The Valley of the Dora Baltea

Challant family decided to build an 18thC palace – you decide if it is bravely innovative or just silly.

Val di Cogne
(detour)

From Aymavilles, carry on up following the signs to Cogne. This wild and beautiful valley marks the edge of the Gran Paradiso National Park. Once the hunting grounds of the Kings of Savoy, it is now a haven for walkers. Couch potatoes, however, will have to be content with the sweeping views from the attractive village of Cogne. Walking itineraries are available at most of the tourist offices, but watch out for the small print, such as 'Warning: it is impossible to get through the Planaval Pass without using ice-axe, crampons and rope'.

Sarre

Back on the main road you pass the stodgy Castello di Sarre, a 13thC castle heavily rebuilt in the 18thC. Vittorio Emanuele II, the first king of unified Italy, bought it by mistake when his agent confused it with the castle of Aymavilles across the river. Making the best of a bad job, he decorated the walls of the interior with an enormous collection of 3,000 pairs of ibex and chamois antlers. There is also an exhibition of royal memorabilia, photographs and family trees (*open 10-12, 2.30-4.30; closed Tue*).

Saint-Pierre

The heavily restored 11thC *castello*, perched high above, now houses a natural history museum (*open 9-6.30*).

Castello Sarriod de la Tour

Under the shadow of St Pierre, below the road to the left, stands this pleasantly intimate castle, built in 1480. It is worth visiting to see the magnificent woodcarving in the great hall (*open 9-6.30; closed Mon*). *From Saint-Pierre head on to Villeneuve.*

Villeneuve

Turn left off the main road to drive through this benign village, perhaps stopping for a drink at one of the tiny bars by the strikingly frescoed church.

Arvier

The narrow street, passageways and gnarled stone houses here conjure up a picture of village life before the onslaught of the 20thC. It also produces an excellent, velvety red wine, Enfer d'Arvier – try some at the Enoteca Caffè du Bourg.

Valgrisenche
(detour)

From here you can take a break from the main road to drive into the quiet Valgrisenche, guarded by the castle of Montmayeur. At the end of the valley lies the high tarn of Lago Beauregard.

Passing Avise, with its brace of hillside castles, you enter the gorge of Pierre Taillée and cross the river. Shortly afterwards Europe's highest mountain comes into sight – the Italians call it Monte Bianco. A few kilometres further on, across the river you can see the village of Derby,

The Castello, Saint-Pierre.

a group of fortified houses huddled around a Gothic church.

La Salle Here the country around is dominated by a lean 13thC tower. Pause in the village to see the unusual collection of sculptures in the church, including fine examples of 15thC and 16thC Flemish work.

Pre-Saint-Didier This small spa town stands at an important crossroads in the valley – the road to the west leads over the Alps by way of The Little St Bernard Pass *(only open June-Oct)*. If too much good living during your driving through Italy has brought you out in spots, the waters here are said to be particularly effective for skin complaints.

Courmayeur The Val d'Aosta's major resort, at the very foot of Mont Blanc, is a Mecca for skiers. As a summer stop it has one star attraction – the breathtaking cable-car ride which takes you from the medieval village of La Palud over the top of the mountains, passing Mont Blanc, to Chamonix in France. Make sure you have your passport with you. Though hardly cheap, it is the least that you can award yourself before the claustrophic drive through the smoggy tunnel.

Liguria
INLAND FROM THE WESTERN RIVIERA

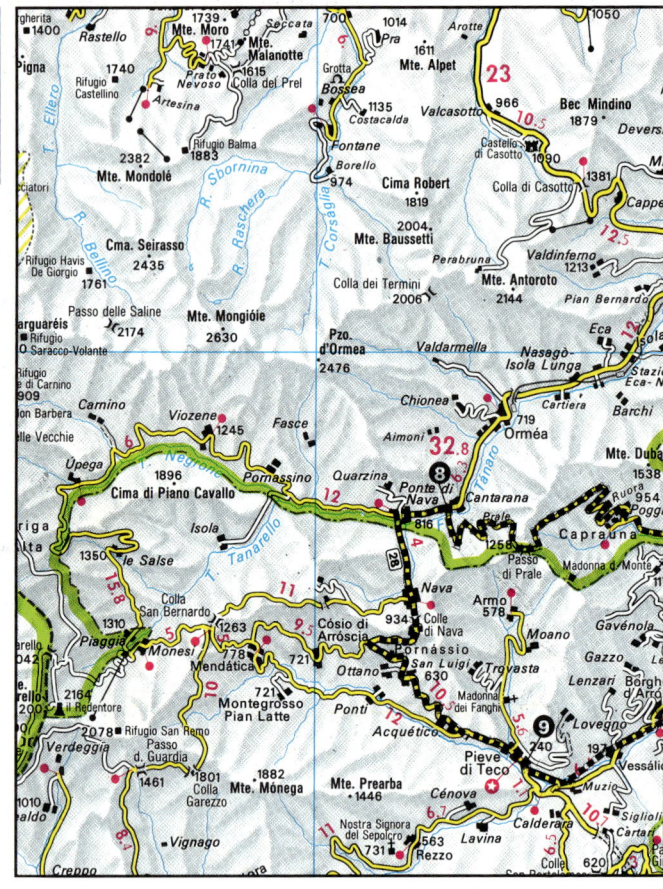

Italy's stretch of the Riviera hardly offers the glamour of its French neighbour, but some may prefer its honest vulgarity to the airs and graces of the Côte d'Azur. Inland, though, it can happily compete with its grand relation. This tour, centred in medieval Albenga, only briefly skirts the coast before heading up ruggedly beautiful valleys into the Maritime Alps. The first loop visits gnarled old villages unsullied by tourism, and a series of caves among whose glistening grottoes are traces of human life dating back 12,000 years. The second route winds through wilder, more isolated country, over high passes, taking in one of Liguria's finest panoramas and some strange goings-on in Alto.

Liguria

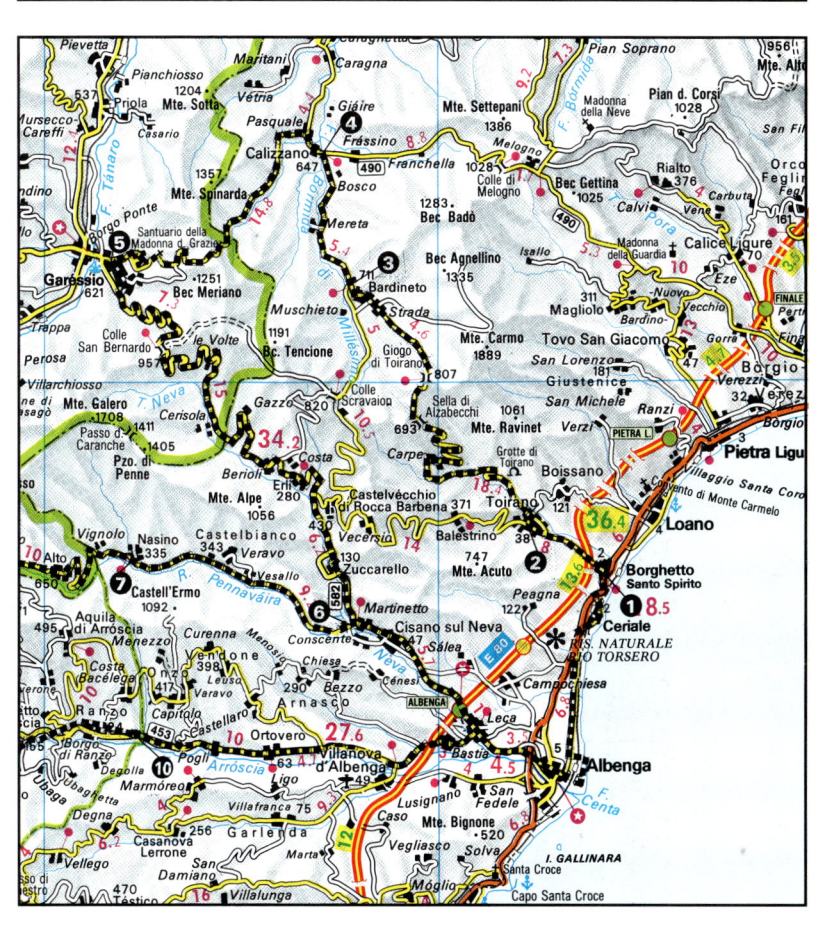

Although the coast has little else other than pizzerie and fast food restaurants, inland there are plenty of culinary treats. Basil (here quite different in flavour to anywhere else), garlic and pine nuts are pounded with Liguria's celebrated olive oil to make the finest pesto in the world. Walnuts, too, are used to make memorable pasta dishes, while the mild climate produces vegetables fit for a harvest festival. For a spuntino (a snack), try a freshly-baked slice of focaccia (a doughy pizza, often topped with a thick layer of sliced onions). For those who demur at the frisky beach life at Albenga, there are a number of pleasant, unpretentious hotels listed along the route.

Liguria: Inland from the Western Riviera

ROUTE ONE: 84 KM

Albenga

The old walled town of Albenga is a jewel set uncomfortably in a modern seaside city. Centuries before the Romans came here, it was home to the Ingaunian tribes whose memory lives on in the name Liguria. The present *centro storico* dates back to medieval times but still follows the original Roman street plan. At its centre, standing shoulder to shoulder, are the survivors of the fifty impregnable towers that jostled for space in the bellicose days of the Trecento, when rival Guelph and Ghibelline families fought it out for Pope or Emperor. In their shadow meekly sits the Duomo, Romanesque to just below the roof. A controversial restoration in the 1960s hacked its stuccoed walls back to the medieval stone while leaving the baroque frescos on the roof. The squat 5thC baptistery, Liguria's earliest Christian monument, sits apart with its peculiar ten-sided exterior and octagonal interior.

With so much to see and enjoy, it is worth staying here overnight. There are plenty of hotels in the modern part of the town, catering mainly for the beach brigade. Eating here is more of a problem. While Ligurian food is excellent, the choice of restaurants in Albenga is not. The best bet is to hunt out one of the half-dozen Neapolitan-run *pizzerie*. It is hardly true Ligurian fare but there are plenty of opportunities to try the best *cucina regionale* along the route.

Albenga - Ceriale

From the main Piazza del Popolo just outside the pedestrian centro storico, *follow the signpost for Stazione FS along the tree-lined avenue. Keep straight on at the traffic lights and turn left at the seafront.* The short strip of sandy beach, as with most beaches in Italy, is carved up into regimented rows of deckchairs and umbrellas and is busy in the high summer – quiet stretches of the coast are few and far between – but after a day on the road, there is nothing quite like being beside the seaside.

At the end of the promenade, turn back under the railway line and right on to the coastal road to Ceriale. Though hardly exciting - the railway obscures the sea view - this stretch avoids the busy main road.

Ceriale

Turn right on to the main SS1, but after only 400 metres take the first right turn to Ceriale's attractive esplanade. The circular tower you pass was meant to guard against Saracen raiders but, when they did invade in 1637, they marched straight past it and carted off the inhabitants to Algeria as slaves.

Carry on to rejoin the main SS1, turning right to Borghetto Santo Spirito. This historic road is the ancient Via Julia Augusta opened in 13 BC. Before then the only route to Rome from Liguria was by sea.

Liguria

The Duomo, Albenga.

Borghetto Santo Spirito

① *Turn left at the sign for Toirano.* The narrow arched streets of the old centro storico, which you pass to the left, have been almost throttled by the modern town but it is still the hub of daily life. Several bakeries sell excellent *focaccia*, here also stuffed with soft local cheese.

Leave heading for Toirano. The plain is silvered with olive groves. Although Ligurian olive oil is celebrated by gourmets as some of the

Liguria: Inland from the Western Riviera

Inside the medieval borgo, Toirano.

best in the world, the olive tree only arrived here in the 12thC.

Toirano

The craggy peaks of the Maritime Alps are the background to this medieval *borgo* which stands securely at the confluence of two rivers. Turn right off the main road and park outside – its enchanting and cobbled central main street is so narrow that only the bravest driver would risk the journey. Note the robustly carved columns which support the porticos, many dating back to Roman times. Half-way along, the small Museo del Civiltà Contadino has an intriguing display of ancient olive presses and farming equipment.

② *Returning to the main road, continue inland and bear right. Now follow the signs for Calizzano.*

Grotte di Toirano *(detour)*

Over 12,000 years ago, these beautiful stalactite-festooned caves were home to Europe's ancestors. The primitive cavemen have left behind hand- and footprints and evidence of strange mystical ceremonies – perhaps designed to ward off the prehistoric bears whose bones have been found in nearby caves. An hour-and-a-half tour takes you through some of the finest caverns. Turn right at the sign just after Toirano village to make this short detour.

The road now enters the barren, rocky valley of the Barescione and begins to snake its way up to the pass of Giogo di Toirano. Stop half-way up at the Bar Royal Panorama for a regal view of the hills sweeping

Liguria

down to the sea. From here the climb is gentler, as the road passes into thickets of acacia and beech. After the pass the road drops down to Bardineto.

Bardineto Apart from the frescos in its 11thC church, there is little to stop for in this unmemorable village. Yellow signs point to trenches dug during the war against Napoleon, though all that remain are a few grassy banks.

③ *After the village, keep on the road for Calizzano.*

Ristorante ai Cacciatori *(restaurant, Mereta)* On the left, just before the village of Mereta, this restaurant blends so well with the surrounding buildings that it is easy to miss. Local ingredients are the cornerstone of the cooking here, with such dishes as salad of local *toma* cheese and walnuts, and tagliatelle with *ortica* (nettles). *Tel 019-790243; closed Mon; price band B.*

Calizzano ④ *Turn left over the bridge to the Piazza San Rocco.* Wild mushrooms provide the reason to stop here. Several shops are dedicated to them and daily licences are available if you fancy your chances at hunting them for yourself. *From the square, continue up the narrow street ahead, over a small bridge and bear left, now following the signs for Garessio.*

Villa Elia *(hotel, Calizzano)* Set away to the right, this is a quiet, friendly and reasonably-priced *albergo*, in a bushy garden. *Tel 019-79633.*

The road now makes its way out of the valley, passing small fields and groves of walnut planted between the woods which clothe the hills up to the Colle Quazzo. Arriving at the pass, you can admire the scenery from the roadside bar. Heading back down into the Val Tanaro, patches of the forest have been planted with a breed of sweet chestnut (*castagna garessina*) which takes its name from the next town.

Santuario di Valsorda The vast, ungainly cupola that quite unexpectedly demands your attention is the Santuario di Valsorda, an anachronistic pile that scores few architectural points. It was started in 1901 to house a miracle-working picture of the Madonna. Today, 90 years later, the work of decorating the enormous blank interior has only just begun. The priest, however, is every bit as optimistic as his predecessors: "they call it the Santuario Bianco", he says, "but one day I'll find our Michelangelo."

Continue on down through orchards to Garessio, passing the ruined Hotel Miramonti, fabled during its short life in the 1930s as one of Europe's most luxurious hotels, only to end its life as a Nazi concentration camp for Slav soldiers. In 1991, just as the building was set to reopen as a hotel, it was destroyed by fire.

Liguria: Inland from the Western Riviera

The main street, Zuccarello.

Garessio
⑤ *Turn left at the crossroads and bear left at the traffic lights to pass through Borgo Poggiolo and arrive at the oldest quarter, the Borgo Antico, of this small town in a dramatic mountain setting. This is the most atmospheric of the three time-worn villages that go to make the town. From here, bear right back on to the main road, signposted for Albenga.*

Colle San Bernardo
This 1,000-metre pass has commanding views northwards over Garessio to the high peaks of the Maritime Alps. In the crystal clear light of the early morning you can see for over 100 km. Later, the mountains are bathed in an intoxicating purple hue. This is excellent walking country – a track takes you from here to the top of Monte Galero, 3½ hrs away by foot.

From here onwards the road drops to the coast, passing through a string of unstarched hamlets circled by terraces of orchards and olive groves.

Zuccarello
The most beautiful village on this route, a single medieval porticoed street flanked by alleyways that seem little changed since the *borgo* was built. Leaving the main road, you can drive straight through the centre, but it is worth stopping to explore on foot. Also search out the Roman footbridge which still spans the river.

Liguria

La Cittadella
(restaurant, Zuccarello)

This classy restaurant specializes in seafood, cooked with aromatic herbs to give it a distinctly Ligurian flavour. *Booking essential; tel 0182-79056; closed Mon; price band D.*

Returning to the main road, continue on in the direction of Albenga. The straight road follows the river, the valley widening out as you approach Albenga.

Cisano sul Neva

⑥ *Passing the bridge at Martinetto, take the second right turn, signposted* centro, *and park just outside the 16thC* borgo *to wander through its lanes and admire the old church.*

The relatively short return to Albenga has few highspots; *if you want to drive the second route without revisiting Albenga, return to the bridge at Martinetto* ⑥.

ROUTE TWO: 61 KM

Return to Martinetto ⑥ *from Albenga, following the signposts for Garessio and turn left over the stone bridge, signposted Nasino.*

Martinetto - Nasino

Passing the rough-hewn castle of Conoscente, the road enters the forgotten valley of the Pennavaira. Around the hamlets of Castelbianco sage, rosemary, and lavender are among the produce of the small roadside market gardens.

Nasino

After passing the slender, single-arched Roman bridge and the waterwheel of the smithy opposite, you see the village around the next corner.

Trattoria Costa
(restaurant, Nasino)

Signora Costa runs her trattoria with matronly efficiency. Her *gnocchi* (the lightest potato and spinach dumplings) with *pesto* or walnut *sugo* (sauce) would put many a grand restaurant to shame, while the *coniglio in umido* (rabbit slowly cooked in herbs and wine) is a delight. She also sells superb olive oil and local *grappa. Tel 0182-77002; price band A/B.*

⑦ *Keep on the main road, bearing left towards Alto, to pass under the village. Briefly leaving Liguria, the road begins a serious climb through sharp bends.*

Alto

Stop in the small square below the abandoned Castello Cepollini. The origins of this mysterious village go back to the dawn of history. In the nearby `Arma du Cupà' cave, archaeologists have found evidence of ritual human slaughter where heads were cut vertically in half. Another cave contains a one-metre high rock phallus. Strange things still go on here, although of a less ghoulish cast; if you are around at 5 pm on the seventh day of the month you will hear the sound of a bell from one of

Liguria: Inland from the Western Riviera

Arroscia valley.

the houses above the square calling you to witness the punctual visits of the Madonna to one of the ladies of the village. Few of the villagers have shared the miraculous vision but word has spread and the house is rapidly becoming a place of pilgrimage.

Caprauna After a tunnel and a couple of bends you arrive at Caprauna, a score of houses and hamlets scattered across chestnut-clad slopes. *Continue along the main road as it zigzags up the hillside.* Above the village there are spectacular views across the mountains and back down through a rocky gorge to Castello Cepollini. The steep grassy slopes were once cultivated; now only the stone walls of the terraces remain.

Colle Caprauna Reaching the brow of the pass, stop to catch your breath in front of the finest view on the tour – mountain cliffs rising up over the valley of the Tanaro and the distant peaks of Monte Mongioie and Pizzo d'Ormea. The road now drops steeply and, before you know it, you are down in the valley.

Tanaro Valley ⑧ *Crossing the bridge at the bottom, turn left along the road by the river.* The stark limestone cliffs that you saw from the top of the pass now tower above you.

San Carlo (hotel, Ponte di Nava) An ordinary, modern hotel with rather spartan furnishing. The majestic surroundings of this valley, however, make it an appealing place to stay. *Tel 0174-391917.*

Liguria

Da Beppe Cagna
(restaurant, Ponte di Nava)

In this small restaurant overlooking the river, you will eat well for surprisingly little. The secret of her delicious menu, confides Signora Cagna, is in the finest raw materials. *On the left of the main street; tel 0174-391924; closed Wed; price band B.*

Bear left to cross the bridge and follow the signs for Imperia. Leaving Ponte di Nava, the route returns to Liguria. Another 4 km takes you to the Colle di Nava on the brink of the wide, wooded Arroscia valley. From here the road weaves down the steep mountainside, passing the vineyards of Pornassio to arrive at the terraced olive groves around Pieve di Teco.

Pieve di Teco

The grand dome of the Oratory of San Giovanni Battista gives the small town a well-deserved appearance of opulence even before you arrive. From its beginnings as a staging post on the Salt Road from the Ligurian coast to Piemonte, it became an important centre for shoemakers. In the porticoed central street where they used to tap away, now only one remains. Judging, though, from the elegant shops which have stepped into their shoes, the town remains as prosperous as ever.

Albergo dell'Angelo
(restaurant, Pieve)

A lovely old hotel founded, as the plaque over the front door proclaims, in Napoleonic times. Some things, including the beautiful frescoed dining-room and the waterworks, haven't changed. But its 1960s-style rooms bring to mind a seaside boarding house. Still, the aged couple and their nephew who run it are very charming – as are the prices. *Tel 0183-36240.*

⑨ *Turn left to Albenga just after the town along the new road. Eventually this highway, yet to be marked on the map, will reach the whole way to Albenga, bypassing the villages on the old route. Although making map-reading more difficult, it will leave the narrow old streets as traffic-free backwaters to be discovered by more imaginative tourists.*

Borghetto d'Arroscia

Turn off here to drive through this timeless *borgo*, then carry on along the old road, passing the mellow Romanesque church of San Pantaleo, the oldest in the valley.

Ranzo

Pause to admire the eye-catching fresco above the porchway of the church. It was painted by the village's own Renaissance master Pietro Guido, who was responsible for decorating many other churches in the valley.

⑩ *Returning to the main road, head back to the plain through peach orchards and vineyards and on to the market gardens of Ponterotto. Once through Ortovero, the outskirts of Albenga begin.*

Emilia
FROM THE PADANA TO THE PIACENTINE HILLS

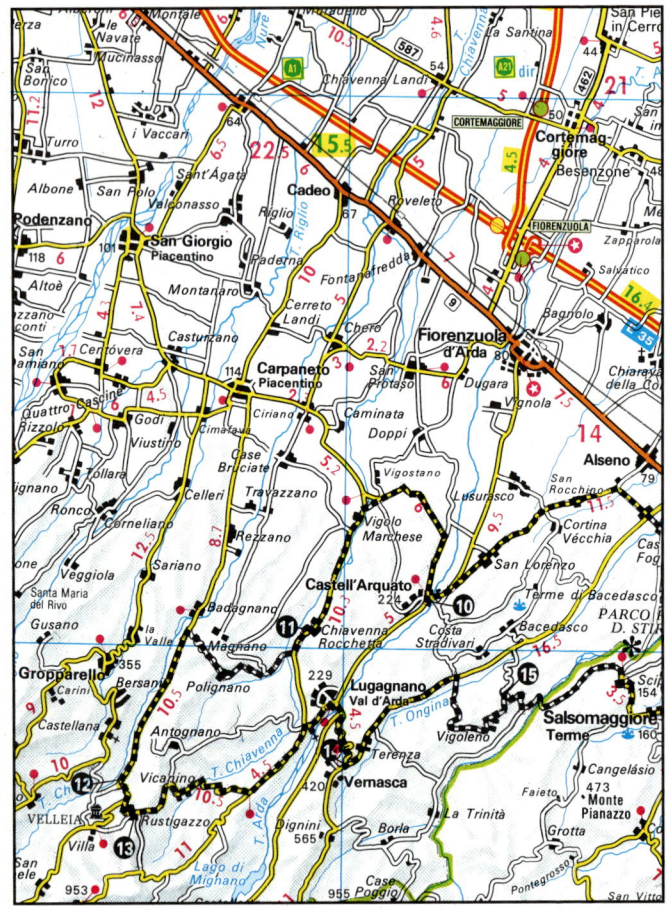

The fine silts of the broad flatlands of the Po, intensively cultivated since Roman times, provide Italy's richest farm land. In the wintry fogs that blight the plain, the landscape is more Dutch than Italian, but in the clear light of summer, the horizon broken by lines of Lombardy poplars, it is assuredly the Italian Padana. Many tourists see it only from the straight and seemingly endless Autostrada del Sole, little realizing its discreet charms.

Landscape apart, the stretches of the Po valley explored in this tour produce two of Italy's great culinary treasures, Parma ham and Parmesan cheese, and the cooking of this bountiful land is amongst the richest in the country.

The tour is centred on Fidenza, one of the more unassuming of the wealthy

Emilia

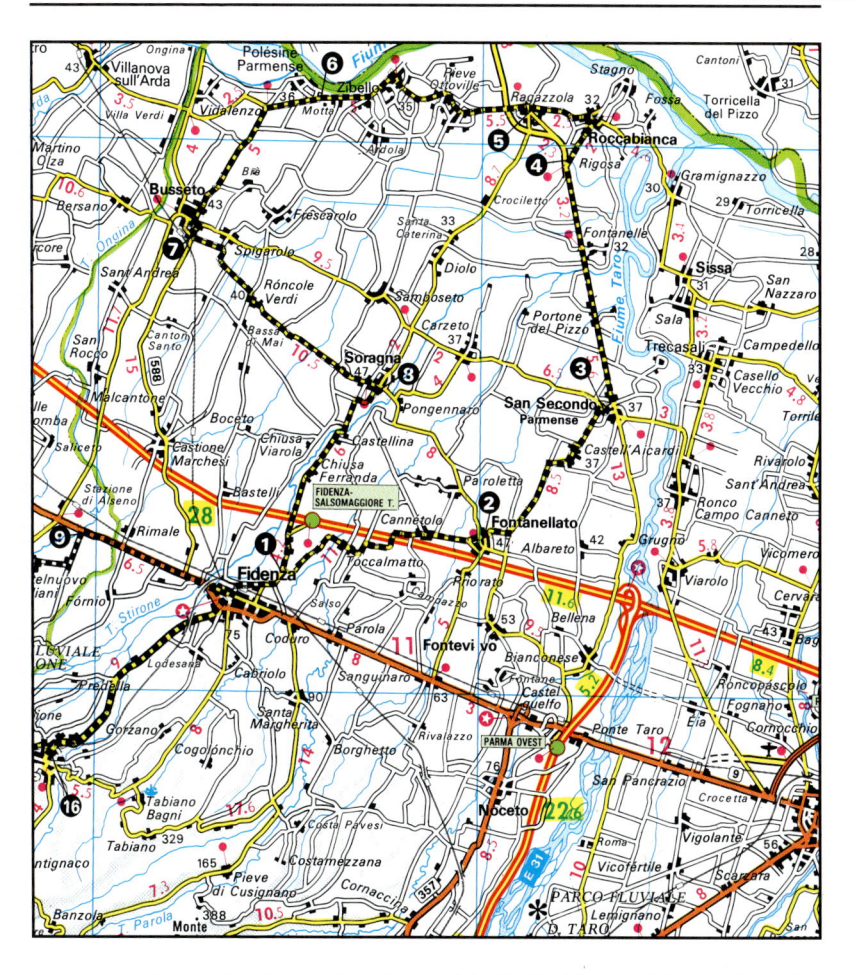

towns standing astride the ancient Roman Via Emilia (the road from which the region takes its name). The first loop charts a course through the grid of long, straight byways that divide up the plain, taking in a handful of elegant castles, the birthplace of Verdi and miles of quintessential Padana countryside where *prosciutto crudo* (cured raw ham) and *parmigiano reggiano* are made. The second, in contrast, is a drive through the gentle green valleys of the Colli Piacentini, the Piacentine Hills that herald the high Apennines. Attractions include a clutch of outstanding medieval towns, Roman ruins and that most Italian of places, a thriving spa town.

Emelia: From the Padana to the Piacentine Hills

ROUTE ONE: 108 KM

Fidenza

This small town is eclipsed by its grander neighbours, Parma and Piacenza. Extensively rebuilt in the wake of wartime bombing, it is, nevertheless, a friendly place that makes a convenient centre for the tour. The two things to see are the splendid 12thC *duomo* and the making of Parmesan cheese. For the latter drop by at the Cooperativa Agrinascente in Via Carducci at around 9 am and ask to see the cheese-makers transform the rich milk of the plains into *parmigiano reggiano* – it takes around 550 litres for each form. The hotels here are rather characterless, though the Due Spade (*tel 0524-523389*) and the Astoria (*tel 0524-524314*) in the centre of town have rooms at middle-range prices.

Trattoria Al Duomo
(restaurant, Fidenza)

Standing in the shadow of the Duomo, this old-fashioned trattoria serves the finest home-made pasta and lovingly prepared main courses. After an excellent pudding, have a generous hunk of young Parmesan cheese. Wine here is drunk, as was once common here, out of terra-cotta bowls. *Tel 0524-524268; closed Mon; price band B.*

Leave on one of the roads which pass under the railway on the northern side of the town, signposted for Soragna or the autostrada. *Continue, following signs for the* autostrada.

① After the Api petrol station, turn right on to the small road for Fontanellato. The pattern of the fields dates back to Roman times. Retired legionaries, given a plot of land as a pension, colonized vast stretches of the Padana. Passing through Toccalmatto, keep taking the signs for Fontanellato. The road crosses over the motorway and runs through the village of Cannetolo.

Fontanellato

A surprise awaits you in the centre of this seemingly ordinary Padana village – in place of the usual piazza stands a magnificent castle encircled by a carp-filled moat. Inside, the Castello di San Vitale boasts richly frescoed chambers, some painted by the area's very own Late Renaissance master, Parmigianino (*closed Mon*).

② Retrace your steps from the square and turn right following signposts for San Secondo. The large, four-square farm buildings that dot the endless plain are solid symbols of the sensible affluence of these rich farmlands – no frills, no unnecessary displays of prestige.

San Secondo

As the road enters the town keep on straight ahead, bearing off the main road. Here you pass another noble castle now housing local council offices. You are welcome to peer inside on any weekday morning. *③ Continue on through the village, turning right at the mini-roundabout, and follow the signs for Roccabianca and Zibello.* The road now runs as straight as an arrow.

④ After about 9 km, turn right to Roccabianca along a ceremonial tree-lined avenue.

Roccabianca The tiny arcaded square of this typical Po village is flanked by another elegant castle, this time used to house a bank. *Leave, following signposts for Busseto.*

From here the road runs along a dyke that marks the edge of the flood defences of the nearby Po — all that is missing are a few Dutch windmills. The river itself, broad and idling, is difficult to glimpse across the fields to the right.

⑤ Passing Ragazzola, bear right following the signposts for Cremona, then turn left at the main road and right towards Zibello. After a few kilometres, turn right again to arrive in Zibello.

Zibello This unprepossessing town is the centre for *culatello* (a cured ham), finer even than the best *prosciutto*, made from tender rump matured for at least a year in the bladder of the pig. You can buy some for a picnic at the Boutique della Carne in the central Piazza Garibaldi, or try it at the Ristorante La Buca in Via Ghizzi.

Leave, following signs for Polesine to rejoin the main road.

The banks of the Po *(detour)* *⑥ Turn off the road at the signpost to the village of Polesine to take this short detour for a rather unexciting glimpse of the Po. Drive through to the end of the village, then turn right and left following the signs for the ristorante Cavallino Bianco. A few metres on from the restaurant, a short track leads to the bank of the broad, sluggish river. Retrace your path back to the main road.*

If you resist the temptation to take the detour, turn left at the sign for Busseto just past Polesine.

Busseto Arriving in the town, bear right towards Piacenza and park at the start of the main Via Roma. This genteel place is unmistakably the town of Verdi. The central Piazza Verdi is overshadowed by his paternal statue and flanked by the grand Teatro Verdi. Down the main street stands the house where the great composer lived, now the Verdi Museum — the elderly custodian gives an enthusiastic guided tour, embroidered with sign language for the foreign visitor. The oddest sight is the Bottega Storica Verdiana, next to the museum, whose entrance is jammed with Verdi memorabilia. It must be the only grocery store in the world with a

Emelia: From the Padana to the Piacentine Hills

visitors' book. Other shops sell Verdi aprons and Verdi beer mats, all displayed in the best possible taste – there is nothing vulgar about Busseto.

I Due Foscari
(hotel, Busseto)

This smart hotel in a Venetian style *palazzo* overlooking Verdi's statue makes a romantic and not over-pricey overnight stop. *Tel 0524-92337.*

Ristorante Pizzeria Teatro
(restaurant, Busseto)

A no-frills establishment with filling *cucina Parmigiana*, this is a convenient place for a quick lunch – a plate of *culatello* (always served with butter) or a substantial pizza. *Price band B.*

Retrace your steps from the car park for 100 metres, then turn right, taking the signs for Fidenza and Roncole.

⑦ Out of the town, turn left just before a level crossing, for Roncole.

Roncole Verdi

As you arrive bear left at the yellow sign for Casa Verdi. This is the small village where Verdi was born in 1813. At the church of San Michele a plaque above the font commemorates his baptism. A few metres further on the simple Casa Verdi has become another museum. For the less Verdi-minded the nearby shop sells excellent Parma hams and cheeses. Head on from here for another 5 km to Soragna.

Soragna

⑧ *Follow the yellow signs on the right to Rocca Santuaria.* The ancient castle was converted into a stately palace in the 18thC – the richly furnished and frescoed rooms open to the public are well worth a visit *(closed Mon, Tue). Leave on the road for Fidenza directly opposite the castle entrance. Passing through a narrow archway and along a straight road, turn right at the cemetery. Then turn left, to drive back over the motorway to Fidenza.*

Parma

Parma, one of the finest cities in Italy, lies 23 km to the east of Fidenza along the fast Via Emilia. Do not try to drive into the centre but park outside and take a bus. Even better, abandon your car for the day and make the journey by train from Fidenza. See the magnificent Duomo, an outstanding example of Italian Romanesque, and the candy pink marble baptistery. The Palazzo della Pilotta houses a fine collection of Renaissance masterpieces, most notably works by the city's own sons, Correggio and Parmigianino. Best of all, just stroll through the gracious streets, try one of the many superb restaurants and indulge in some window shopping – you will soon understand why many consider Parma to be one of the most civilized cities in Europe.

Emilia

Typical marketplace of the region.

ROUTE TWO: 87 KM

Leave on the main Via Emilia heading westwards towards Piacenza. After roughly 4 km pass the impressive gateway to your left that leads through a tree-lined avenue to the castle of Fontevivo.

⑨ *Turn left immediately afterwards on the small road to Castelnuovo Fogliani and leave the racing traffic behind.*

Castelnuovo Fogliani This handsome village, on the first hummock to break the flatness of the Padana, is dominated by a sturdy castle. *In the centre turn right. After another 500 metres, cross a main road following signposts for Castell'Arquato.* The road begins to undulate as it edges away from the plain towards the Colli Piacentini, the foothills of the Apennines. Finally Castell'Arquato rises ahead of you on a steep slope crowned by the romantic ruins of its citadel.

Castell' Arquato *Entering the town, cross the bridge. You can drive up to the top when it is not too busy, otherwise leave your car at the foot of the hill and walk.* This defensively sited town started life as a Roman garrison guarding the Arda Valley. It reached its zenith in late medieval times under the dominion of a succession of famous military *condottieri* (mercenaries), including the great Colleoni, immortalized in Verrocchio's famous equestrian statue in Venice. The *rocca* at the top is more of a self-contained village than a castle and is built with great panache. Note the swallow-tail Guelph crenellations that decorate the Palazzo Pretoria,

85

Emelia: From the Padana to the Piacentine Hills

evidence of its Papal allegiances during the feuds of the 13thC (the anti-Pope brigade – the Ghibellines – always built square battlements). Also visit the mellow Romanesque church for its austere interior and the enormous 8thC font in the far corner.

This attractive town has a number of good restaurants – Da Franco (*price band B/C*) is an amenable choice up by the castle. Down at the bottom, the Leon d'Oro (*price band B*) serves excellent pasta and salumi with a broad selection of local wines.

The soil of the Colli Piacentini produces a wine that is often *frizzante* and slightly sweet, ideal company for the rich local food. *Gutturnio* is a typical example – buy some at the local *enoteca* half-way up the hill.

⑩ *Return to the traffic lights and turn left to follow the River Arda. After about 6 km turn left to Vigolo Marchese.*

Vigolo Marchese

This matter-of-fact village has a gem of an 11thC church that lies to the right of the road. The font inside its little circular baptistery is carved from an ancient Roman capital.
Keep on the same road, following the valley of the Chiavenna. Passing a ramshackle watermill on the left, cross the river and drive past strips of fields marked off by drainage ditches. On the other side of the valley, vineyards take up any spare space on the wooded slopes.

Pass through Chiavenna Rocchetta.

⑪ *After 1 km turn right in front of the bar. The road crosses two small bridges. Bear left past a church and carry on through Prato Ottesola and Polignano. The road now climbs over the hill into the next valley. Passing through the hamlet of Tabiano - you will see the aeroplane poised in flight over the pizzeria car park - turn left on to the main road running along the valley, following the signs for Velleia.*

⑫ *After 7 km turn left out of the valley and up to the village itself.*

Velleia

In this lonely spot lie the ruins of the small but affluent Roman town of Velleia, built with money donated by the Emperor Trajan. Apart from the foundations of the forum, temple and amphitheatre, little else remains but, like so many of the little-visited Roman sites that dot Italy, it is an atmospheric spot. You will find the rather hidden entrance to the ruins just after the Antica Locanda restaurant.

⑬ *Carry on up the hill and turn left. Now take the signs for Lugagnano. Leaving the valley of the Chero, the road crosses another valley before dropping back into the Val d'Arda.*

Emilia

Lugagnano The pretty valley here is marred by the large chemical works upstream. Ignoring it, cast your gaze over the delightful vale on the other side of this ridge road. As you drop down, the unmistakable silhouette of Castell'Arquato comes into view again, standing sentinel at the end of the valley.

At the signpost marking your arrival at Lugagnano, turn right following signposts for Piacenza and bear right skirting the town. Another right turn takes you over the bridge. Carry straight on towards the tedious village of Bore. As the road climbs out of the valley, notice how the rows of vines are planted closer together – it is too steep to work the soil between by tractor.

⑭ *After 4 km, just before Vernasca, turn sharp left back on yourself towards Alsena. After another 5 km, turn right just after the IP petrol station. The road is signposted for Becchi and eight other places - the yellow sign to Vigoleno, the next stop on the route, is hidden in the grass - Italian signposting at its most teasing. Carry on following clearer signs for Vigoleno.*

Vigoleno Anywhere else, this breathtaking medieval hamlet would be surrounded by a sea of coach parks. Here in Italy, it is just another of those unsung hidden corners that make exploring the Italian countryside such a delight. Fine Guelph crenellations enclose a huddle of houses, a post office and a pair of simple restaurants. At the far end of the two tiny cobbled squares stands its oldest building, a pearl of a Romanesque church with squat columns and an early fresco of St George and the Dragon. *Leave on the road just by the castle entrance, signposted for Salsomaggiore and the SS9, which takes you down under the walls towards the valley.*

⑮ *Turn right and carry on following signs for Salsomaggiore, passing through Scipione.*

Salso- After Vigoleno this is a surprise of quite another sort. This fashionable,
maggiore sprawling spa resort stands as a monument to an Italian obsession that
Terme dates back to the days of ancient Rome. The rust-coloured waters here are rich in iodine and bromine salts and are claimed to cure a host of disorders from rheumatism to sterility. For the traveller passing through, the star attraction is the Terme Berzieri, the grandiose bath house built in 1923 – a heavily ornamented building standing architecturally somewhere between Liberty style and an Indian temple.

⑯ *Leave, following signs for Fidenza and Piacenza, to return to base.*

Northern Tuscany

Well to the north of Tuscany's Chianti country lie the genteel hills at the foot of the lonely Garfagnana mountains. The local tourist board leaflet, using an apt neologism, calls them 'humanly-suited' - a claim proved by the glittering array of history's more colourful characters who have made themselves at home here. The most vivid perhaps was the faintly comic figure of Napoleon's sister, who set up her Ruritanian court just outside Lucca.

The centre of the tour is Pescia, a lively, tourist-free town, celebrated for cut flowers and outsize asparagus. The first short loop lies to the west weaving through Lucca's 17thC version of Beverley Hills, thick with grand villas and some of Italy's most splendid gardens. The second circuit is a lazy drive through a landscape whose beauty owes more to nature than man, as the road heads up hill and over dale to end in the valley of Lucca's once fashionable spa resort, Bagni di Lucca.

Tuscan food epitomises Italian culinary flair, with its knack for taking the finest raw ingredients and transforming them with a minimum of fuss into some of the best cooking in the world. Many Tuscans prefer soups to pasta, followed by grilled or roasted beef or game. This is a land of passionate hunters who love nothing more than to crunch their way through plates of roast *tordi* and *allodole* (thrushes and skylarks).

ROUTE ONE: 61 KM

Pescia

Italy's cut flower capital makes an ideal centre for this tour. Start with a drink on the terrace of one of the bars in the central Piazza Mazzini. From here you can look up to the medieval Palazzo del Vicario spangled with heraldic crests and down the patrician street-like square to the pure lines of the Quattrocento church of the Madonna Piè di Piazza. In the nearby church of San Francesco, the piercing eyes of St Francis stare out at you from his earliest known image. The work of the Luccan master Bonaventura Berlinghieri, it was painted in 1235, only nine years after the saint's death. Students of architecture or human folly can search out the town's prime example of fascist grandeur, the former party headquarters now crumbling into decay opposite the Town Hall, its doorway flanked by a pair of enormous fasces.

Villa delle Rose *(hotel, Castellare di Pescia)*

Just outside the centre of Pescia, this comfortable if large three-star hotel has the luxury of a swimming-pool and garden at modest prices. *Tel 0572-451301.*

Northern Tuscany

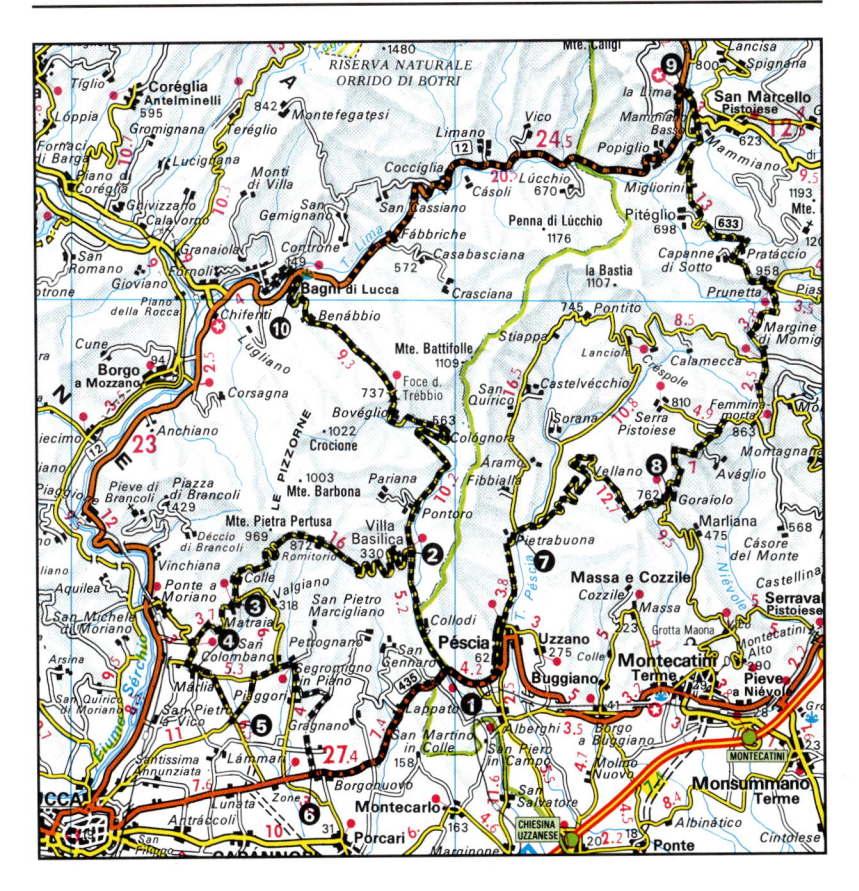

Cecco
(restaurant, Pescia)

In season this is the place to try Pescia's celebrated king-sized asparagus. For the rest of the year you are not likely to be disappointed with the excellent *cucina Toscana* in this smart restaurant. For dessert don't miss the home-made ice-cream with a warm fruit sauce. *Tel 0572-477955; closed Mon; price band C.*

Leave the town, heading south to follow the signs for Lucca. Put together a picnic before you leave – there are very few restaurants on the first route.

① *After 4 km, turn right at the sign for Collodi and Villa Basilica.*

Collodi and Villa Garzoni

Ahead you catch your first sight of the baroque gardens of Villa Garzoni, some of the finest of their epoch in Italy. The single central axis of this imposing garden is an arpeggio of sweeping stairs, statues and

89

Northern Tuscany: The Threshhold of the Garfagnana

sculptural hedges climbing a steep hillside, complete with a theatre and bath house. On sultry afternoons, the guests of the Garzoni family would relax in segregated bathing areas while an orchestra played from a discreet distance (*open daily 8-sunset*).

If the name Collodi sounds familiar, it may be because Carlo Lorenzini took it as his pen name before creating Pinocchio. His mother came from here and Carlo passed much of his childhood in the little village. Children will love the modern park dedicated to the world's most famous nose, watched over by Lorenzini's statue and decorated with scenes from the adventures of Pinocchio.

Continue along the same road for another 3 km.

② Turn sharp left at the signpost for Villa Basilica and continue to follow signposts for Villa Basilica.

Villa Basilica Turn off the road to see this village's star turn, a Romanesque church set in a striking sloping square. The fine façade is in the Pisan style, an eclectic rendering of Romanesque that characterizes the early churches of the region – note the eight columns, each different to the other, that top the frontage. Inside, peer through the gloom at another Berlinghieri masterpiece over the altar dedicated to the Crucifixion.

Returning to the road, carry on upwards to wind through woodland, punctuated by occasional glimpses of the vast plain of Pisa below. There are plenty of cool, leafy picnic spots on this stretch.

Pizzorne This small resort on the slopes of Monte Pietra Pertusa is a rather dull collection of modern buildings strung out in an attractive woodland setting. *Take the left fork here and follow the signs for Lucca.* The road starts its descent, dropping quickly towards the plain with Lucca stretched out before you in the distance.

Matraia -
Villa Reale

③ Bear right at the wooded junction above the village on to an unexpected one-way system. From here to Villa Mansi follow the directions with extra care - it is a confusing labyrinth of roads, some unsignposted or not marked on the map. At the traffic lights turn right through the narrow main street of Matraia, then right at the signpost for Lucca. From here, bear left, descending the hill and bear left again before a small bridge. Continue to follow signs for Lucca. Leaving the wooded hillside the road passes pocket handkerchief fields and olive groves. Passengers can look back for the view of Monte Pietra Pertusa, from where they have just come.

Arriving almost at the plain, the road divides at the high wall of the hidden Villa Cittadella. Bear right, following the line of the wall, passing the Renaissance church of San Pancrazio and bearing left until you arrive at the

Northern Tuscany

The Piazza, Pescia.

Northern Tuscany: The Threshhold of the Garfagnana

entrance. Here you can cast a covetous glance at the villa, before the road heads away to a T-junction 50 metres on. Ahead of you, through the wrought iron gateway, is the tantalizing vision of another stately pile, Villa Oliva, built in the late-16thC Florentine style. Sneak a look across its magnificent topiary and manicured lawns. *Turn left and continue to follow the walls of Villa Cittadella to its other entrance. Here, turn right, driving away from the villa.* Around the next corner, passing the wall of a third villa, you are at Villa Reale, arriving by the side entrance.

Villa Reale   Napoleon's imperious sister, Elisa Bacciochi, made this opulent villa one of the most famous around Lucca. When she bought it in 1805, Count Orsetti is said to have so regretted the sale of his family home to such a parvenue that he spent the purchase money on silver plate. Sending her a message that the villa was about to pass under her window, he loaded the silver on to ox carts and drove them past her palace. During her short residence here, Elisa, too, seemed capable of grand gestures. Calling herself the Queen of Etruria, she even kept a small private army with her tin soldier husband as Commander-in-Chief and Minister of War. The magnificent gardens which still surround it, laid out in the 17thC, are set like a series of rooms in thick woodland and include a beautiful open-air theatre and an epic cast of statues. They now also play host to Lucca's Summer Music Festival. *There are hourly guided tours; closed Mon, July and Aug closed also Wed, Fri and Sat, when the owners take up their summer residence.*

④ *Leave along the main tree-lined approach, but turn left after 300 metres and bear left again, following the wall of the villa. At the war memorial take the second right turn down a straight road (you will see a group of umbrella pines over the road ahead) and go straight on at the junction. Here the road does not tally with the map.*

⑤ *After 2 km turn left at the traffic lights towards Segromigno in Monte and drive through the hamlet of San Colombaro, bearing right to continue along the main road.*

At Segromigno, turn left at the roundabout and follow the road until you arrive at the village's main street, Via Piaggori. Turn left here and then right at the T-junction at the end, signposted Villa Mansi. After another 300 metres the entrance to the villa is marked to the left.

Villa Mansi   This High Renaissance villa has grown old gracefully, sitting in a grassy
(Segromigno)   clearing amidst an over-mature park. At one time it was surrounded by a magnificent formal garden, laid out by the Sicilian architect Juvara. Now only its water gardens remain, trimmed with lichen-encrusted balustrades and forlorn statues. *Open 10-12.30, 3-6.*

Northern Tuscany

> **Lucca**
> In urbane Tuscany, Lucca is one of the most urbane cities of all. Even the celebrated walls which still frame it are set in elegant lawns – hardly the menacing spectacle of Tuscany's other medieval towns. Its serenity is perhaps a reflection of its resilience – while others fell, it managed to pass relatively unscathed through its long history, remaining for the most part an independent state. Top of the long list of delights are the remarkably ancient Duomo, dating back to the 6thC, and the Torre Guinigi, bizarrely topped out with an oak tree. But the greatest pleasure is to meander through its streets whose palaces, porchways and passageways make it one of Italy's great cities. For all its beauty, it has yet to be discovered by the hordes of coach trippers who are suffocating the rest of the area.

Return to the main road and turn left, bearing left again after 100 metres. Keep on straight ahead as far as you can go, passing a number of junctions, and finally entering a narrow lane. Ahead you can see Villa Torrigiani.

Villa Torrigiani (Camigliano)
Park by the grand, rusticated gateway which stands at the end of a long avenue of needle-thin cypresses. The gardens, designed by Le Nôtre of Versailles fame, incorporated *giochi d'acqua* (water games) – in the garden to Flora where the host would take his guests for an after-dinner *divertimento*. He would trap them by switching on a wall of water. As the guests fled backwards, he would switch on more fountains which pursued them into the Temple at the far end where they would get a final drenching from Flora herself (*open daily*).

Carry on past the old stables; turn right at the roadside crucifix. Follow the road for several kilometres until you reach the main road back on the plain.

⑥ *Turn left along the SS435 to complete the remaining 8 km of the route back to Pescia. Alternatively turn right to visit the stately walled city of Lucca, 7 km away.*

ROUTE TWO: 95 KM

Leave Pescia, following signs for Abetone, crossing the last few kilometres of flat plain before the beginning of the foothills of the southern Garfagnana. Here you pass acres of greenhouses; millions of flowers are despatched daily during the season from the town's enormous Mercato dei Fiori.

⑦ *At the small village of Pietrabuona cross the bridge and turn right, on the road signposted for Abetone.* The road begins to climb steeply, passing olive groves and vineyards. The slopes are too steep here to cultivate

Northern Tuscany: The Threshhold of the Garfagnana

by plough and the farmers scythe the hay by hand and gather it into stooks for their animals.

Vellano — Pause here to take in the grandstand view of the Pisan plain below and to wander about the village's narrow stone streets before continuing on to Macchino.

Trattoria Lina *(restaurant, Macchino)* — The *padrona* of this simple old-style trattoria is justly proud of her home-made pasta dishes which she follows with generous plates of succulent grilled meat. You will find it in a terrace of houses on the left of the road. *Tel 0572-409155; closed Wed; price band A.*

Goraiolo — This modern little resort is little more than a collection of uninspiring restaurants and hotels in a hushed country setting.

⑧ *Bear left at the junction, continuing towards Abetone.* The road threads through intimate woodland scenery, passing several holiday villas before emerging on to a ridge with commanding views. Why the little hamlet of Femminamorta – dead woman – should be thus named is a mystery.

Le Lari *(hotel, Prunetta)* — After the anonymous hotels a little way back, this historic *albergo* is a welcome change, though if you want luxury you should look elsewhere. Its atmosphere is more that of a friendly boarding house, with matching prices. According to the *padrone*, Signore Valiani, the building once housed the Knights Templar. Behind it there is a cool garden. *Tel 0573-672931.*

Heading on through Cecafumo and Pratacccio, the landscape shows a wilder face as you look towards the heights of the Garfagnana. Descending towards San Marcello Pistoiese, you see ahead of you the deep valley of the River Lima which leads to Bagni di Lucca.

San Marcello Pistoiese — Down in this beautiful green valley, a catwalk of a footbridge stretches over the torrent of the Lima, forming a bloodcurdling 220 metre walk.

Continuing through the village and back on to the main road, you arrive at the hamlet of La Lima.

⑨ *Turn left, now following the signs for Lucca, crossing the bridge and into the valley of the Lima for the finest scenery of the tour.*

Popiglio — Its fine Romanesque church stands on the edge of a small square, and is viewed to greatest effect over a chilled Campari – try it *liscio* (without soda) at the nearby bar. On the far side of the river the hills roll up to the pint-sized peaks of La Bastia and Monte Battifolle.

Northern Tuscany

Ponte Coccia　Here the road follows the river deep into the valley which, after several hamlets, narrows into a sombre gorge, hemmed in by sheer cliffs before arriving at Bagni di Lucca.

Bagni di Lucca　Something of the Queen of Etruria still haunts this faded little spa town. It reached its apotheosis under her patronage and its air of northern gentility makes it seem quite un-Italian. Along with the Tuscan princes a host of foreign poets, including Byron, Shelley and Heine, came to take the sulphurous salty waters. Later, Europe's first legal casino, built in 1838, became an added attraction. The number of English expatriots grew so considerably that they made themselves at home with their own Anglican church and cemetery. Here you will find the tombs of Louise de la Ramé – better known as Ouida, the English romantic novelist whom Trollope loved to hate – and Rose Marie Cleveland, sister of the American President, Stephen Grover Cleveland.

Bridge Hotel　The English name is the only reference to Bagni di Lucca's past at this
(hotel, Bagni di small, modern, family-run hotel, just by the river. Still, it has three-star
Lucca Terme)　rooms at less than the usual three-star prices. *Tel 0583-87147.*

Locanda Maiola　This recently converted farmhouse, tucked away on the quiet slopes above the town, in Via Controneria, serves Tuscan food with a south-
(restaurant, ern Italian touch. The more tradional dishes include *zuppa di verdure*
Bagni di (Tuscan vegetable soup) or *papparadelle alla lepre* (ribbons of pasta in
Lucca)　a thick hare sauce) which might be followed by succulent pork roasted with fennel or *coniglio in umido* (a rich rabbit stew). *Tel 0583-86296; closed Tue; price band B/C.*

⑩ Leave the town, following the signs to Abetone, crossing back over the bridge on which you arrived. Then, almost immediately, turn right at the sign for Villa Basilica and Benabbio. The road now climbs steeply up the wooded flank of the valley.

Benabbio　You arrive at this rustic village after 5 km, passing the 13thC Castello Lupari. *Carry on along this up-country road to the Passo di Trebbio where the road begins its descent through a string of sleepy hamlets. Passing the junction for Villa Basilica ②, rejoin the road along which the first route started. Just past Collodi, turn left at the main road ① and coast back to Pescia.*

Western Tuscany
VOLTERRA AND THE METAL HILLS

Western Tuscany

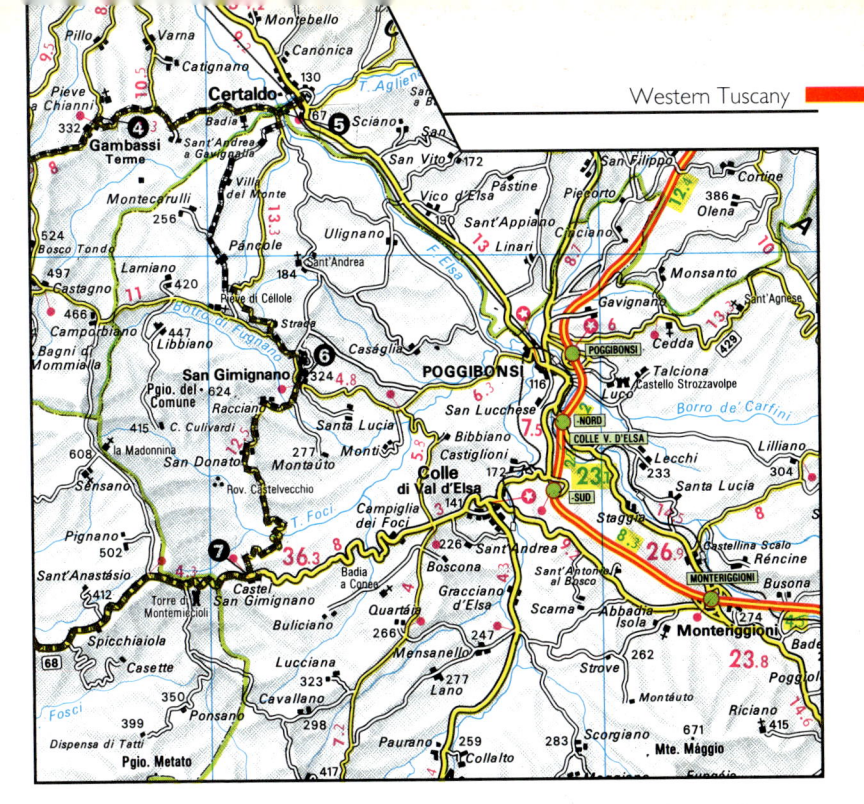

The gentle Colline Metallifere, the Metal Hills, run down to the sea from the heart of classic 'Chiantishire' with curves as sensuous as a Rubens nude. Tourists flock to San Gimignano and braver members of the herd might make it to Volterra. Otherwise these uplands remain one of the few corners of the idyllic Tuscan countryside yet to be discovered by the pack. From Etruscan times these hills have been mined for lead, tin and copper and, since its foundation 2,700 years ago, Volterra has been fought over for its mineral wealth. Today, however, the wounds of ancient mining and industry have largely healed over and only at Lardarello is there much evidence of the exploitation of the area's underground riches. The first loop of the tour briefly joins the more conventional tourist circuit with a visit to the towers of San Gimignano but leaves the throng behind with a pilgrimage to a 16thC 'Jerusalem' and a drive through unspoilt quintessential Tuscan countryside. The second circle explores the altogether wilder landscape of the Metal Hills, with a passing glimpse of one of the most unusual geological phenomena in Europe - the volcanic geysers and gurgling mud pools at Larderello. Here a labyrinth of stainless steel pipes harness geothermic energy to generate electricity. Glinting in the sun, they slide through the lush woodland like a megalomaniac modern sculpture.

Western Tuscany: Volterra and the Metal Hills

ROUTE ONE: 95 KM

Volterra

A sombre, lordly town perched on a windswept bluff, it ranks as one of the oldest cities in Italy. As the Etruscan Velathri, it was one of the leaders of the Dodecapolis, the powerful confederation of 12 Etruscan cities that held sway before Rome took over. Something of these ancient times still haunts you as you wander through the gaunt medieval streets. The archaeological finds in the Museo Guarnacci, too, vividly bring to life the city's past. See the enormous collection of carved funerary urns, each decorated according to the quirk of the artist – some witty, some grotesque – and marvel at the tall Giacometti-like 2ndC BC bronze, L'Ombra della Sera. After walking down to the Porta all'Arco, the worn Etruscan gate that pierces the town's inner walls, stroll back up to see Volterra's medieval gem, the Palazzo dei Priori in the equally splendid piazza with the same name. A glimpse of the nearby Duomo with its rich blue and gilt ceiling and alabaster windows would not be wasted. For centuries the city has been famous for its alabaster work and there are plenty of shops selling everything from small pots for a few thousand lire to the grandest of sculptures.

There are several appealing hotels which would make an ideal base for the tour, although parking is a headache in this impossibly positioned place. The Hotel Etruria in the central Via Matteotti (*tel 0588-87377*) is a comfortable, medium-priced choice. Those on a tight budget might prefer the 15thC Monastery of Sant'Andrea (*tel 0588-86028*) just outside the centre, with simple airy rooms leading off a magnificent, frescoed hallway. Guests must be in by 11pm, though, and in April/May school parties are liable to shatter the calm. But at least you can park outside.

Sacco Fiorentino
(restaurant, Volterra)

Although there are many restaurants in Volterra, most are undistinguished. This smart trattoria serving a modish, refined version of Tuscan cookery is an exception. You will find it in Piazza XX Settembre. *Tel 0588-88537; closed Wed; price band B/C.* For lunch on the hoof, stick to generously-stuffed rolls from a *paninoteca*, or sandwich bar – you will find a decent one in Via Matteotti.

① *Leave the city wall at its westernmost point, following signs for Pisa and Pontedera.* The road drops down, briefly skirting the remains of the venerable Etruscan walls.

Le Balze

Le Balze – 'the cliffs' – are marked by a yellow sign to the left just outside the town. The unstable clay that surrounds the town is slowly but inexorably crumbling away, leaving these dramatic sheer cliffs. The views are enticing but do not get too close – even the viewing platform has become a victim. *Returning to the road, continue down into the valley.*

Western Tuscany

The evening constitutional, Volterra.

Western Tuscany: Volterra and the Metal Hills

② *Turn right over the River Era, on to the road signposted for Firenze. After crossing the bridge, immediately turn left, and left again after 200 metres for Villamagna. Passing through a placid valley, turn right after 3 km into Villamagna, then bear left and right for Montaione.* The road now enters the characteristic, treeless grasslands that surround Volterra; the eerie silhouette of the city stands to the right. For a few kilometres the road is unmetalled. *Carry on through the hushed village of Iano and the wooded hunting reserves until you arrive at San Vivaldo. Ahead of you at the junction a yellow sign directs you to the monastery.*

San Vivaldo With an eye to armchair pilgrims, Franciscan monks created a miniature Jerusalem in this green and pleasant land in the opening years of the 16thC. Chapels – 34 of them – dotted about the wooded slopes faithfully followed the configuration of the principal shrines of the holy city. Only 17 remain, each depicting episodes of the Passion with life-like polychrome terracotta figures set against frescoed backdrops. Today, the once thriving community is reduced to a pair of ageing friars – ring the bell and one of them will show you around. You would be wise to see this magical place before it gets discovered.

③ *Leaving the monastery, turn right and right again, following the signposts for Montaione, then turn right at the sign for Gambassi along a short stretch of unmetalled road. Keep following signs for Gambassi, turning first right then left through a perfect Tuscan avenue of cypress and umbrella pines.*

Gambassi Terme This small spa town (you pass the modern thermal baths in the square to your right as you drive down to the older part of town) has a pretty enough medieval centre but little else to tempt you to stop.

④ *Passing through the town, turn right at the easily missed sign for Certaldo. Follow the road down the ridge through a patchwork of vines and olive trees until you cross the River Elsa and the railway line and drive into Certaldo.*

Certaldo It is possible to negotiate the narrow streets up to the hilltop medieval *borgo*, but you might prefer to leave the car in the large car park in the more modern town and make the stiff climb on foot. Giovanni Boccaccio spent the closing years of his life here. You will find his house in Via Boccaccio, the main street of this red-brick and rather over-restored, fortified town. His body lies in the nearby church, though surely the author of the lusty Decameron could not have had such a stern face as that carved on his tomb. There is a rather different face in the glass sarcophagus nearby – that of the Blessed Giulia of Certaldo, now reduced to a grisly, toothy mask.

■ 100

Western Tuscany

Il Castello Housed in a historic medieval *palazzo* at the far end of Via Boccaccio in
(hotel, Via della Rena, this is an atmospheric hotel with satisfactory rooms at
Certaldo) fair prices. *Tel 0571-668250.*

> ⑤ *Leave, following signs for San Gimignano, returning over the railway and river, this time bearing left. Shortly afterwards turn right off the main road at the signpost for Pancole, along a reasonable but unmetalled road.* To your left you catch your first glimpse of the memorable skyline of San Gimignano punctuated by its famous towers. Travelling along a road flanked by cypresses, past a perfect villa, this is Tuscany *par excellence*. Here several producers sell the best of the famous white Vernaccia wine of San Gimignano – even just a couple of bottles – at prices lower than you will find in the town. Buy some to help down a picnic under one of the olive trees along this stretch of road.

Le Renaie Far enough away from San Gimignano not to charge inflated prices, this
(hotel/restau- smart country hotel has airy if rather precious rooms, and the finest
rant, Pancole) Tuscan cooking in its inviting restaurant. *Just before the village, up a concealed right turn after the tennis-courts. Tel 0577-955044; price band B/C.*

Pancole The road passes right underneath the parish church of this small village. *One kilometre on, turn left and drive down the hill to turn right on to the main road and into San Gimignano.*

San The outstanding beauty of this medieval town has made it vain and in
Gimignano its greed to exploit tourism it is fast losing its charms, considerable though they are. The moment you see the place from a distance, its bristling towers make an unforgettable impact. Built by feuding families in the 11thC, both as defensive strongholds and as symbols of power, they give the city the look of a medieval Manhattan. Once inside, its streets are immaculately preserved but thronged with coach parties. Almost every shop is given over to souvenirs and the pulse of real Italian town life is weak.

As you would expect, there are plenty of restaurants, though the sin of greed is here committed by the proprietors rather than the customers. Best choices, if expensive, are Le Terrazze in the Hotel La Cisterna in the main square, and Dorada in Vicolo d'Oro, a restaurant with 'ancient Etruscan cuisine'.

> ⑥ *Leave San Gimignano on the road to Volterra.*

Cinque Gigli
and Pescille A few kilometres outside, on the left, this restaurant, attached to a
(restaurant/ decidedly elegant hotel, has the best views of San Gimignano that you
hotel, San will find. The high-class refined Tuscan menu includes *sorpresa di coniglio*
Gimignano) – the surprise being tender cooked rabbit inside a small loaf of bread.

Western Tuscany: Volterra and the Metal Hills

The bill, too, is a surprise, though not so pleasant. *Tel 0577-940186; price band D.*

Continue on through alternating vineyards and stands of evergreen oak, passing the high-tech prison.

⑦ Turn right on to the main road to approach the gentler, less eroded face of Volterra.

ROUTE TWO: 104 KM

Leave Volterra on the SS68 taking the signs for Larderello and Cecina. The road winds down, passing several alabaster works, to arrive at the hot brine springs of Saline di Volterra, one of the most important sources of salt in Italy.

⑧ Turn left for Massa Marittima and cross the railway. Immediately bear right, following the signs for Larderello and Pomarance. Below you lie the government salt works – salt is still a state monopoly in Italy.

Pomarance In the middle of this modern village there is an attractive enough old centre – the little piazza makes a good stop for a coffee as there are few others on the route. The bronze statue by the square of a blind-folded man is a moving tribute to the Italian Resistance that was so strong in Tuscany during World War II. Continue along the road for Larderello. The ruined castle of Silana stands high in the distance to your left while ahead an incongruous cooling tower looms up over the crest of a wooded hill – your first taste of the science-fiction landscape around Larderello.

Larderello If you begin to tire of Tuscany's monuments to the past, here is the perfect antidote – 60 km of gleaming stainless steel pipes darting across the landscape, harnessing super-heated underground vapours which generate around 500 megawatts of pollution-free power. The place has a surreal beauty despite the cooling towers and enormous generating plants that dominate the valley. The town takes its name from Francesco de Larderel, a Frenchman who first tapped the *soffioni* – awesome pools of mud, billowing sulphourous steam – in 1818, to produce borax. The museum, housed in his original works, is filled with sepia photographs of frowsty old aristocrats posing in front of improbable machines, wooden models in glass cases and everything else that an old-fashioned museum ought to have; it is also free. Nearby, you can also see a real live *soffione*.

Aia del Diavolo *Continuing on the same road, head south through Castelnuovo di Val di Cecina.* You now pass below the chestnut-clad slopes of the Aia del

Western Tuscany

Olive pruning, western Tuscany.

Diavolo, the Devil's Porchway. From here Old Nick sat brooding over the valley. When he had failed to drag the inhabitants into Hell, he brought the inferno here in revenge. But the story has a happy ending. When God saw how unperturbed the people were, He invested the geysers with a wealth of minerals.

⑨ *Some 9 km on from Castelnuovo, turn right to Sasso Pisano.*

Sasso Pisano The road, if you were to follow it, goes straight into the dead-end, tiny central piazza. *Bear to the left, instead, following the yellow signposts for the* fumarole e putizze. *A few hundred yards further on, a yellow signpost directs you into a little car park beneath a slope of fumaroles.* At first they resemble nothing more than a smouldering slag heap. At closer quarters you can see that it is a mass of steaming vents in an encrustation of salts. Further along the road, following the signs for Pomarance, plumes of steam (the *putizze* of the signs) begin to appear in the strangest

Western Tuscany: Volterra and the Metal Hills

places – from the middle of vegetable plots, vineyards and front gardens. Neighbours chat over the fence, oblivious to the hiss of the steam and the smell of sulphur that hangs in the air.

Continue along this road heading north through olive groves and dark woods, passing below the hamlet of Leccia.

⑩ *After about 9 km turn left, taking the signs for Serrazzano.* The chestnut woods gradually give way to evergreen oak and aromatic Tuscan scrub and, just when you think you are back in unadulterated Tuscany, two more cooling towers pop up – don't worry, they are the last.

Lustignano
(detour)

This pretty little hill village, 2 km off the road to the left, has a bar with food.

The road now begins to head northwards again, skirting the gentle slopes of Monte di Canneto.

⑪ *Just before the village of Canneto, turn right following signs to Cecina and Volterra.*

Canneto

It is well worth stopping to stroll around this fortified ancient hamlet two tiny streets and a church huddled within its walls. *Continuing on, the road drops down to the open valley of the Sterza.*

Just after the road up to La Sassa, a simple roadside bar will make you up solid sandwiches to be eaten on the shady terrace with a glass of thick red wine, produced nearby on the slopes of Montescudaio.

⑫ *About 6 km after the turn for La Sassa, turn right at the signpost for Querceto and Volterra.* The town above you to the right is the impressive hill town of Querceto, worth the detour if you are not pushed for time.

⑬ *At Ponteginori turn right on to the SS68 but turn left off this main road after 2 km, signed Montecatini.*

Buriano
(hotel/restaurant, Buriano)

This simple country hotel is well signposted off to the left. Set amongst vines and olive groves and commanding magnificent views across to Volterra, it is an inviting place to eat or stay, with very fair prices. The unfussy Tuscan food in the homely restaurant includes fresh pasta (made on the premises) and game. *Tel 0588-37295; price band B/C.*

Montecatini

Approached through vineyards scattered with volcanic boulders, this lofty hill town is topped by a noble medieval *borgo*. Leave your car in the car park below and explore the quiet lanes above.

From here the road heads on to Volterra.

⑭ *At the SS439, turn right then left, after 1 km, following signs for Volterra.* The naked slopes of the grasslands around Volterra return to escort you back to the gaunt city, teetering high above you on the brink of the dramatic *balze* (cliffs).

The Northern Marche

THE LANDS OF MONTEFELTRO

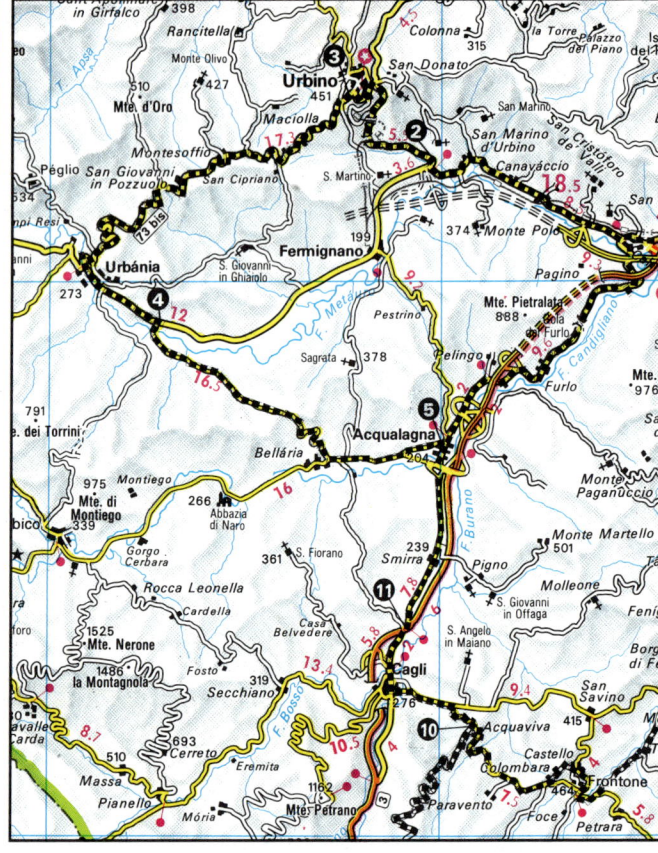

Inland from the cheap and cheerful coastal resorts of the Adriatic Riviera lies a secret land of great beauty. Shielded from the west by the high peaks of the Central Apennines, it is well fortified against the invasion of tourists that has so altered neighbouring Umbria and Tuscany. Few of the 'sun 'n' sand' holidaymakers venture far from the crowded beaches. The first loop of the tour is an easy drive that allows plenty of time to explore Urbino, a perfect example of an Italian Renaissance town preserved like a fly in amber. The second passes through contrasting landscapes of oak-clad limestone mountains – the haunt of wild boar and golden eagles – and fertile river valleys bristling with fortified hill towns, many still well preserved.

106

The Northern Marche

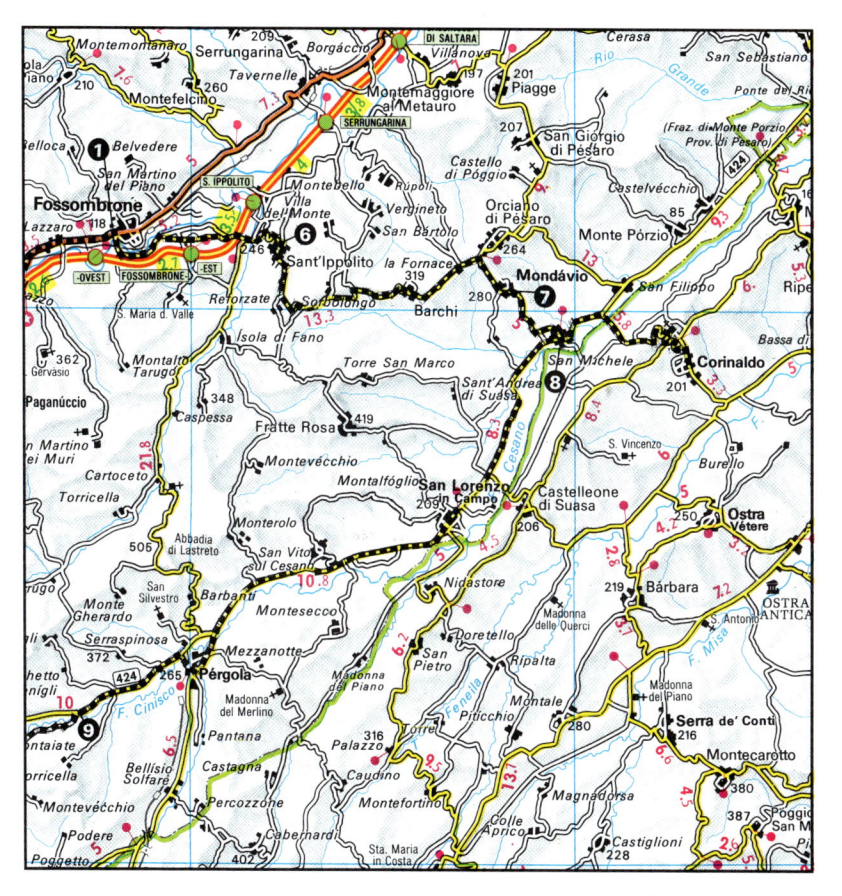

At the flowering of the Renaissance, these lands were the domain of the great Duke Federico Montefeltro. Their glory was short-lived, however, and the leaden hand of the Papal States, that lasted until the Unification of Italy in 1870, left the Marche a forgotten backwater of Italy, a legacy that remains to this day. Enjoy this tranquil corner of Italy before it gets put firmly on the tourist map.

The Marchigiani eat more meat than anyone else in Italy and it shows in the menus. Meat *alla brace* (charcoal grilled) is a staple along with *coniglio in porchetta* (roast rabbit stuffed with wild fennel), excellent cured pork – *prosciutto, salami* and *lonza* – and *piccione ripieno* (stuffed pigeon).

The Northern Marche: The Lands of Montefeltro

ROUTE ONE: 67 KM

Fossombrone

This small town, once the Roman Forum Sempronii, looks splendid on the slopes of the Metauro valley. Although it has no single outstanding monument, it is a delightful collection of buildings and streets that bear witness to a long and prosperous past. The town is crowned by the ruins of a gaunt castle built by the powerful Malatesta family, and boasts a pair of arcaded streets lined with gracious, small-scale Renaissance palaces. The Albergo Al Lago, 2 km west of the town on the old Via Flaminia, has clean, reasonably-priced rooms with all mod cons in a rather sterile, motel-style establishment. *Tel 0721-726129*. You might prefer to base yourself in Urbino or at the spectacularly-sited Ginestra hotel in Furlo (see *page 111*).

① *Leave Fossombrone on the old Via Flaminia going west in the direction of Roma and Urbino. Outside the town, continue straight on. Ignore the left-hand turn to Rome and follow the poor signposting to Urbino.*

Fermignano

② *Passing the junction for Fermignano, keep on the main road for Urbino.* If you are driving in early April you may catch the annual *Palio della Rana*, when the more athletic citizens of this small town race through the streets balancing frogs in wheelbarrows. It is one of the few times when the place is really jumping.

Round a few more bends you enjoy your first views of the pink-bricked city as you wind up – very slowly if you are behind a lorry – to Urbino.

Urbino

Bear left as you reach the town and skirt the walls until you arrive at the large car park below the palace. For a brief 40-year span in the later part of the 15thC Urbino vied with Rome as the artistic hub of central Italy. Duke Federico Montefeltro, the Renaissance man *par excellence*, gathered around him the greatest poets, thinkers and painters of his day and housed his glittering court in an idyllic palace. Its fairy-tale towers still watch over twisting cobbled streets that seem little changed since the heyday of this stunning city. Inside the Palazzo Ducale much of the original decoration remains, including the Duke's little study, entirely decorated with exquisite, *trompe l'oeil* inlaid woodwork. It provides the perfect setting for a significant collection of paintings which includes works by Raphael and the great Renaissance master Piero della Francesca. Raphael himself, born in 1483, was a product of the city. His birthplace in Via Raffaello is now a charming museum.

With much else to see, Urbino deserves at least a day to itself and there are a number of good hotels to choose from. Inexpensive choices are the Italia, in Corso Garibaldi, *tel 0722-2701*, and the San Giovanni in Via Barocci, *tel 0722-2827*, both small, unostentatious *alberghi* in the heart of town.

The Northern Marche

The old quarter of Fermignano.

Urbino is a good spot to try the full range of Marchigiano food. Le Tre Piante in Via Foro Posterula offers good regional food as well as proper *pizzas* at economical prices. At Agripan in Via del Leone you can taste the robust peasant cooking of a bygone age, while Vecchia Urbino in Via Vasari offers classic cooking at classic prices.

③ *Leave Urbino heading southwest on the road signposted for Arezzo and S Giustino, heading for Urbania.* The road now has spectacular views of the high Apennines to the south and a distant glimpse of the jagged triple peaks of the republic of San Marino to the north.

Urbania On arrival follow signs for *centro*, cross the bridge and park in one of the little squares. This historic small town retains many of its fine medieval and Renaissance buildings and warrants a stop. Monuments to note while strolling in the shade of the arcaded streets include the Bramante Theatre (Urbania is one of two cities claiming the great Renaissance architect as one of its sons) and the imposing Ducal Palace, containing an engrossing collection of ancient maps, globes and paintings. Hunt out the Chiesa dei Morti in Via Ugolini to see a dozen leathery mummified corpses standing in a row of glass-fronted cabinets – children will love it.

The Northern Marche: The Lands of Montefeltro

* *Urbino skyline with the duke's palace prominent, centre.*

Acqualagna *Leave Urbania on the road marked for Fano.*

④ *After 3 km turn right onto the SS257 signposted for Acqualagna. At the junction just before the hamlet of Pole turn left for Acqualagna and Roma. After 3 km bear off to the right following signposts for Acqualagna.*

Most of the old buildings in this not unattractive small town were destroyed in the last war and you probably won't be tempted to stop. However, on the last weekend of October and the first two weekends of November, Acqualagna becomes the most important market for the Marche's greatest treasure the truffle; the smell of these underground fungi greets you before you arrive. Look out in the restaurants on the route for any dish described as *con tartufi* to experience their special flavour. Look out, too, for the price.

⑤ *Keeping on the main road, pass through the town and bear left at the stop sign.* You are now travelling on the route of one of the oldest and most important Roman roads in Europe, the Via Flaminia. Along it marched the cohorts of Rome's great army on its way to its northern

The Northern Marche

	empire. *Ignore turnings to the right on to the modern dual carriageway and keep to the old road heading for Furlo.*
La Ginestra *(hotel/restaurant, Furlo)*	On the right, just before the Furlo Gorge, you will find this modern restaurant and hotel, with superb views and justly renowned for its food. In the autumn when the truffles and wild mushrooms are at their best, Italians flock here from afar, happy to pay high prices for these delicacies. At any other time of year you are unlikely to be disappointed by the refined regional cooking. Airy rooms set apart from the restaurant are reasonably priced and the hotel has tennis courts and a swimming-pool. *Tel 0721-797033; restaurant closed Mon; price band C (more con tartufi).*
Furlo	If your purse does not stretch to the Ginestra, stop at the open air snack bar before Furlo on the right at the Abbey of San Vincenzo. Here you can sample a *piadina* – a flat bread, filled with salami or cheese, only found in this part of Italy. While eating you can admire the massive stones of the nearby Roman bridge.
Furlo Gorge	The Furlo Gorge marks the highspot on the tour. Sheer naked limestone cliffs rise up on either side, leaving barely enough room for the road to pass. At one point the route becomes a tunnel hewn by hand (you can still see the chisel marks) through the hard rock in 76 AD – a remarkable feat of Roman engineering. If you are lucky you may see a golden eagle wheeling overhead.
Furlo Fossombrone	As the gorge ends abruptly the road enters a wide, wooded valley where the Metauro and the Candigliano rivers meet. *Keep following the signposts for Calmazzo staying on the old Via Flaminia rather than the modern dual carriageway. At Calmazzo turn right at the junction then, after 4 km, turn left returning to Fossombrone.*

ROUTE TWO: 90 KM

① *Leave Fossombrone, crossing the old bridge over the Metauro to the west of the town, following signposts for Barchi and S Ippolito. After 3 km, cross over the dual carriageway and keep on the road following sign for S Ippolito, Barchi and, further on, Mondavio.*

Sant'- Ippolito	The road snakes up through a series of hairpin bends with peaceful views before arriving at Sant'Ippolito. This airy village still preserves a good proportion of its medieval walls and the romantic ruins of its castle.

⑥ Carry on following signs for Barchi.

111

The Northern Marche: The Lands of Montefeltro

Sorbolongo Some 4 km on from Sant'Ippolito the road passes the tiny medieval borgo of Sorbolongo huddled within its ancient walls. Pause to stroll through this unsanitized place with washing and crumbling stucco at every turn and admire the 360-degree views of the smiling Marchigiano countryside.

Sorbolongo - Mondavio *Keeping on the main road to Mondavio, pass through Barchi* – another pretty medieval village worth a pause if you are not in a hurry. You are now driving on a magnificent crest road with sweeping views on either side of the well-worked slopes of the valleys of the Metauro and Cesano rivers. *As you arrive at Orciano turn right for Mondavio.*

Mondavio Bright geraniums and spreading conifers add a graceful touch to this beautifully preserved, red-brick medieval hill town. The imposing fortifications were built by Francesco di Giorgio Martini, one of Italy's most celebrated Renaissance military architects, and still stand guard over the place. They now house an entertaining 'living museum', portraying life when the *Rocca* (the fortress) was built for the powerful Della Rovere family; youngsters will particularly enjoy the grisly torture chamber (*open daily am and pm*). Wander round the compact centre of the town and stop for an ice cream and fine views at Al Giardino in the little park near the square.

La Palomba Mondavio is a tranquil place to break your journey. This small, friendly *(hotel/restaurant, Mondavio)* *albergo* opposite the fortress has modestly-priced rooms with lovely views. The simple restaurant offers above average *piatti tipici* including *tacconi*, a pasta made from broad bean flour and only found in this town. *Tel 0721-97105; price band A.*

⑦ *Leave, following signs for Pergola to head down to the valley of the Cesano.*

⑧ *Pass through the shady village of San Michele al Fiume and turn right onto the main road for Pergola unless you want to make the detour to Corinaldo.*

Corinaldo At ⑧ turn left onto the SS424, then turn off to the right after a couple *(detour)* of kilometres, following signposts for Corinaldo. This fortified hill town contains some of the best-preserved 15thC battlements in Central Italy. It also boasts the much visited shrine to Maria Goretti, the town's own 20thC saint, murdered in 1902 at the age of 12.

The route now meanders along the green valley of the Cesano, a patchwork of family-sized fields, vineyards and nurseries with some good straight driving.

The Northern Marche

San Lorenzo in Campo

This attractive roadside village is typical of the more comfortable habitations that lie in the fertile valleys of the northern Marche. It also boasts two off-beat curiosities a museum of African ethnography and a room entirely covered in mosaics made from 97,000 postage stamps. There is also a low-key archeological museum and a well-restored little 18thC theatre, all housed in a medieval palace (apply to the parish priest at 50 Via Vittorio Emanuele II). Continue on the main road to Pergola.

Giardino
(restaurant/hotel, San Lorenzo in Campo)

On the left, 2 km on from San Lorenzo, the Giardino stands back from the road amidst an unpromising cluster of houses and light industry. Do not be put off – padrone Massimo Biagiali provides some of the most imaginative food in the northern Marche. Ask for the *menu degustazione* to try a string of lovingly-prepared courses and choose one of his green-tinted Verdicchio wines from the encyclopaedic wine list. The price to quality ratio is very much in your favour. You can also stay the night in one of the inexpensive, comfortable rooms – the swimmimg pool is a rare treat. *Tel 0721-776803; closed Mon; price band C.*

About 5 km on from San Lorenzo you will see the unpolished medieval village of San Vito sul Cesano on the slopes of the valley to your right. Arriving at the edge of Pergola turn left following the signposts for Centro.

Pergola

This shapely small town set in a vineyard-dotted valley has many noble buildings and a distinctly 18thC air. It also has, at the time of writing, the celebrated Bronzi Dorati. These extraordinary Roman gilded bronze statues dating from the first century AD are at the centre of a long-running row between the Pergola town council, who want to keep them here, and the regional authorities who want to cart them off to Ancona. In the meantime they remain shamefully closed from public view. Console yourself with an excellent ice cream at the Gelateria Antica in the main corso or a bottle or two of Vernaccia, a rich perfumed red wine peculiar to the town. Leave, following signs for Cagli. Back at the SS424, turn left towards Cagli and Frontone.

Pergola - Frontone Castello

⑨ *After 5 km turn off to the left following the clear signs for Frontone.* You can now see the *castello* of Frontone stark against the treeless peaks of Monte Catria and its sister Acuto. Agriculture along this idyllic stretch of road is still a small-scale affair that has changed little over the centuries. *Keep on main road passing through the modern roadside town of Frontone. At the end of the town cross the bridge and bear right on to the road marked with a yellow sign for Castello.*

Frontone Castello

Turn sharp left at the crossroads below the castle and drive in low gear up to this gusty eyrie. The panorama from the medieval stronghold is breathtaking and the Malatesta Rocca (fortress) looks as sturdy as when it was first built.

The Northern Marche: The Lands of Montefeltro

Taverna della Rocca
(restaurant, Frontone)

A convenient lunch stop, this convivial trattoria in the old stables under the castle has cheap and simple fare, mostly meat cooked on a huge charcoal grill. *Price band A.*

Frontone - Cagli

At the crossroads below the castle turn left following signs for Cagli. At the T-junction turn right. The road now travels in the shadow of the craggy mountains passing the small villages of Colombara, Buonconsiglio and Acquaviva. The last of these harboured *partigiani* Resistance fighters during the Second World War and was consequently razed to the ground. At every turn there are spectacular views of the highest peaks in this section of the Apennines. Monte Catria, marked by a cross on its summit, rises to over 1,700 metres.

Monte Catria
(detour)

⑩ *The road off to the left by the petrol station in Acquaviva snakes up after 16 km to the summit of Monte Catria. Even if you don't have time to go all the way to the top, it is worth taking this empty road for only a few kilometres to enjoy the giddy views. The flowery meadows are a picnicker's heaven. At the T-junction after Acquaviva turn left for Cagli.*

Cagli

You may well be surprised that this jewel of a town is not yet on the tourist circuit. An important staging post on the ancient Via Flaminia, it still retains its Roman street plan and a score of notable medieval buildings. After visiting Mondavio you may recognize the hand of Francesco di Giorgio Martini in the dramatic defensive tower 100 metres from the central square. Hunt out the fresco of the Madonna and Child by Raphael's father, Giovanni Santi, in the church of San Domenico near the hospital and ask at the medieval Town Hall to see inside the 19thC theatre, a miniature 'La Scala' look-alike. It is only a shame that there are no decent hotels in town.

Di Luchini
(restaurant, Cagli)

The Cagliese are noted for their love of snails, and with any luck *lumache* will be on the menu at this unpretentious and inexpensive *trattoria* by the hospital. Other specialities are the home-made *tagliatelle* and *coradella d'agnello* (a sauté of lamb offal that is much tastier than it sounds). *Tel 0721-787231; closed Fri; price band A.*

Leave, following signs for Fano and pause to admire the Roman bridge as you cross the river at the edge of the town.

Cagli - Fossombrone

⑪ *At the fork in the main road some 2 km from the centre of Cagli bear off left following signs for Smirra and pass under the flyover. You are now back on the old Roman Via Flaminia running parallel with the modern dual carriageway and in for a slightly bumpy ride. Some 3 km after passing through the village of Smirra, bear right then immediately left for Acqualagna just before the large agricultural silos. Keeping to the road, head on to Acqualagna. Carry on past the town and* ⑤ *rejoin the route you took*

The Northern Marche

• *Mountains of the Apennines rising near Cagli.*

to return to Fossombrone on the first route. You will not regret this replay of the awe-inspiring drive through the Furlo Gorge.

The Flaminian Way
FROM ROME TO ASSISI

The Flaminian Way over the Apennines was the key to ancient Rome's control over its vast northern empire. Built by the Consul Gaius Flaminius in 220 BC, it became the main route from Rome to the rest of Europe. In medieval times the Papal States, understanding its importance, garrisoned it with equal determination. They also lavished attention on the decoration of its churches, for by now it had also become the pilgrim route to the shrine of Italy's patron saint, St Francis of Assisi.

Today, motorways cut effortlessly through the Apennines, leaving much of the old Via Flaminia as a quiet backwater still strung with sturdy Roman bridges and well fortified hill towns.

This tour abandons the usual figure-of-eight and provides an unhurried route for those driving from Rome to Assisi and on into the heart of Umbria. After a succession of poetic Roman ruins and atmospheric medieval towns, it ends at the tomb of St Francis of Assisi.

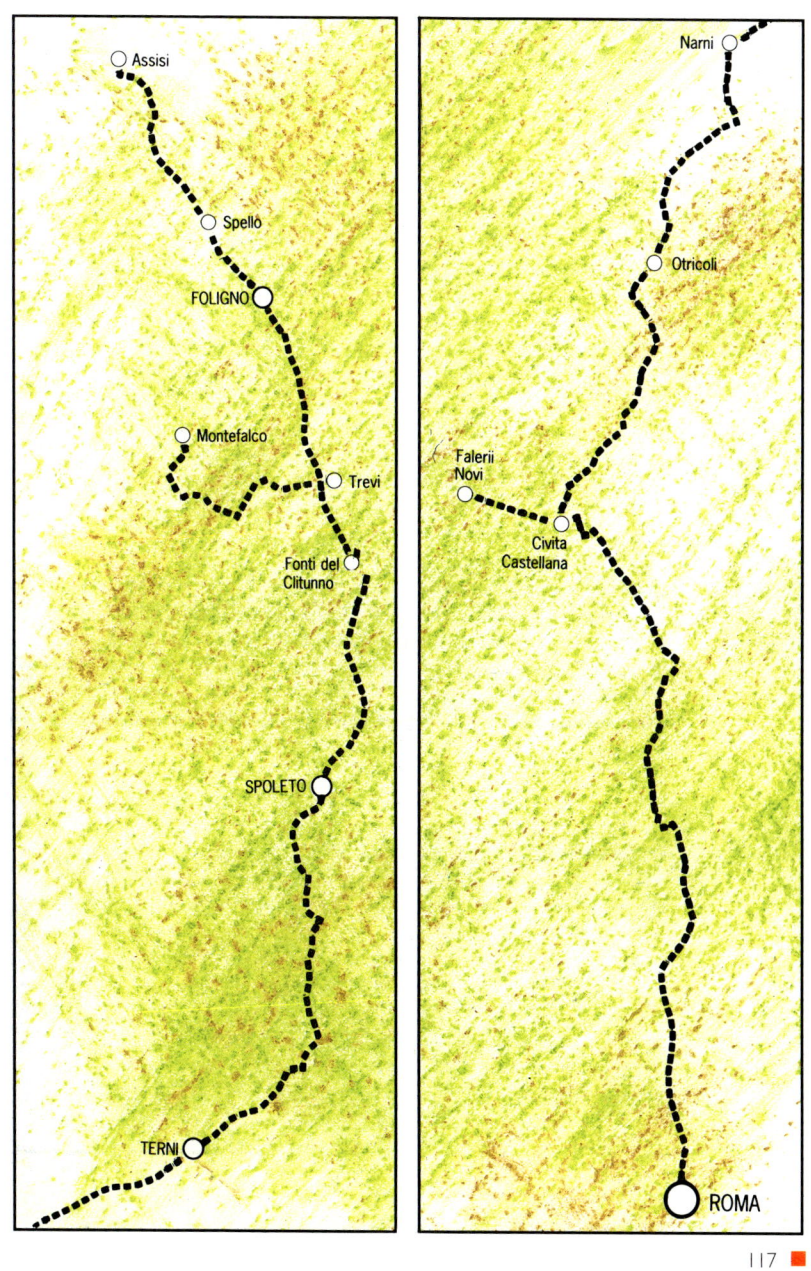

FROM ROME TO ASSISI

- Assisi
- Spello
- FOLIGNO
- Montefalco
- Trevi
- Fonti del Clitunno
- SPOLETO
- TERNI

- Narni
- Otricoli
- Falerii Novi
- Civita Castellana
- ROMA

The Flaminian Way: From Rome to Assisi

ROUTE: 132 KM

The interest starts at Civita Castellana some 50 km from Rome, but *if you are driving from the capital leave the frantic Grande Raccordo ring road due north of the city at the Flaminia exit.*

Civita Castellana
Built on the heights at the confluence of two rivers, this is the site of the ancient town of Falerii Veteres. In 241 BC the Romans, seeing how impregnable such a position might be, destroyed the town and resettled the Faliscan people on the nearby plain at Falerii Novi. There they stayed until the troubled 8thC when they crept back to the safety of the ancient site. Today, the town, though frayed about the edges, has a modest elegance and an interesting medieval core. Stop and have a coffee, and a glance at the portico of the 12thC *Duomo*.

Falerii Novi
(detour)
Leave Civita going northwest towards Fabrica di Roma for this worthwhile detour. The eerie vision of the almost intact walls of the Roman city looms up on your left in the midst of farmland after about 6 km. The beautiful arches that pierce the massive blocks of moss-covered tufa are now guarded only by trees.

Civita Castellana - Otricoli
The Flaminia here has fine views of the foothills of the Apennines. After about 7 km the road passes under the ivy-clad ruined castle at Borghetto. Look out for the roadside stall selling local cheeses including the freshest mozzarella – with a few tomatoes and a crusty loaf it makes a good picnic to eat amidst the Roman ruins coming up ahead. After crossing the mainline railway you pass over the Tiber and the border of Lazio and Umbria.

Otricoli
The chief delight of this medieval village is outside at the romantic collection of ruins of the Roman Ocriculum. A tree-lined track on the left, immediately before the right-hand fork off the Flaminia into the town, leads to the site. Standing amidst trees festooned with vines, the impressive stones are the remains of a town without walls, built more as a pleasure garden than a defensive site. Where once Imperial Rome's patricians strolled you can now wander freely – no guides, no admission charge, just sheep.

Otricoli - Narni
The Via Flaminia now climbs up through olive groves. *Follow signs for Narni and Terni. Just after the turning for the village of Vigne bear right following signs to Narni.*

Narni
This typical Umbrian hill town stands on a spur over the valley of the Nera River commanding a grandstand view of the wide plain. Its lanes and small squares preserve much of their medieval air and are flanked by graceful *palazzi*. Climb up to the *Rocca* for panoramic views and

FROM ROME TO ASSISI

• Remains of Roman Ocriculum, outside the medieval village of Otricoli.

follow the signs to the bottom of the town to see the mighty ruins of the Ponte d'Augusto, one of the many bridges on the Flaminia that the Emperor Augustus built in the first century AD.

Terni The smell of sulphur as you approach will warn you that this is not a place to linger. Once a fine medieval town, it became a major arms and steel centre destroyed in the Second World War. Lovers might, however, want to make a pilgrimage to the Basilica of the legendary St Valentine 2 km before reaching the city. He was bishop of Terni until martyred in 273 and lies buried here.

Terni - Spoleto Leaving the industry of Terni quickly behind you, the road runs through densely wooded rolling hills dotted with fortified hamlets.

Spoleto The first view of this outstanding hill town is dominated by the 80-metre high arches of the Ponte delle Torri and the towering *Rocca*. The modern-day Flaminia passes under the town through a tunnel but it would be a shame not to stop. It is best, though, to leave the car outside the centre. Set in the rolling wooded hills of Southern Umbria, this is no backwater. From mid-June to mid-July it hosts the Festival dei Due Mondi, one of Italy's premier annual arts jamborees, and with its art galleries and smart restaurants it has a decidedly sophisticated air. Though popular with tourists, the atmosphere is not suffocating. If time

The Flaminian Way: From Rome to Assisi

• *Trevi's piazza.*

is short make sure you see at least the *Duomo* with its beautiful frescoes by Fra Filippo Lippi. The great artist lies buried here having been poisoned in 1469 after seducing the daughter of a local noble family.

Gattapone
(hotel, Spoleto)

If you want to spend more time exploring the beguiling town try this small four-star hotel set in a flowery garden. Not cheap, but worth the money. *Via del Ponte; tel 0743-36147.*

Il Tartufo
(restaurant, Spoleto)

Definitely the place to try the best Umbrian cooking, including plenty of dishes laced with truffles, as its name suggests. You get above-average cooking at above-average prices. *Piazza Garibaldi; tel 0743-40236; closed Wed and mid-July to 5 Aug; price band D.*

Leaving Spoleto the road opens out into a wide valley whose olive covered slopes have made the area famous for its oil.

Fonti del Clitunno

Some 11 km out of Spoleto, a less than picturesque stretch of the Flaminia hides the source of the river Clitumnus, a sacred site in ancient times. Amidst tall poplars the waters of this small river bubble up into a crystal-clear rock pool whose magical properties washed cattle to a dazzling white, ready for Roman sacrifice. Poets from Virgil to Byron have praised this charmed spot. Nowadays, however, you will need a healthy

FROM ROME TO ASSISI

imagination not to have the spell broken by the numerous school parties. For the poetically-minded, better perhaps to carry on 1 km to the Tempietto, a very early Christian building but looking for all the world like a miniature classical temple. To see it ring the bell at the gate.

Le Casaline (hotel/restaurant, Campello sul Clitunno)
Just before the springs, turn right off the Flaminia to Campello. This small country *albergo* and restaurant lies amidst olive groves 2 km after the village on the road to Poreta. Benedetto Zeppadoro and his family offer genuine rural hospitality and a serious restaurant where even the bread is home-baked. Try his range of unusual *salumi*, cured meats made from goose, deer, goat and horse. The inexpensive rooms are much in demand so book ahead if you want to stay. *Tel 0743-521113; restaurant closed Mon; price band C.*

Trevi
Set in acres of olive groves this shimmering hill town tumbles down its slopes above the Flaminia. It is a delightfully unspoilt example of a medieval garrison town, with plenty of crumbling stucco. On your way up, stop at the church of the Madonna delle Lacrime to see the Adoration of the Magi fresco by Perugino, Umbria's native Renaissance master. *From here either take the following detour or continue on to Foligno.*

Montefalco
From Trevi take this loop to the west of the Flaminia to visit Montefalco, La Ringhiera dell'Umbria – the Balcony of Umbria. This crow's nest commands the finest views of Umbria on this tour. Before strolling through the airy streets of the *centro storico*, walk round the walls to admire the views. Chief delights here are a cycle of frescoes and an unusual wine. The Life of St Francis, in the church of San Francesco, painted by the Florentine fresco painter Benozzo Gozzoli in the mid-15thC, is one of the most spirited accounts of the saint's life in Italy. Secular tastes are well satisfied with Sagrantino Passito, a sweet and heady red dessert wine with an alcoholic kick.

If you have taken this loop, head on to rejoin the Flaminia at Foligno, the last town on the Via Flaminia that this tour visits. You could appreciate the views as you drive down to the valley or take a siesta under an olive tree, depending on how liberal you have been with the Sagrantino.

Foligno
This is one of the few historic towns of Umbria not built on a safe hilltop and it has suffered for it. Badly bombed during the Second World War, it is now a busy commercial centre with little of its past to be seen. It is only worth stopping on the second Sunday of September when the different quarters of the town battle out, on horseback, the 17thC Giostra della Quintana – not quite up to the *Palio* at Siena but very exciting. As you pass by you might like to know that the first edition of Dante's Divine Comedy was printed here in 1472, the first book in Italian ever to be printed in Italy.

The Flaminian Way: From Rome to Assisi

- *The Arch of Augustus at Spello.*

From Foligno the route bids farewell to the Flaminia and heads northwest pausing at Spello before reaching its goal at Assisi. Plenty of signposts to both places; you are not likely to get lost.

Spello

This gem of a hill town lies about 3 km after Foligno. Although it has been a bit distorted to accomodate the tourists it is still enchanting. Once the Roman town of Hispellum, its streets abound with testimony to each era of its history. Note the Roman Porta Consolare, still the main gate that pierces the town's walls to the south, and see the recently restored, stunning frescoes by Pinturicchio in the first chapel to the left in the church of Santa Maria Maggiore. Make the short sharp hike up from the 13thC Palazzo Comunale to the Torre Belvedere for your first view of Assisi and the overgrown Roman amphitheatre directly below. In the main square there is a *cantina* selling the best local wines, a red Merlot di Spello for the serious and a much cheaper Rosso di Spello for the rest of us.

FROM ROME TO ASSISI

La Cantina
(restaurant, Spello)

Work up a good appetite for lunch at this excellent restaurant in an old wine cellar. The short menu depends much on the mood of the cook and what is in season and features the best Umbrian *cucina casalinga* – tagliatelle with a hearty *sugo* (pasta sauce) of goose, rabbit cooked with wild fennel and rosemary, or roast goose. *Via Cavour; tel 0742-651775; closed Wed; price band B.*

From Spello follow signs for Assisi, 11 km further on.

Assisi

In high season avoid driving up to the centre. Park in one of the car parks below the town – the first as you arrive has a convenient escalator up to the centre. Twinned with (where else?) Bethlehem, this opera-set hill town seems bathed in heavenly light even when all around is grey. Apart from Rome, it is Italy's greatest place of pilgrimage and you may either be deeply moved by the devotion to the humble St Francis or thoroughly disgusted by the tawdry cashing-in on his name. Goethe was of the latter mind. But you would have to be a hardened cynic not to be moved by Giotto's celebrated cycle of frescoes on the life of the saint. You will find them in the Upper Basilica of the double-decker church that houses the saint's remains and towers over Assisi. Committed pilgrims should visit the church of Santa Maria degli Angeli which stands on the plain below. Here Francis and his companions pushed back the brutal Dark Ages with a new way of life based on love and poverty. The small primitive chapel, the Porziuncola, where the little community worshipped, stands incongruously in the centre of the great domed basilica.

If St Francis leaves you cold, search out the Temple of Minerva in the main square. Although now converted into a church, you are not likely to mistake it for a Christian building. It is an uncompromisingly grand Roman temple with a magnificent *portico* of lofty Corinthian columns. With time to spare you can explore the excavations of the old Roman forum under the square with not a pilgrim in sight.

Umbra
(hotel, Assisi)

To see Assisi at its best, stay the night and avoid the day-trippers. This small hotel with a much-praised restaurant just off the main square offers tranquillity and a shady pergola at prices that will not overtax a small budget. *Via degli Archi; tel 075-812240.*

Northern Lazio:
ROME'S VOLCANIC LAKELAND

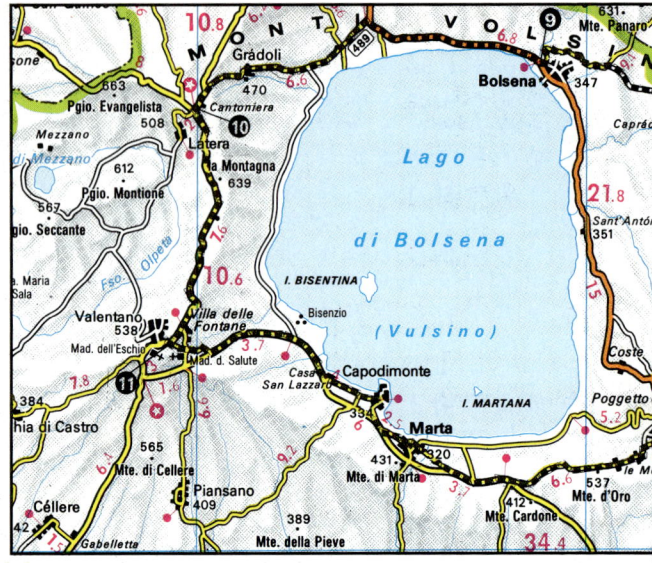

Since the days of Imperial splendour this gentle countryside has been a playground for jaded Romans. Today they flock here on summer weekends, but for the rest of the time it is an uncrowded corner set with a trio of delightful lakes, cupped in the craters of extinct volcanoes. The tour encompasses the contrasting rural landscape of chestnut-clad hills and open lakeland views, yet also includes impressive Roman ruins, gems of late Renaissance extravagance, and a score of unpolished medieval villages waiting to be discovered.

The provincial capital Viterbo, a city with Roman airs and one of the most outstanding medieval quarters in Italy, provides a vivacious centre for the tour. The first loop of the natural figure-of-eight winds through the Cimini mountains to circle Lago di Vico, the prettiest of the lakes, and takes in the finest surviving 16thC garden in Italy. The second route makes a lazier circuit of the largest lake, Lago di Bolsena, with a 'dying city', and some outstanding wines on the way.

The gastronomic treat here is the much prized fish from the pure lake water – one of Dante's victims was sent to hell for overindulging in Lake Bolsena eels. The flowery white wines produced from the volcanic soil are their ideal counterpart.

Northern Lazio

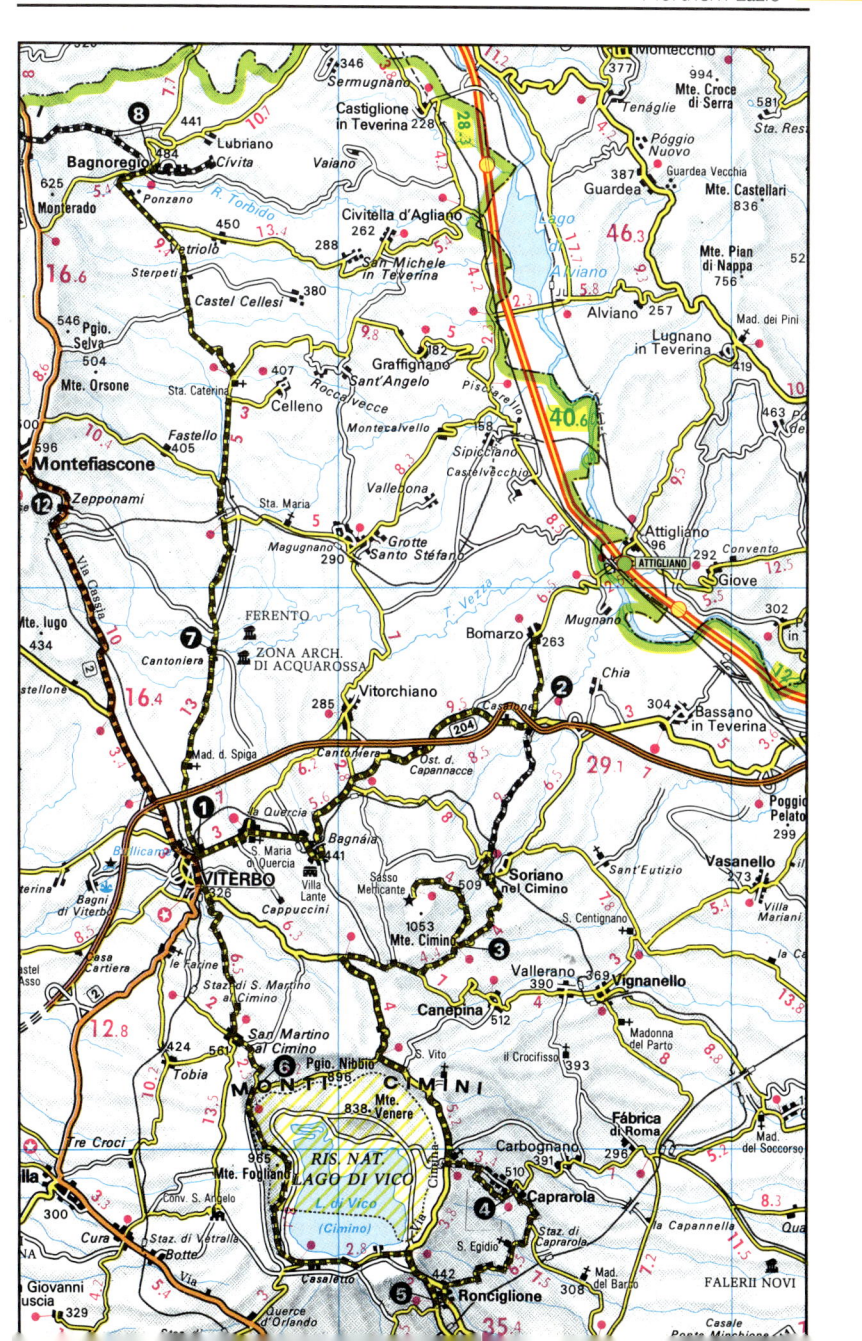

Northern Lazio: Rome's Volcanic Lakeland

ROUTE ONE: 82 KM

Viterbo Celebrated for its fountains and beautiful women, Viterbo needs time to reveal its secrets. At its heart lies a remarkable medieval core that has been largely untouched by later centuries. Many regard it as the best-preserved example of its kind in Italy and a stroll along the Via San Pellegrino is a must. The narrow street is a warren of arches, towers, terraces, open staircases and passages, best experienced on a warm summer's night. Nearby, in Piazza San Lorenzo, the 13thC Papal Palace is celebrated both for its Gothic architecture and its illustrious history. For around twenty years in the 13thC it was the centre of the Christian world when the papacy left a feuding Rome to set up court here. The palace also witnessed the election of Pope Gregory X; after two years and nine months the assembled cardinals only reached agreement when the people of Viterbo tore off the roof to force a decision.

As for fountains, the city is littered with them – don't miss the watery medieval masterpiece in the Piazza Fontana Grande. For beautiful women, head for the smart Corso Italia at dusk when it comes to life as the Viterbese take their *passeggiata*, mingling with the soldiers from the large army barracks outside the town. A word of warning – Viterbo is also famous for its witches.

The Leon d'Oro, *tel 0761-344444*, in Via della Cava is a pleasant enough *albergo* in a city not well endowed with attractive hotels. The Milano (*tel 0761-340705*) in the same street is a budget choice – you get what you pay for.

Trattoria Porta Romana
(restaurant, Viterbo)

Tina Pallucca offers authentic Viterbese cooking in this simple *trattoria* off the tourist beat near the Porta Romana gateway. Amongst the down-to-earth dishes, try the *lombrichelli alla amatriciana* (literally 'little earthworms', suggested by the shape of this pasta), *zucchine ripiene* (stuffed courgettes), and the *bollito di manzo* (boiled beef with onions). Finish off with the local sweet biscuits, *tozzetti*, with honeyed Aleatico wine from nearby Gradoli. Honest food at honest prices. *12 Via della Bontà; tel 0761-237118; closed Sun; price band B.*

① *Following signs for Orte and Villa Lante, cross railway line to northeast of town.*

Santa Maria della Quercia

The massive, austere façade of this Renaissance church looms up in front of you shortly after you leave Viterbo. Pause to look at the three blue and white Andrea della Robbia terracotta reliefs above the main doors. If you have time to spare, ask the priest to show you the curious museum of *ex voto* paintings on wood dating from 1490.

Continue on to Bagnaia and Villa Lante.

Northern Lazio

• *Waterworks with charm at Villa Lante, near Bagnaia.*

Villa Lante — A classic late-Renaissance garden where nature has been thoroughly knocked into shape, it looks much as it did when it was laid out by the mannerist master Vignola in the late 16thC. Its five terraces on a steep slope are linked by flights of steps and elegant fountains all framed by manicured hedges of box and yew. *Closed Mon; guided tours only.*

Bagnaia — The attractions of this small town are put in the shade by Villa Lante but it is worth ambling round the old part behind the little main piazza. Flanking the square is Il Beccorosso, a medium-priced restaurant that offers typical local dishes in a grand 15thC palazzo. *Tel 0761-289730; closed Wed.* Continuing on the main road look out for the houses built into the *tufa* (volcanic stone) cliff face as you leave.

Bagnaia - Bomarzo — *After about 3 km when you arrive at the main junction, take the road signposted for Orte. On your right you pass a couple of clean-cut tufa quarries; the easily-worked stone has set the architectural tone for the whole area. ② Turn left taking sign to Bomarzo just before the bridge that crosses the busy main road.*

Bomarzo — *Go through Bomarzo bearing right and drop down round the back of the village to follow the signs to Parco dei Mostri. Here you will see the*

Northern Lazio: Rome's Volcanic Lakeland

• *Monster mask at the Parco dei Mostri, Bomarzo.*

strangest sight on this tour. At the end of the 16thC a bastard son of the rich Orsini family created a late-Renaissance Disney World, piling a host of enormous *tufa* sculptures on the slopes of a natural amphitheatre. Decidedly the product of a rampant imagination, his Sacro Bosco is filled with strange monsters and fantastical beasts all on a huge scale – three-headed dogs, an elephant crushing a soldier, a giant mangling a woman. Dali loved it. Try and see it early on a misty morning avoiding the school parties. *Open daily dawn to dusk; entrance L8,000.*

As you leave, the view of the village above is dominated by the Orsini Palace. *From Bomarzo bear right following signs for Soriano.*

Bomarzo - Soriano nel Cimino

② *Back at the crossroads, this time continue straight on over the main road for Soriano. The road is poor and potholed though metalled – do not drive too fast.* The sombre *tufa* castle of Soriano, standing to the east of Monte Cimino, comes into view several kilometres before you arrive. The neatly-coppiced plantations that flank the road are chestnut and hazelnut, a major staple of the local economy.

Soriano nel Cimino

At the entrance to the town stands the Palazzo Chigi-Albani whose inner courtyard hides the Papacqua fountain, a masterpiece of 16thC mannerism by Vignola. It is closed for restoration and guarded by Alsations, but you may get a glimpse by telephoning the custodian; *tel 0761-222531*. If not, climb up to the lively little square in the centre of town and on up through the gates to the commanding *rocca*.

Northern Lazio

La Bastia *Pass through town continuing on the main road. After traversing the main*
(hotel, *square carry on straight up the hill following the hard-to-spot signs for La*
Soriano) *Faggeta and pass under the arched gateway leaving the town.*
On the right just outside town, up a well-signed track. This smallish
hotel in modern Italian style is a bit precious, but sound value. Come
here if you want a room with a spectacular view of the Tiber plain and
the Apennine foothills. *Tel 0761-729062.*

Soriano - The road now climbs up the slopes of Monte Cimino with sweeping
Caprarola views of the plain to the left. Ancient plantations of decapitated
chestnuts line the twisting road.

Monte ③ *When you are 4 km out of Soriano, turn sharp right at the first junction*
Cimino *to take this detour up to the summit of the mountain.* The road winds up
(detour) through more chestnut and hazelnut woods which give way to an
ancient beech wood – La Faggeta – that crowns the peak. At the top
there are good picnic spots and a *pizzeria* with a picture-postcard view.
As with any beauty spot in Italy, it is packed at weekends and deserted
for the rest of the time. *Return to the main road.*

A couple of kilometres further on, 6 km outside Soriano, take the right turn
signposted Roma and Viterbo, then after 2 km take the left turn for Roma
and Ronciglione. You are now on the old Roman Via Cimina. Keep
following clear signs for Caprarola and Villa Farnese.

Villa You first glimpse the palace to your left as you approach. Don't be
Farnese tempted to turn off towards it but keep on the main road, dropping
down to the lower part of town. Cross the bridge over the gorge,
then turn left up the main street, signposted *centro storico*. Park at the
bottom and walk up to the palace – you won't miss it. This huge imposing villa is one of Italy's best examples of the Renaissance ideal, past its
sell-by date. No expense was spared on the lavish wall-to-wall frescoes
– mostly to the glory of the Farnese family. The whole effect is an object
lesson in the expression of power and disdain. The guided tour is obligatory. Highlights include the Scala Regia – a spiral staircase that puts
others in the shade – and the Mappamondo room with its colourful
mapping of the world as it was then known. Vignola, as at Villa Lante,
was the architect behind the extravaganza with the virtuosi Zuccari
brothers and an army of other artists providing the frescoes. *Closed Mon.*

④ *Leave town heading south on the road signposted Roma and*
Ronciglione. After about 2 km bear right following signs for Ronciglione. By
now you will be used to the pretty hazelnut groves that line the road.

Ronciglione Although Dickens described this town as 'a large pig-sty', nowadays it is
little worse than worn at the edges. Its little square is oddly hemmed-in

Northern Lazio: Rome's Volcanic Lakeland

by a ruined church and castle. *Leave taking the narrow Via Plebiscito on the opposite side of the square from the Duomo, then turn right up the main street out of town. Keeping straight on you arrive at a turning to the left for S Martino al Cimino.*

Lido dei Pioppi
(restaurant, Ronciglione)

Just outside the town as you reach the lake, take the well-marked track to this favourite haunt of epicurean Romans. Sitting on the terrace with the wavelets lapping at the table legs, it is a good place to try delicate lake fish such as perch, pike and eel. *Tel 0761-612029; closed Mon; price band C.*

Lago di Vico

After a string of holiday homes you get your first real views of Lazio's prettiest volcanic lake. Shady lay-bys provide ideal picnic spots except when the day-trippers invade at weekends in high summer. Keep bearing right to continue on around the lake. The road begins to leave the banks and rises up on to the crest of the volcanic crater. Stop and admire the sweeping views of the whole lake spread out below. ⑥ *You soon reach a turning to the left signposted for Viterbo and S Martino al Cimino.* Viterbo now lies before you on the plains.

S Martino al Cimino

Before returning home pause here to admire the austere 13thC Gothic Cistercian abbey that crowns the town; it is a good antidote to the excesses of Villa Farnese. Look out for the street of identical terraced houses that runs down the hill parallel to the main *corso* – a fine example of enlightened 17thC town planning. *Leave following signs for Viterbo.* On your way back, the striking modern building to your right is Viterbo's new high-rise hospital.

ROUTE TWO: 109 KM

① *Leave, as before, on the road signposted for Orte and Villa Lante but immediately after crossing the railway line, turn left following signs for Bagnoregio.*

Acqua Rossa

⑦ After a couple of kilometres a track to the left marked by a rusty yellow sign directs you to the archaic Etruscan settlement of Acqua Rossa – though you will be hard pressed to find much trace of the rudimentary ruins thickly overgrown with broom. Much more impressive are the Roman remains at the next stop, Ferento.

Ferento

Turn off the main road at the well-signposted turning on the right. After about 2 km you will come upon the ruins of the Roman town of Ferentium dotted about the fields. The remarkably intact theatre, circled by 26 tufa arches, is an impressive sight. *Open am; closed Mon; but even when closed there are good views of the ruins.* The city was

Northern Lazio

• *Well preserved remains of the Roman theatre at Ferento.*

founded by the Etruscans, destroyed then rebuilt by the Romans and finally razed to the ground by the Viterbese in 1172 for alleged heresy. Return to the main road and turn right for Bagnoregio.

Bagnoregio The main reason for coming to this medieval village is to see the startling sight of Civita di Bagnoregio, La città che muore, 'the dying city'. The town stands a couple of kilometres outside Bagnoregio perched on a dizzy pinnacle of golden tufa which is slowly, but inexorably, crumbling away. The only way to reach Civita is over an exhilarating roller-coaster of a footbridge. Once inside you can admire the beautifully restored houses that have become weekend retreats for well heeled Romans – clearly somebody is hoping the place will not die too soon.

⑧ *Returning to Bagnoregio, drive along the one-way system until you arrive back at the main road, then take the left turn signposted Viterbo. Drive back past the old gateway until you reach the unsignposted turning on the right by the unusual large pyramid war memorial.* After about two kilometres turn left at the T-junction, taking signs to Bolsena. After passing over the busy main road you will catch your first glimpse of Lago di Bolsena as the road snakes down through olive groves.

Northern Lazio: Rome's Volcanic Lakeland

• *Capodimonte across Lago Bolsena.*

Bolsena Although a thriving resort noted for its mild climate, this old town has not been tempted to make too many concessions to tourism. It is well worth spending an hour or so wandering through the steep alleyways and narrow streets to work up an appetite for a superb fish lunch in the *centro storico* or on the waterfront.

Da Picchieto One of the best and most reasonably priced places to eat the fish from
(restaurant, the lake. In a cool vine-covered courtyard you could try the spaghetti
Bolsena) dressed with a fish sugo, stewed eel and grilled goregone, a fish similar to wild trout and found only here and in Lake Como. In the lower part of the old town in Via Porta Fiorentina; *tel 0761-799158; closed Mon; price band B.*

⑨ *Leave Bolsena on the Siena road going west and skirting the lake. Here there are a number of hotels and camp sites set amidst olives and vines that, although popular in summer, are nevertheless attractive. After 7 km the road heads away from the lake. Take the left turn here for Gradoli along the SS489. Stay on this road, bearing right.*

Gradoli A small town topped by another of the imperious Farnese palaces that dot the area. Stop here to buy a bottle or two of Aleatico di Gradoli, a sweet white dessert wine which is pure nectar.

Gradoli - ⑩ *At the T-junction after the village follow the signpost to the left for*
Capodimonte *Valentano then turn left again after 1 km onto the SS312. You are now*

Northern Lazio

driving along the rim of the volcanic crater with, to the right, spectacular views of the lake – the largest of volcanic origin in Italy – and the plains to the left. ⑪ *Just before entering the town of Valentano, bear left, following signposts for Capodimonte, heading back to the lake unless you want to stop here.* Valentano is not a major attraction – just an ordinary Lazio town – and perhaps that is its charm.

At the junction on the main road, turn left to follow signs for Viterbo. Your view of the lake is now dominated by its two islands, Bisentina and Marta, and the wooded promontory of Capodimonte.

Capodi- *As you arrive at the lake, take the left turn off the main road to*
monte *Capodimonte.* As you drive along the straight approach bordered by the lake, once again a grand Farnese castle rules the skyline. This is a good spot to picnic and swim in the unpolluted lake, though it is busy at summer weekends. With time to spare you can take the twice-daily, two-hour boat trip out to Isola Bisentina and see... another Farnese palace.

From Capodimonte head back on main road to Viterbo. After 500 metres turn off left to Marta.

Marta This lakeside medieval town is watched over by a 13thC tower and is notable for not having a Farnese palace. A good reason to stop here is to eat in one of the string of fish restaurants on the waterfront. Fillets of smoked eel, richer even than smoked salmon, are worth the rich price.

Leave, taking signs for Viterbo and Montefiascone. After 2 km fork left off the main road to Montefiascone. You are now in the heart of Est Est Est vineyard country.

Monte- Arriving at this noble hill town topped by its Duomo and ruined *rocca*,
fiascone follow signs for the *centro*. Park in the main square and walk up to the *belvedere* for some of the finest views of the lake on this route. At the bottom of the town, on your way out, stop to see the church of S Flaviano – actually two churches built one on top of the other. In front of the high altar rest the remains of Canon Johannes Fugger of Augsburg. Legend has it that, travelling to Rome, he sent his valet ahead with instructions to write "est" on the door of taverns where the best wine was to be drunk. At Montefiascone the servant enthusiastically scrawled the word three times. So much was the wine to the canon's liking that he died from drinking too much of it and Est! Est! Est! it remains to this day.

⑫ *Leave Montefiascone, following signs for Viterbo and make a speedy return on the main road that follows the course of the old Roman Via Cassia.*

Abruzzo:
THE PEAKS OF THE GRAN SASSO

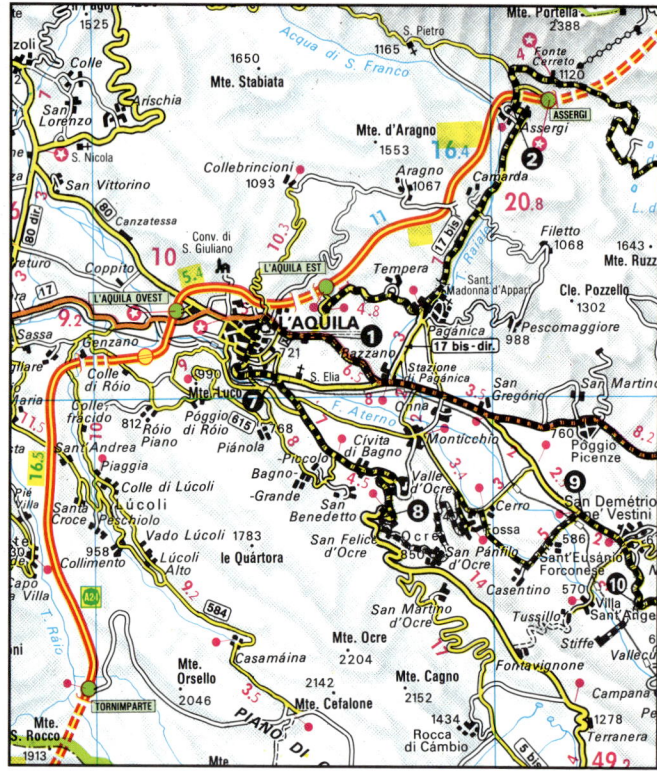

Italy's 'Big Rock', The Gran Sasso d'Italia, takes centre stage on this journey. The crests of these mountains, the highest in the Apennines, loom over the landscape at every turn and provide the backdrop to this rugged corner of Italy. L'Aquila, a self-sufficient city with the air of a frontier post, provides an intriguing base for the tour. The first loop ventures through the lonely desolation of the Campo Imperatore, a high plateau hemmed in by the crags of the Gran Sasso and a ski resort in winter, and a string of isolated villages where strangers are rare – check your petrol tank before leaving L'Aquila. The second explores the more genial valley of the Aterno, guarded by a chain of sombre medieval castles and boasting a succession of beautiful small churches and an outstanding complex of caves.

The simple *cucina casalinga* of the area owes more to south-

Abruzzo

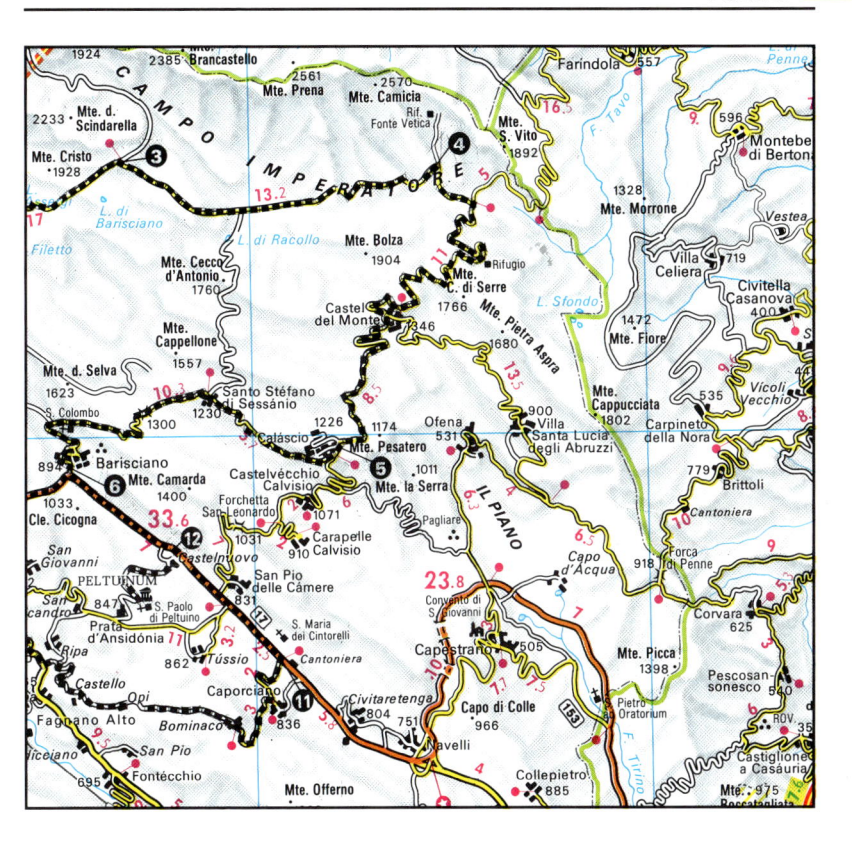

em Italy than to the north. *Diavolicchio* (the local name for chilli) features in many dishes and vegetables play a leading role in the regional diet. Cheeses, too, are important – *scarmozza*, a delicious mild soft cheese, is often served grilled as a light main course. The wines of the Abruzzo are a pleasant surprise – with lunch try Cerasuolo dry rosé and a heavy red Montepulciano d'Abruzzo for dinner (Valentini's vintage is one of Italy's top wines).

ROUTE ONE: 109 KM

L'Aquila   After the brashness of many Italian cities, the understated charms of L'Aquila come as a refreshing change. The open-faced robust people of this provincial capital seem less obsessed with appearances and are happy that their magnificently-sited home town remains a private secret.

Abruzzo: The Peaks of the Gran Sasso

The airy streets and small squares centred on the gracious arcades of the main Corso Vittorio Emanuele are best explored on foot. Pick up a town plan at the helpful tourist office half-way up the Corso and dedicate a day to discovering the place. Sights for special attention are the church of San Bernardino, where the great Sienese saint rests, the white and pink marble facade of the basilica of Santa Maria di Collemaggio, and the Fontana delle 99 cannelle, a medieval fountain with 99 carved spouts. Explore the dark alleyways of the ancient Santa Giusta quarter and peer into the courtyards of the noble *palazzi* that line Via Sassa. There is no shortage of restaurants – try the *spaghetti alla chittara* at San Biago on Via Sassa or go where the Aquilani go for a special meal at Ernesto, in Piazza Palazzo.

Duomo
(hotel,
L'Aquila)

Hotel Duomo (tel 0862-410769), just off the central Piazza del Duomo, is the most attractive small hotel in the centre of town. It offers stylish, modern, if rather cramped, rooms at reasonable rates in a recently renovated 18thC palace. If your purse is light try the decrepit Aurora (tel 0862-22053) in nearby Via Cimino – high on atmosphere but low on comfort.

Leave the city on the SS17 signposted for Funivia and Gran Sasso d'Italia. ①
After leaving the city proper, take the clear signs for Campo Imperatore and Paganica. Most of the heavy traffic around you will shortly be joining the motorway, leaving you in peace. *Keep following the signs for Paganica and Funivia.*

Da Pellicola
(restaurant,
Tempera)

About 4 km out of L'Aquila you arrive at the village of Tempera and surely one of the strangest restaurants in Italy. Trout and crayfish are reared in the streams that surround the long wooden barn where you eat, and the two ingredients form the basis of the simple menu. Do-it-yourself is the order of the day – from fetching your wine from the flasks cooling in the river outside to taking your plates to the kitchen. Then for the oddest part. The elderly padrone Vincenzo Pellicola, ringing the bell by the counter, will launch into a homily "Dio disse..." (God said...) or perhaps a little quiz on the Book of the Apocalypse. Though he sounds a touch puritanical, the flow of wine is decidedly catholic. For the full bizarre experience, go there when its busy at weekends. The restaurant is very difficult to find – turn sharp left after the Fiat garage on the right on to a single-track lane. Then follow the easily-missed little red signs for da Pellicola which you arrive at after 1 km. *Tel 0862-68655; closed Mon; price band B.*

Tempera -
Fonte Cerreto

Leaving Tempera, the road passes the little town of Paganica, noted for its dried beans. From here you enter a gorge cut by a rushing torrent that runs off the Gran Sasso. Stop to admire the sanctuary of the Madonna d'Appari carved into the rock. A few kilometres on, the road

• *Mellow Camarda, seen leaving L'Aquila.*

skirts Camarda, a sturdy example of an Abruzzo hill village, with spectacular views of the peaks of the Gran Sasso. Make the most of the trees that line the road here, as they are the last you will see for some time.

② *After passing Assergi, a fine old village with a handsome Romanesque church, keep straight on for Campo Imperatore. The sign here tells you in four languages if the road ahead is open. Shortly afterwards bear right and drive up to Fonte Cerreto through a rocky, blasted landscape dotted with scrubby trees.*

Fonte Cerreto This attractive, small ski resort crouches under the Corno Grande, the highest summit of the Gran Sasso. For those in search of peace and fine scenery, it makes an excellent alternative centre on this tour. Even if you are just passing, don't miss an ear-popping ride up the *funivia (open daily all year)*. It rises 1,000 m in around 10 minutes to reach the highest part of the Campo Imperatore and some of the finest mountain views south of the Alps. It was from here that the imprisoned Mussolini escaped in 1943, thanks to a daring raid by German airmen. You can see the room where the dictator stayed in the recently restored Albergo Campo Imperatore. You can even stay here yourself if you can bear the awesome silence more than 2,000 metres up.

Abruzzo: The Peaks of the Gran Sasso

• *The Tuscan tower at Santo Stefano.*

Fiordigigli
(hotel, Fonte Cerreto)

A modern chalet-style hotel, the Fiordigigli, *tel 0862-606171*, stands in a spectacular setting, a stone's throw from the bottom of the *funivia*. It has pleasant rooms at fair prices.

The Cristallo and Nido dell'Aquila, the other two hotels here, are equally attractive.

Campo Imperatore

Continuing on from Fonte Cerreto the road climbs gently up to the Campo Imperatore, first skirting Monte Cristo. A turning off to the left after about 10 km takes you up to the ski lifts on the mountain; stay on the main road to arrive, after 7 km, at the Campo Imperatore.

③ At the junction here the road to the left would take you up to its western extreme – at the top of the *funivia* from Fonte Cerreto – but beware of trying it as snow regularly lies well into June. *Bearing right the route now skirts the bleak but atmospheric landscape of the Campo*

Imperatore, a prehistoric dried-up lake bed some 27 km long and at an average height of 1,700 metres. The only signs of life are the few ruined shepherd's huts rapidly returning to the rocky ground from which they came. In early summer, the finest time to be driving the route, vivid mauve drifts of wild crocuses vie with the dazzling white patches of snow still lingering in the keen air. After about 4 km, carry straight on past the right-hand turn for S. Stefano di Sessanio.

④ *At the next junction, some 8 km on, turn right then, after 1 km, right again, following signs for Castel del Monte. You are now leaving the high plateau by way of Monte Capo di Serre and driving down to the town of Castel del Monte.*

Castel del Monte   The first of a string of lonely Abruzzi hill villages with long, often violent histories, Castel del Monte is worth a visit to see the austere medieval fortified borgo at its heart. Tourists are rare here; don't be surprised if people stare at you. Leave the town on the road marked for Calascio heading south.

Calascio   The 13thC castle here is the finest on this route. Perched 1,400 metres up, its towers dwarf the village below. Turn off to the right just before the town, signed Rocca di Calascio, to see the ruins close up – you will have to walk the last kilometre or so. Your reward is a magnificent view back to Castel del Monte. Returning to the main road, turn right to skirt the village below.

⑤ *Bear right following signs for Santo Stefano di Sessanio.*

Santo Stefano di Sessanio   After around 6 km the partly abandoned village of Santo Stefano suddenly and strikingly comes into view, this time ruled over by an elegant round tower built by the Tuscan Medici dynasty. Like a hill town in some early Renaissance painting, the fields around are still worked right up to the medieval walls. To the left as you arrive, a yellow sign directs you, round a very sharp turn, to the Torre Medicia. Park, and clamber through the warren of weed-infested steps and passages, looking out for the Tuscan touches that abound in this picturesque, if sadly deserted, place.

Leave Santo Stefano heading for Barisciano. The wild rugged country that has kept you company since leaving L'Aquila begins to give way to the fertile valley of the Aterno as you approach the modern fringes of Barisciano. Spoilt by the Rocca Calascio, you will probably not be tempted to stop at the few vestiges that remain of the medieval castle here.

⑥ *At Barisciano turn right on to the main SS17 signed for L'Aquila.* There is

Abruzzo: The Peaks of the Gran Sasso

a petrol station at this junction, your first after the long traverse of the Campo Imperatore.

Barisciano - L'Aquila

Although this is a main road, the return to L'Aquila is not unduly busy and there are fine views of the surrounding mountains as you drive along the valley floor. Only for the last few kilometres of this tree-lined, straight road is there much modern development as you arrive back at L'Aquila, entering the city through the Porta Napoli. *(If you are staying at Fonte Cerreto turn off to the right at Bazzano following clear signs for funivia to avoid L'Aquila.)*

ROUTE TWO: 86 KM

Leave L'Aquila through the Porta Napoli at the southern end of the city. The road, once you find it, is signposted for Sulmona, but beware as most of the signposting in L'Aquila pushes you on to the by-pass that skirts the town to the north. The road you want passes close by the church of S Maria di Collemaggio. *If you do find yourself taking the by-pass, turn off to the right at Bazzano and head back to L'Aquila and turn off to the left at ⑦.*

⑦ *A couple of kilometres after passing the Porta Napoli, turn right on to the SS5-bis signposted for Bagno and Avezzano, leaving the traffic behind. Pass Civita di Bagno, keeping to the main road, following signs for Avezzano.* The road begins to twist and turn as you leave the verdant valley floor and climb into wilder mountain country.

Castello d'Ocre

⑧ *Some 5 km on from Bagno turn left off the main road at the sign for San Panfilo d'Ocre, and drive through the small hamlet of San Felice d'Ocre.* Ahead of you to the left stand the imposing ruins of Castello d'Ocre. More a medieval fortified town than a castle, it is perched on a long, high mountain ridge, guarding the valley way below to the north. *Just before you arrive at the village of San Panfilo d'Ocre take the turning off to the left marked by a yellow sign for Castello d'Ocre.* At the junction just below the castle carry straight on to see the ruins at close quarters – although you will not be able to get further than the main gateway – or continue on the tour, bearing left, following signs for the Convento di S Angelo.

Convento di Sant'Angelo

In just under 3 km the narrow, tortuous road brings you to this hallowed spot. The 12thC Franciscan monastery of Sant'Angelo clings tenaciously to a sheer rock face with staggering views across the valley to the distant peaks of the Gran Sasso. Birdsong and the tolling of the bells are the only sounds that break the silence. Ring the bell and the friars will show you around. From the monastery, head on down the hill towards the broad valley and Fossa.

• *Gran Sasso, backdrop to this tour.*

Fossa Turn off sharp left as you arrive above the village, doubling back and winding down to the patch of earth that serves as the town square. This dusty little medieval village tottering on the steep slopes of the valley may not tempt you to stop – you will have seen all there is to see of the ruined castle as you arrived. However, the town's crusty centre hides a delightful cycle of 13thC frescoes. From floor to ceiling, the church of Santa Maria ad Cryptas is decorated with the story of the Last Judgement. Like innumerable other spots in Italy, it is reputed to have provided inspiration for Dante's Divine Comedy. You may need to do some vigorous miming, though, to find the priest to open the church. To leave, you can drive through the little cobbled main street – watch out for sleeping dogs and surprised inhabitants – but you are well advised to return to the junction above the village where you arrived, turn left and then, after 300 metres, left again on the unmarked new road that will take you down to the main road. Either way turn right at the T-junction on the main road. The road now runs through the rich agricultural lands on the valley floor.

Fossa - Stiffe *After about 1 km bear to the right then, another kilometre further on, bear left following signs for Sant'Eusanio.* Ahead of you stand the rather melancholy ruins of the Rocca di Sant'Eusanio Forconese, a small forbidding castle much knocked about by earthquakes. The town itself is a prosperous place with little of the air of abandonment that characterizes so many Aquilan towns. *Passing Sant'Eusanio, cross the railway line and ⑨ immediately turn right at signs for San Demetrio which appears after*

Abruzzo: The Peaks of the Gran Sasso

• The village of Fossa: a crumbling centre hiding 13thC frescoes.

less than 2 km. There is not much to stop for in this comfortable town; as you arrive keep on the main road, following signs for Molina and the Grotte di Stiffe.

⑩ *After a couple of kilometres, take the well-marked right turn to Stiffe. You now have some of the most attractive pastoral countryside on the tour and plenty of tranquil picnic spots.*

Grotte di Stiffe

You will now see ahead of you the white gash in the limestone bluff above the hamlet of Stiffe where the waters from a remarkable series of caves rush out into the valley. Just before the village, follow the signs for the *grotte* to arrive at the entrance. These caverns have only recently been opened to the public and should not be missed even by those with mild claustrophobia. They are a rare example of an 'active' chain of caves – the underground river that has formed them is still very much at work. Along with the visual delights of beautiful stalactites, the roar of the rushing waterfalls and rapids is unforgettable. The guided tour lasts just under an hour, so dress warmly. *Open Sat and Sun, daily in July and Aug.* If your Italian is up to it, you can arrange to see the caves when they are closed by telephoning *0862-61554*.

Leave Stiffe heading back on the road you came on. Arriving back at the T-junction on the main road turn right, following signs for Molina. After a couple of kilometres, take the sharp turning on the left signposted for Ripa, Fagnano, Castello and Opi, then 1 km on bear right to Bominaco. This delightful road now takes you, in just under 10 km, to Bominaco and the star attraction on the tour.

Bominaco This dust-blown collection of houses is an unlikely setting for two of the most delightful churches in Abruzzo. The rude façade of the little oratory of San Pellegrino hides resplendent floor-to-ceiling 13thC Byzantine frescoes, including an enchanting almanac of the seasons. Just up the hillock stands the church of Santa Maria Assunta, a gem of the 12thC Romanesque style with the most sublime stone carving inside. The two ancient buildings are all that remain of a rich and powerful Benedictine monastery destroyed when the monks rebelled against monastic rule. To get the custodian to open the churches ask at the bar/pizzeria alongside.

Bominaco - *Return to the road that skirts the village and turn left to continue on to*
Peltuinum *Caporciano*, another half-derelict Abruzzo hill village worth exploring if you have time on your hands. *Drive through the village taking the sharp dog-leg to the left to leave it.* The road now heads down to the green chequerboard of fields in the plains below. The striking ruined castle that you see on the far side of the valley is the Rocca of San Pio.

⑪ *Arriving at the main SS17 turn left following signs for L'Aquila.* The dead straight road, flanked by defensively sited villages, passes the saffron fields of the Navelli plains, the only area in Italy to grow this rare spice.

Peltuinum ⑫ *Some 5 km on, turn left off the main road at the village of Castelnuovo*
(detour) *to see the meagre but atmospheric ruins of Peltuinum.* A few upright piers of masonry are all that remain of this ancient pre-Roman city. You will see them on your left, 3 km after the turn-off – a romantic spot for a picnic. A fair walk to the south stands the abandoned Romanesque church of San Paulo di Peltuino, built entirely from the stones of Peltuinum.

La Cabina In an area where restaurants are thin on the ground, La Cabina is a
(restaurant, welcome oasis. You will find it on the roadside at the junction. Don't be
Castelnuovo) put off by the drab dining room; the seasonal local cooking is excellent and very reasonably priced. This is one of the few places where you can taste *farro*, a kind of grain prepared as a thick soup that was once a peasant staple. Also try the roast *scarmozza* cheese served with *prosciutto. Closed Wed; price band B.*

Follow the SS17 to return to L'Aquila. Some 8 km on, pause at Poggio Picenze to see some fine, intimate architecture in its medieval core.

Southern Lazio:
THE CIOCIARIA

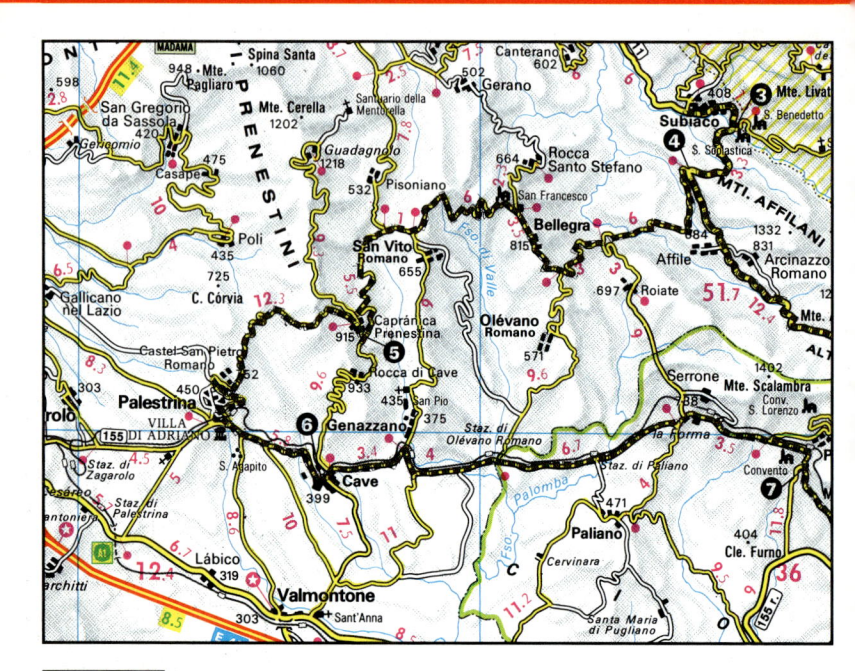

The *ciocie*, the humble sandals once worn by the peasants hereabouts, have given this hilly corner of Lazio its name. Yet the history of this absorbing area is far from humble. Long before Rome held sway, the bellicose Hernici tribe peopled the area. Their legacy is a series of towns still encircled by walls of massive five-sided blocks of stone, 'Cyclopean' defences unlike anything to be seen elsewhere in Italy. Rome, too, has left its mark with the substantial remains of the Temple to Fortune at Palestrina, while in medieval times at Subiaco St Benedict founded the monastic order that so profoundly influenced the course of European history. History apart, the jumble of wooded hills, fertile valleys and wild *karst* scenery – limestone eroded by percolating ground waters and underground streams – makes this a compelling and varied tour that should not be hurried. Apart from abundant highlights and attractions, both routes offer glimpses of many small medieval hill towns little changed in 600 years. Sadly, the modern Roman habit of dumping dead domestic appliances in the pristine countryside is a constant reminder that the Eternal City is never far away. Both routes are designed to avoid Roman dodgem car driving as much as possible.

Southern Lazio

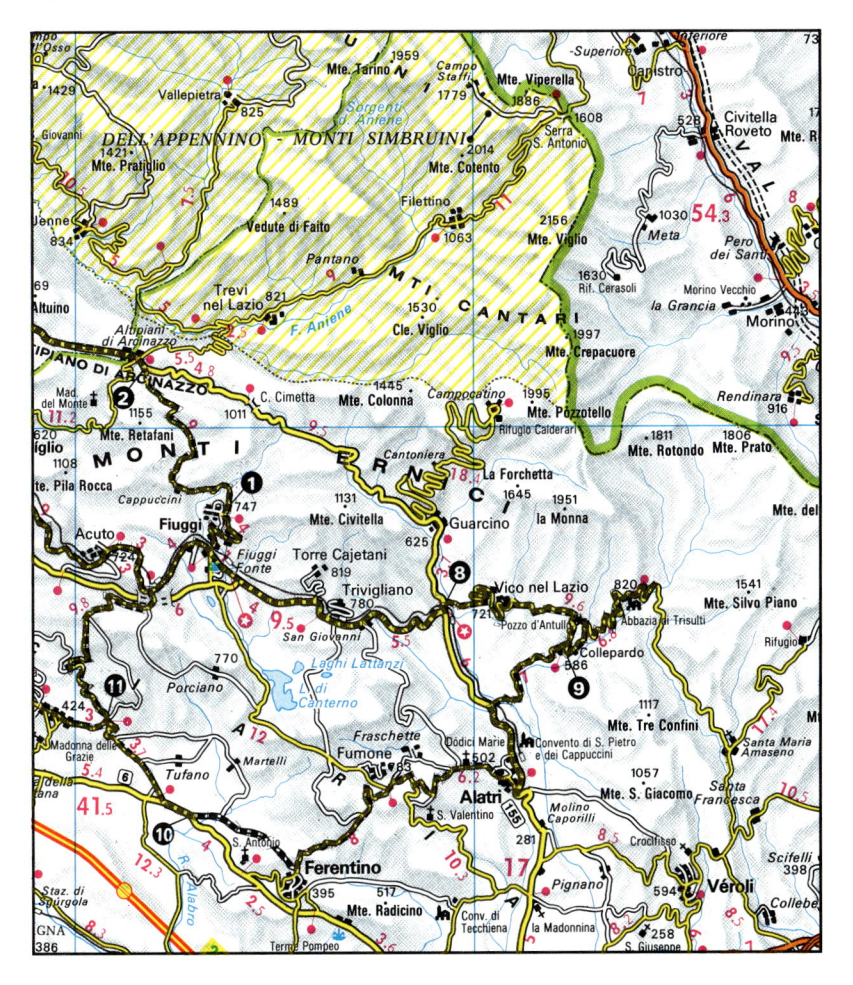

However, it is best to avoid July and August when the tour's centre, the spa town of Fiuggi, is besieged by legions of health-seeking holidaymakers.

ROUTE ONE: 114 KM

Fiuggi Michelangelo was just one of the famous visitors who came to seek a cure at this famous spa town – in his case for gallstones – and in high summer the place is packed with health-conscious Italians. A cross

145

Southern Lazio: The Ciociaria

Southern Lazio

• *Worn fresco at the church of Sacro Speco, Subiaco.*

between an expensive private hospital and a smart seaside resort, the lower town around the two springs, known as Fiuggi Fonte, has an ersatz chic that you might prefer to avoid. Head, instead, to the medieval town of Fiuggi Città, a 4 km twisting drive up from Fiuggi Fonte. Although not outstanding, it makes a quiet centre for this tour and the small square is a pleasant place for an evening stroll and dinner.

Anticoli
(hotel, Fiuggi Città)

If you decide to stay in Fiuggi, this small hotel in the old town is a reliable alternative to the rather expensive spa establishments down in Fiuggi Fonte. Although furnished like an old people's home, it is excellent value and well signposted as you drive up to Fiuggi Città. *70 Via Verghetti; tel 0775-55667.*

Fiuggi - Altipiano di Arcinazzo

① *Leave Fiuggi Città (the upper old town) and head north following signs for Subiaco and Arcinazzo.* As the road climbs up into the Ernici Hills you very quickly leave behind the sprawl of Fiuggi.

Altipiano di Arcinazzo

After some 8 km driving through rocky country you arrive at the edge of a high limestone plateau, the Altipiano di Arcinazzo. ② *At the small, mock-Swiss mountain resort of Altipiani di Arcinazzo turn left at the T-junction signed for Subiaco and head across the plain.* A singular landscape of open meadowland dotted with rocky outcrops and stunted trees, this *karst* landscape looks like the wild background to an early Renaissance painting. In the days of Imperial Rome it was a popular summer resort for patrician Romans escaping from the heat and squalor of the capital. Some 3 km into the plain the sorry remains of a grand villa from the time of Trajan stands at the side of the road (look out for the yellow sign Villa Romana). Reaching the edge of the plateau the hilltown of Affile surrounded by steep terraces of vines, olives and vegetable plots can be seen in the distance. This is one of the three centres for Cesanese wine, the best red that Southern Lazio has to offer.

Altipiano di Arcinazzo - Subiaco

After your first glimpse of Affile take the well-marked turning off to the right for Arcinazzo. This little loop on the route offers a good bird's-eye view of the plain and a glance at the little village of Arcinazzo Romano. Continue on from the village to rejoin the main road and turn right for Subiaco.

Passing the turning for the small medieval town of Affile bear right for Subiaco and after 3 km bear right again, keeping on the main road. Subiaco briefly comes into view before the road enters a short tunnel.

Monastero di San Benedetto

③ *Immediately after the tunnel take the sharp turn to the right signed for Monasteri Benedittini and double back on yourself* – be prepared for this junction as it is a very tight turn. In the closing years of the 5thC the youthful St Benedict chose a lonely cave on the wooded cliffs above

Southern Lazio: The Ciociaria

Subiaco to shut himself away in prayer. Three years later he emerged and founded the first twelve religious communities of the monastic order that was to single-handedly drag Europe out of the Dark Ages. Before visiting the town itself, make the pilgrimage to the cave where it all began. The road first passes Santa Scolastica, the only surviving monastery of the original 12 and worth visiting to see the fine Gothic cloisters. More interesting, though, is the Monastery of San Benedetto, built around the Sacro Speco – the grotto where Benedict lived in solitude. Here two churches, all of a piece with the rock to which they cling, are covered with luminous frescoes framing the bare rocky cavern. It is an intensely moving place and even the sceptic might feel swayed to say a prayer in honour of the patron saint of Europe.

Nero's Villa Retracing your steps from the Sacro Speco, shortly before arriving back at the main road for Subiaco, you pass on your right all that remains of a great palace built by Nero (you will also have passed it on your way up). The lavish villa was reflected in the waters of artificial lakes from which Subiaco – Sublaqueum – took its name. Tacitus describes how Nero was nearly killed here when lightning cleft the table at which he was dining. It was the gods, too, who finally swept away the villa and lakes when the dam across the river broke. *Now return to the main road ③ and turn right to Subiaco.*

Subiaco This attractive small town was originally built to house the workers constructing Nero's villa. Wander around the neat medieval quarter to work up an appetite for lunch – the Aniene right in the centre near the church of Sant'Andrea offers simple Lazio fare at modest prices.

Retrace your steps along the road on which you arrived, passing ③ the turn for the monasteries and continue on for around 3.5 km.

Subiaco - Palestrina ④ *Turn right towards Olevano and Bellegra.* From here to Palestrina the route twists through a switchback of wooded hills dotted with medieval hill towns; stop at Bellegra for the view and San Vito to explore its old quarter. *Winding up to Bellegra keep bearing right. After Bellegra bear left following signs for San Vito. After 6 km the left fork in the road leads to the centre of San Vito; take it if you have time to explore its small ancient centro storico, otherwise bear right at the fork signed for Tivoli. Just over 1 km on, turn off left following signs for Capranica.*

⑤ *At the isolated village of Capranica Prenestina leave the mini-roundabout at 9 o'clock, taking the road signposted for Roma, not the lower turn for Rocca di Cave.*

After Capranica have a picnic or a siesta in the shade of the cypresses that stand by the road. This is your last chance to savour this appealing

Southern Lazio

countryside before descending into hectic Palestrina.

Castel San Pietro Romano Shortly before arriving at the built-up fringes of Palestrina you will see this ancient village to your right. The ruin of the Colonna fortress that crowns the place marks the site of the acropolis of the ancient city of Praeneste.

Palestrina As you arrive at Palestrina stay on the main road bearing left to find yourself under the impressive *portico* of the 17thC Palazzo Barberini. Roman Praeneste boasted a vast temple to the goddess of Fortune. Although the celebrated oracle was finally stilled at the close of the 4thC, her voice still haunts you as you wander round the town. The modern-day centre follows the plan of the four terraces in the enormous pagan complex and at every turn remains of the temple emerge to delight the eye. First visit the museum in the Palazzo Barberini on the spot where Fortuna held sway from the top terrace. Having seen the beautiful mosaic of the Nile in Flood and studied the model reconstruction of the temple, pick up a copy of the helpful town guide and amble down through the terraces.

Stella Explored at night, Palestrina is an even more evocative place. A small,
(hotel/restaurant, Palestrina) well appointed albergo in the central Piazza della Liberazione, the Stella has comfortable modern rooms at reasonable prices. The *cucina casareccia* – home cooking – in the restaurant is well above average, as is the choice of wines. *Tel 06-9558172; price band B.*

Leave from the bottom of town following signs for Fiuggi. You are still in the province of Rome so be prepared for unpredictable Roman driving. You have now left the grandeur and tranquillity of the hills behind. In recompense, the return to Fiuggi offers a chain of old towns noted for their wines and one of Southern Lazio's most outstanding restaurants.

Cave Lying in the folds of the foothills of the Ernici Mountains this is a well-proportioned small town, its stuccoed buildings emitting a distinctly Roman air. ⑥ *Continue on the main road for Fiuggi.*

Genazzano The hill town of Genazzano shortly comes into view as the road passes through a more rural setting. This attractive place marks the edge of the Cesanese red wine area. Some 2 km after the town you pass the large Cantina Sociale – stop here to see a winery at work. There are also a number of small private producers selling their wine – look out for the rough painted signs 'Vino'. You are usually made very welcome, though they will expect you to buy at least a couple of bottles.

Passing the solid citadel at Paliano you arrive at La Forma. You have now left the province of Rome and might just notice an improvement in the driving. Heading for Piglio the road has some fine hilly views.

Southern Lazio: The Ciociaria

• *Atmospheric Collepardo.*

Southern Lazio

Piglio The best of the Cesanese wines come from here and the ancient centre is worth a visit, if only as an example of a typical, small Ciociaria town. Apart from the red DOC Cesanese del Piglio, it is certainly worth tasting Passerina de Frusinate, a smoky, full-bodied white wine. *Return to the main road and turn left, continuing on towards Fiuggi.* ⑦ *At the next junction bear left and climb to Acuto and the heart of the Ernici hills.*

Acuto The best reason for a stop here lies on the main road to your right as you leave the village - an unprepossesing white building that hides one of the finest restaurants in Southern Lazio. It may prove to be a long stop.

Colline Ciociare *(restaurant, Acuto)* Salvatore Tassa, a rising young star amongst Lazio chefs, is a serious cook, and his elegant but unfussy restaurant is for serious eaters. Have the *menu degustazione*, eight courses combining to make an unforgettable meal, and a bottle of red Cesanese del Piglio. Although not cheap, it is remarkable value for the quality. *Tel 0775-56049; closed Mon and Tues lunch; booking essential; price band D.*

Leave heading for Fiuggi and bear left at the main junction. The hotels of Fiuggi Fonte now lie before you.

ROUTE TWO: 69 KM

Leave Fiuggi Fonte (the lower spa town) heading east, following signs for Frosinone and Alatri. Passing the small hill villages of Torre Cajetani and Trivigliano, ⑧ *you arrive at a junction to the left signposted initially for Subiaco. Beware as there are two roads off to the left – you want the second which has an easily-missed sign for Vico nel Lazio.* Happily, you are now on a much quieter country road heading towards real mountains.

Vico nel Lazio A series of hairpin bends brings you to this hushed medieval village with much of its original wall intact. Park by the tower-flanked gateway and stroll about. From here the road continues to twist up into the mountains through a landscape dotted with a few sheep, the odd cow – and inevitably the occasional abandoned fridge.

Pozzo d'Antullo *Some 9 km on from Vico a battered little yellow sign directs you to the left to the Pozzo d'Antullo.* This enormous, sheer chasm, some 200 m wide, is a dramatic example of a limestone pothole. Hung with fantastically shaped stalactites, and echoing with raucous bird calls that warn you not to venture too close to the fearsome pit, here is an enlivening spot for a picnic.

Collepardo Leaving the *pozzo*, this inviting hill village soon comes into view. Stop to admire the inspiring views of the Ernici Mountains and wander through

Southern Lazio: The Ciociaria

- *Above, the cyclopean or giant walls at Alatri.*
- *Right, hillside Ferentino.*

the dark lanes lit by shafts of brilliant sunlight. You will also give the old widows in black something new to gossip about: "Ma, chi sono?" they will whisper as you pass.

Certosa di Trisulti (detour)

This detour, 12 km there and back, to the Carthusian monastery of Trisulti is definitely worth the journey. ⑨ *Leave Collepardo following signposts for Certosa and Grotte dei Bambocci.* The ancient abbey dates back to 1204 and clearly the monks had an eye for a memorable setting. The highspot is the lavishly decorated 18thC pharmacy with its topiary garden. Fountains, palms and grandstand views over the wooded hills complete the scene. You can also taste and buy monkish liqueurs.

Returning to Collepardo, you pass a turning to the Grotte dei Bambocci, a series of impressive caves much appreciated by children (open daily July-Sept; weekends only, Oct-June).

Head on from Collepardo following signs for Frosinone and Alatri and turn left at main road for Alatri.

Alatri

One of the best-preserved examples of a pre-Roman town in Italy, this Hernici stronghold is still girded by its cyclopean walls built over 2,400 years ago. Negotiate the brutish fringes of the modern town and leave

152

Southern Lazio

Southern Lazio: The Ciociaria

• *Domestic details, Ferentino.*

your car by one of the chunky gates at the bottom of the *centro storico*. Star billing here goes to the Acropolis, the monolithic Hernici fortress crowning the town that looks much as it did when built in the 4thC BC. The rest of the town is not miserly with its charms — wander through the sombre streets hemmed in by gaunt *palazzi* or, even better, stay the night.

Rosetta (hotel/restaurant, Alatri)

The pretty pink Albergo Rosetta stands right opposite the massive walls of the Acropolis and offers inexpensive, modest rooms. Its restaurant, popular with the townspeople, is well known for its excellent Lazio cooking. *Tel 0775-450068; closed Fri; price band B.*

Leave Alatri following signs for Ferentino and Fumone negotiating a slippery one-way system. Around 2 km after leaving Alatri keep on the main road bearing left to follow signs for Ferentino.

Ferentino

This too was a Hernici stronghold, though its massive walls were much meddled with in Roman and medieval times. Walk up to the Roman remains that stand on the site of the old Acropolis at the top of the town and have a glance at the fine marble pavement in the adjacent Cathedral. The views from up here are an added bonus.
Leave the town following the green signs for the Roma-Napoli motorway,

then follow the signposts for Anagni. ⑩ *Turn right when you arrive at the main road, the ancient Roman Via Casilina. After 2 km turn right off this rather busy highway.* ⑪ *At the next stop sign, turn left for Anagni.*

Anagni As you arrive look out for the hospital and park nearby. A short walk to your left brings you to the Cathedral, a glorious Romanesque church with a crypt paved with sensual, inlaid marble. From here the main Strada Vittorio Emanuele winds down through the town – look out for the austere 12thC town hall and the Casa Barnekow, just two of the appealing buildings lining this elegant street. This gracious town produced a handful of 13thC popes, headed by the overweening Boniface VIII. Pushing the temporal power of the Papacy as far as it had ever been pushed before, it was here that he met his nemesis when the forces of Philip the Fair of France took him prisoner. Although released after three days by his fellow Anagnini, he died a month later a broken man. Ring the bell at the nunnery now housed in the Palazzo di Bonifacio VIII and the sisters will show you the room where the Pope calmly awaited his capture, dressed in full Papal regalia.

Del Gallo This simple *trattoria* in a distinguished old palace offers superb *fettuccine*
(restaurant, (the Roman version of tagliatelle) and an excellent *brasato* (pot-roasted
Anagni) meat with a piquant dressing). The prices, though, are a mite higher than they ought to be. It also has a few very cheap rooms without bathrooms. *Tel 0775-727309; closed Thurs; price band C.*

Leave Anagni on the road by which you arrived. ⑪ *After about 1.5 km, bear left following signs for Acuto and Fiuggi. The pleasant country road winds through olive groves with pretty views back to Anagni. Some 3 km further on keep to the main road, bearing right to follow signs for Fiuggi. Arriving at the T-junction, turn right onto the SS155, the old Roman Via Praenestina which will take you back to Fiuggi Fonte.*

Campania:
THE CILENTO PENINSULA

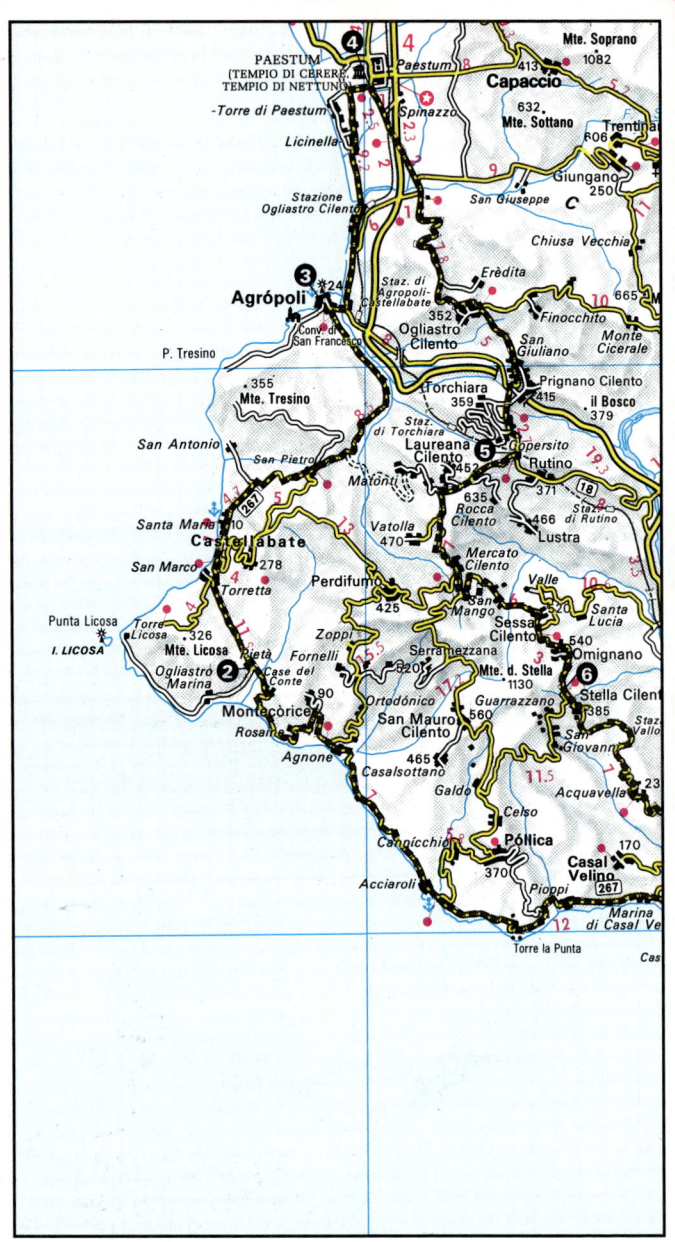

Campania

A voiding the northern coast of the Bay of Salerno around Amalfi —undeniably beautiful but a tourist honey-pot – this tour sets out to explore the lesser-known Cilento peninsula that forms the southern arm of the bay. Along the coast a handful of modest resorts play host to Italian family holidaymakers for the brief summer season. For the rest of the time they return to being typical small Mediterranean fishing harbours. Inland, the wild mountain country is largely undiscovered by all but the most pioneering traveller.

The first route meanders along the rocky coastline, visiting the prettiest of the Cilento seaside towns before briefly joining the tourist circuit to visit the outstanding temples at Paestum, the

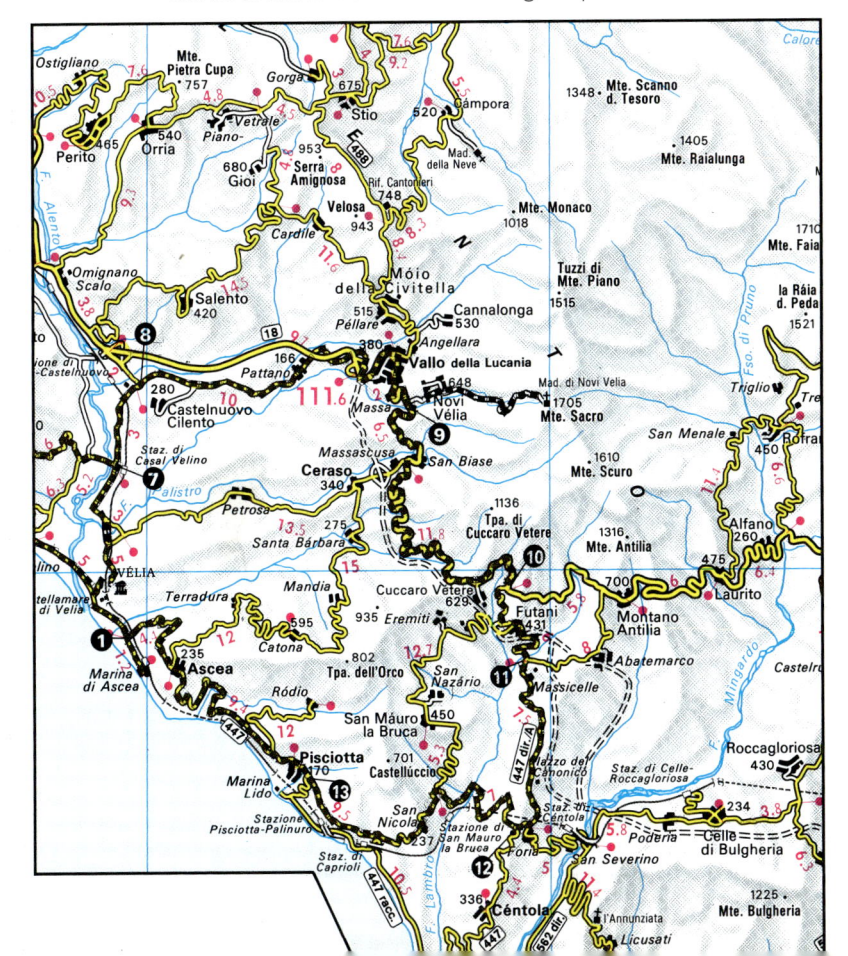

Campania: The Cilento Peninsula

finest Greek ruins in Italy. A switchback drive through the interior takes you back to the centre at Marina di Ascea. The second loop spends more time winding through the lonely high southern slopes of the peninsula with a shorter stretch of pure Mediterranean coastline to end the day.

Inland restaurants are few but there are plenty of picnic spots. On the coast, however, there is no shortage of charming *trattorie* serving superb fish and shellfish. Pizzas, too, are a good alternative – the proximity to Naples guarantees the real McCoy.

ROUTE ONE: 125 KM

Marina di Ascea

This little family seaside resort typifies the Italian idea of fun in the sun – a bit seedy but quite animated. There is a good sandy beach and a pair of small, low-key campsites. The handful of hotels has no particular appeal and you may do better staying at one of the other resorts described on this route. August apart, you should not have any difficulty finding a room.

Leaving Marina di Ascea, turn left following signs for Salerno.

① *After just under 2 km turn left again for Acciaroli and, following the coast road northwards, cross the wide Alento valley. At the next junction keep straight on, following signs for Pioppi and Acciaroli.* The road edges ever closer to the sea, skirting a string of charming coves set amidst umbrella pines and prickly pear – you would have to travel far to find such an undeveloped stretch of the Mediterranean.

Pioppi

At the heart of this enchanting little resort with its shingly beach is a small, working fishing harbour with the smell of the catch everywhere. This endearing spot makes an ideal alternative centre for the tour.

La Vela
(hotel/restaurant, Pioppi)

This small hotel near the beach offers unassuming, inexpensive rooms from March to October. It also boasts a pergola-covered terrace where you can eat the freshest of fish overlooking the sea. *Tel 0974-905025; price band C.*

After the village, the road continues along the coast passing Torre la Punta, a watchtower whose picturesque remains lie below the road. *After a few kilometres turn off to the left into Acciaroli.*

Acciaroli

One of the most attractive resorts on the Cilento, this small working port was much admired by Hemingway. Despite its decent sandy beach and a handful of small, pleasant hotels, tourism is still secondary to the

Campania

• *Acciaroli*

village's fishing trade.

Leave on the coast road for Agropoli and, after 7 km, hugging the coastline, bear left, again following signs for Agropoli. Off to the left there are striking views of the Licosa peninsula.

② *Carry straight on for Agropoli.*

San Marco & Santa Maria di Castellabate
Returning to the sea, before long you catch sight of the medieval hilltown of Castellabate on the horizon, a huddle of houses around a 12thC castle reached by tortuous hairpins. Modern-day life centres on the two satellite resorts of San Marco and Santa Maria down on the

Campania: The Cilento Peninsula

• *Interior of the Temple of Neptune at Paestum.*

coast below. Both are still thriving and authentic Mediterranean fishing ports of great charm, though liable to be crowded in high summer. If you enjoy exuberant fun and games join the young Italian holidaymakers for a few days at the L'Approdo, *tel 0974-966001*, at San Marco, a scaled-down 'Club Med' that offers, as its leaflet says, "a full-time holiday". At Santa Maria, you can virtually climb out of bed straight on to the sandy beach at the Hotel Sonia, *tel 0974-961172*. Neither will empty your wallet. Even if you decide not to stay, at least try the excellent ice creams at Santa Maria. *Leave, continuing northwards, following the signs for Agropoli.*

Campania

* *Temple of Neptune at the ruined Greek city of Paestum.*

Agropoli

Traffic can be a nightmare in the cramped centre but it is worth stopping here. *Carry straight on as you arrive at the inauspicious outskirts if you want to visit the town. Otherwise, turn right following the signs for Paestum and Lungomare.* The compact old quarter, perched on a hill that splits the working port area from the rather seedy beach resort, is a delight to explore. There are several *pizzerie* and restaurants with superb views over the Bay of Salerno – on a clear day you can catch a distant glimpse of Capri. If you decide to stay here, the town has an aggressively vital *passeggiata* and a touch more sophistication than the other resorts on the Cilento.

Carola
(restaurant/hotel, Agropoli)

An attractively faded hotel, its airy inexpensive rooms have good views over the harbour. It also has an excellent restaurant – fresh tuna and a fine *zuppa di pesce* feature on the menu. The other bonus is the hotel's car park. *Tel 0974-826422; price band C.*

Agropoli - Paestum

③ *Leaving the centre of Agropoli you have to contend with an obtuse one-way system but signs for Lungomare and Paestum will get you to the coast road heading north.*

About 3 km further on turn left, following the yellow sign for litoranea *(coast road) to continue skirting the sea.* Look out for the lumbering buffalo in the grasslands to your right – Italy's finest *mozzarella* cheese is made from their milk. The thought of a fresh *mozzarella* dressed simply with olive oil and pepper – ask for one as a light second course in any Cilento restaurant – will take your mind off the scruffy camp sites that blight the sandy beaches to your left. Before too long, though, you arrive at Paestum.

Campania: The Cilento Peninsula

- *Cilento coastline.*

Paestum Visiting here in 1787, Goethe felt stupefied in front of the ruins of the ancient Greek city. You may feel the same. Lost in malarial marshes for more than 800 years, the remarkably intact ruins of these Doric temples are the finest testimony to the greatness of Greek civilization in Italy. Founded in the 7thC BC, the city was named Poseidonia after the Greek sea god. Later colonized by the Romans who gave it its modern name, it finally slipped into oblivion in the 9thC, wiped out by Saracen raids and the anopheles mosquito. As you wander through the august Temple of Neptune, the most perfect of the trio, try to imagine what it was like covered in the brightly coloured *stucco* that once encased it. The adjacent museum houses outstanding finds from the site including rare examples of Greek wall painting – the Tomb of the Diver has a particularly frank rendering of a *symposium*, the Greek drinking party made respectable by Plato. Both the museum and site are *open daily except Mon.*

Martini To appreciate the ruins at their best, avoid the coach parties and
(hotel, stay overnight at this comfortable hotel by the site. The rooms, little
Paestum) bungalows in a garden setting, are modestly priced and peaceful; *tel 0828-811020.* Across the road, actually in the archeological zone, is the Nettuno restaurant with honest local food and an excellent view; *tel 0828-811028; closed Mon; price band B.*

④ *Leaving the entrance to the ruins, carry straight on over the traffic lights*

Campania

heading south, following the sign to S Venere. After 2 km along a perfect Italian avenue of umbrella pines, the road crosses a railway bridge where you bear right, then left, following signs for Giungano and Ogliastro. Keep straight on at the next two junctions continuing to head for Ogliastro.
The road rapidly leaves the coastal plain, climbing round a series of sharp bends. There are sweeping views ahead of the northern slopes of the Cilento mountains and back across to the Bay of Salerno.

Ogliastro Cilento

The first of a string of Cilento hill villages on this route, Ogliastro has little to offer, though it is typical of these isolated, unblest habitations. After the bustle of the coast, it comes as a welcome contrast – the late 20thC has some catching up to do here. The real attraction of this stretch of the tour, however, is the rugged mountain countryside with wide-ranging views around every corner.

Drive through the winding main street of Ogliastro and head on to Prignano Cilento. At Prignano follow the signs for Rutino keeping to the main road. **⑤** *Turn right 2.5 km on from Prignano onto a small road marked for Laureana, San Martino and Mercato Cilento.*

San Martino Cilento

At this small hamlet, turn left to take a short detour up through chestnut woods to Rocca Cilento, one of the prettier of these villages with the ruins of a 9thC castle and fine views down to Agropoli. Otherwise continue along the main road which skirts Laureana Cilento and Vatolla to arrive, after 5 km, at Mercato Cilento. Here, at the end of the village, keep straight on ignoring the right turn for Perdifumo and, shortly afterwards, bear left at the sign to S Mango.

Monte Stella

Ahead of you stands the chestnut-clad slopes of Monte Stella whose timber props up the local economy. At 1,131 metres this is the highest peak in the northern section of the Cilento mountains and offers some splendid virgin walking country. Circling the mountain the route passes through the villages of San Mango and Sessa Cilento. At Omignano, follow the road through the arch in the middle of the village. A pause in any one of these small hill towns provides a thought-provoking if rather grim glimpse of life in these lonely hills.

⑥ *After Omignano, turn left at the junction for Stella Cilento. Then, passing through the village, turn right for Acquavella, the last of the hill villages. From here on, the road drops rapidly to the fertile and developed plain of the Alento. About 3 km on from Acquavella bear left. After another 1 km turn left at the sign for Vallo della Lucania and Salerno.* The road shortly crosses the Alento river. **⑦** *Turn right onto the main road following signs for Ascea and Palinuro.*

The road now heads towards the sea through market gardens – mostly

Campania: The Cilento Peninsula

tomatoes and artichokes – before arriving at the main coast road. The round medieval tower you see ahead is Castellamare di Velia. *Turn left as you arrive back at the coast road and shortly afterwards right, to return to Marina di Ascea.*

ROUTE TWO: 90 KM

① *Leave Marina di Ascea and turn left on to the main coast road signposted for Agropoli and Salerno. After about 1 km turn right up a rough track at the easily missed sign for Scavi di Velia.*

Velia

Here, at the side of the main Napoli-Reggio railway, are the remains of the Greek city of Elea. Founded around 540 BC, its name lives on in the Elean school of philosophy. As you wander amongst the ruins, try unravelling Zeno's famous paradoxes – a tortoise given a handicap can never be outrun by Achilles, or an arrow in flight is in fact at rest – for it was here that he thought them up. Even if Zeno leaves you cold, the site is an atmospheric spot with lizards sunning themselves on the sun-baked stones which lie among wild flowers and dry grasses. Don't miss the Porta Rosa, the landward gate to the old city that stands a few hundred metres above the main ruins and the earliest Greek round arch in existence. The ruined medieval citadel of Castellamare above the city marks the site of Elea's Acropolis.

Turn right on leaving the site, then bear right again to follow the signs for Salerno.

Velia - Vallo della Lucania

Heading up the valley of the Alento, you pass through rather dull agricultural lands sprinkled with light industry. *Continue, following the signs for Salerno until you arrive at Vallo Scalo.*

⑧ *At the stop sign here turn right for Castelnuovo Cilento.* You are now on a much more inspiring road winding up the hillside with fine views ahead of the inland Cilento. *Keep on the main road, following signs for Vallo della Lucania, and pass through the village of Pattano. After some 12 km you arrive at Vallo della Lucania.*

Vallo della Lucania

The main market town of the Cilento, this is unmapped territory for the tourist. Although low on major attractions – the church of Santa Maria delle Grazie and the little museum are of minor interest – it is the only real town in inland Cilento and a good place to watch animated southern daily life. If it is lunchtime, hold on – there is a restaurant a few kilometres further on well worth waiting for.

Leave the town's central square, following the main road to the right, then

Campania

• *Ruins of the Greek city of Elea at Velia.*

bear right again. There is a rather haphazard one-way system here and a paucity of signs but you cannot get too lost. If you are on the right road you will arrive at the village of Massa shortly after leaving the town.

La Chioccia d'Oro
(restaurant, Vallo della Lucania)

This simple *trattoria* set in chestnut woods by the junction for Novi Velia comes as a welcome surprise. Crowded with locals at the weekend, it offers genuine cooking of the region – *gnocchi* with a concentrated meat sauce, excellent lamb and *castrato* (kid), and an unusual cheese made from a mixture of sheep and goat's milk. *Tel 0974-65085; closed Fri; price band B.*

Madonna di Novi Velia
(detour)

This 30-km round trip to the ancient sanctuary on the summit of Monte Sacro, the highest mountain in the Cilento, has some hair-raising driving but rewards you with some of the finest views you are likely to find in the whole of Southern Italy. ⑨ *Just after Massa, turn left at sign for Novi Velia.* The road begins well enough. After several kilometres, however, it becomes an obstacle course with enormous boulders from the winter landslides littering your path – it is not a drive for the faint-hearted. Arriving as far as the road will take you, it is a 10-minute walk up to the sanctuary of the Madonna perched on the summit. A place of pilgrimage, this rather eerie spot is festooned with crutches and bandages left by the infirm. The sanctuary is open from late May to October. The views of the whole of the Cilento from this 1,700-metre

Campania: The Cilento Peninsula

- *Porta Rosa, the landward gate of the old city of Elea.*

Campania

high holy mountain are staggering. Pray, however, for good weather – there is no point making the journey if there is cloud about.

Even if you don't want to brave the full drive up, take the first couple of kilometres of the detour to visit the ancient *borgo* of Novi Velia with its medieval Longobard tower. Just on from the village there are some exhilarating picnic spots by a rushing mountain torrent.

⑨ *From Massa keep on the main road following signs for Sapri.* After the village of San Biase the route twists and turns through the foothills of Monte Sacro. Some 10 km on you pass the hoary village of Cuccaro Vetere perched on its hill off to the right.

⑩ *After a couple of kilometres, turn off to the right at the signpost for Futani and Palinuro.* Passing through beech woods you arrive at fly-blown Futani. *From here, follow signs for Palinuro.*

⑪ *Bear right at Massicelli, still following signs for Palinuro.* Look back for the spectacular views of Monte Sacro as you drive through this attractive open countryside at the head of the Lambro valley. Over to your left the imposing bulk of Monte Bulgheria soon looms into view with its striking eroded limestone bluffs.

⑫ *Shortly after your first view of the mountain bear right, following signs for Palinuro, then turn right at the major road junction some 500 metres on (unsignposted). After 6 km turn left at the sign for Pisciotta and drive down to the coast.*

Capo Palinuro

To your left you soon have distant views of the coast down to Capo Palinuro. This cape takes its name from Palinurus, the helmsman of Aeneas who, so Virgil's story goes, fell overboard off the cape and was slaughtered by the native Lucanians when he swam ashore. The modern day inhabitants of Palinuro are much more welcoming and in fact the town has become the busiest of the Cilento resorts – this route avoids it and heads back along the *corniche* road to Pisciotta.

Pisciotta

This handsome little town, dominated by its citadel, has a sleepy fishing harbour at the marina below. It is a difficult, twisting drive down to the port but there are some sheltered rocky bathing spots when you arrive.

Da Sofia
(restaurant, Pisciotta)

This modern *trattoria* on the left just after the town is the local choice at weekends and offers the best of the catch at low prices. The sea views are an added bonus. Tel 0974-973462; price band B.

⑬ *Continuing along the coast, enjoy the quintessential Mediterranean views as you drive the next 10 km to Ascea. Then follow the signs for Salerno before taking the left turn back down to Marina di Ascea.*

Northern Puglia
THE GARGANO PENINSULA

The mountainous spur on Italy's boot is one of the few places where you can still find the quintessential Mediterranean coastline largely unspoilt by the inroads of mass tourism. Holidaymakers do come here every year in greater numbers, but the season is short and outside July and August you will not have to fight for space on its beautiful, unpolluted beaches. Facilities for tourists are still simple and, apart from Vieste, do not unduly mar the scenery. May, June and September are the ideal months to visit, when the dependable weather may tempt you to stay in some of the most enticing campsites that you will find in Italy.

The first loop of the tour takes in the finest stretches of the coastline before plunging into the deep forest that clothes the

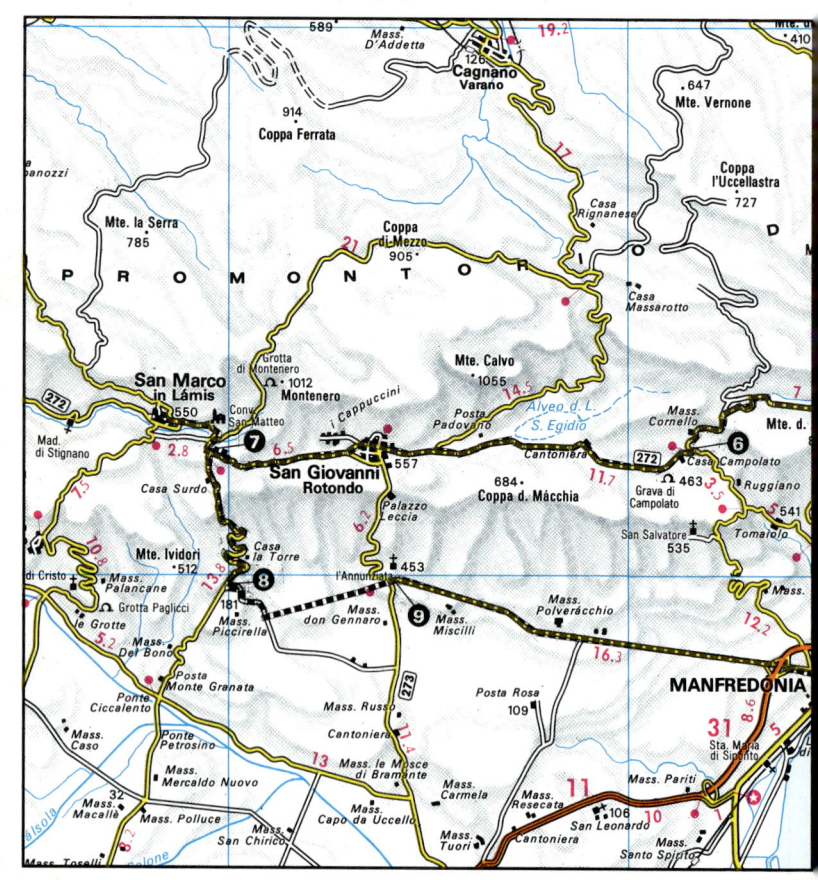

Northern Puglia

Northern Puglia: The Gargano Peninsula

heart of the peninsula. The second route follows in the footsteps of the pilgrims who came here centuries before the modern-day sun worshippers, to visit Monte Sant'Angelo, the tour's centre. Pilgrimage still plays a part with the faithful now flocking to the modern sanctuary of Padre Pio at San Giovanni Rotondo.

Few make the pilgrimage to Puglia for the food but it does offer superb raw ingredients, simply prepared. On the coast the fresh fish is of the finest quality, while inland plain grilled meats are the order of the day. Puglia's favourite pasta, the little ear-shaped *orecchiette*, is a permanent fixture and invariably homemade.

ROUTE ONE: 130 KM

Monte Sant'Angelo

The Archangel Michael's appearance here some time around 490 made it one of the earliest shrines in Christendom. For centuries pilgrims trekked across Europe to visit this lonely, high place, and it was an obligatory halt for crusaders heading for the Holy Land. On the 8th of May, the Feast of the Apparition, the town is still packed with faithful but for the rest of the time it is a sleepy town that makes an ideal centre for the tour. The star attraction is the sanctuary to St Michael, whose gothic portals look like the entrance to any other church – except, perhaps, for the Latin inscription above: "Awesome is this place. This is the house of God and the Gateway to Heaven". Once inside, a long flight of worn steps leads down to the dank cavern where the Archangel first appeared 1,500 years ago – an elemental place that was a centre for pagan worship long before Christianity took over. The town has many other charms – take time to wander through the blindingly white medieval Junno quarter below the shrine, originally built to lodge the numerous pilgrims, and climb up to the Norman castle for the panoramic views over the whole Gargano peninsula. There are plenty of restaurants here, mostly serving identical menus at identically low prices – *orecchiette* for *primi* and charcoal grilled lamb for *secondi*. One of the best is Al Grottino in the Corso Vittorio Emanuele in the centre of town.

Rotary
(hotel, Monte Sant'Angelo)

An anonymous small modern hotel but in a spectacular setting – all the comfortable bedrooms have sweeping views down to the Gulf of Manfredonia. Prices, too, are very moderate. It lies a couple of kilometres out on the road to Pulsano and is well signposted from the town. *Tel 0884-62146.*

Leave, first following signs for Manfredonia and Mattinata, then, at the roundabout, follow signs for Mattinata. The road now descends rapidly

Northern Puglia

• *Picnic fare for sale at Monte Sant'Angelo.*

through ancient terraces of almond trees with your first heady views of the Mediterranean. Finally, after about 14 km, you will see the bay of Mattinata set in a forest of olive trees.

① *At the junction turn left for Mattinata.*

Mattinata Mattinata has yet to be swamped by tourism and remains the most

Northern Puglia: The Gargano Peninsula

• *The natural arch of Architello near Pugnochiuso.*

appealing of the Gargano coastal villages. It has no special sights but a stroll through its old white-painted centre stacked up the hillside is a memorable experience. In the small *piazza* visit the Enoteca Bisceglia to buy the best local produce – olive oil, the pick of Puglia's under-rated wines, a host of *antipasti* under oil and fresh local farm cheeses.

Papone
(restaurant, Mattinata)

Just outside the town on the SS89 in the direction of Vieste, try traditional Pugliese cooking with a touch of imagination at this popular restaurant in an old olive oil mill. *Tel 0884-4749; closed Mon; price band B.*

Leave Mattinata heading down towards the sea, then bear right following signs for Vieste Littoranea and Pugnochiuso – do not take the alternative inland route for Vieste via the SS89. Off the road to the right a small track leads down to the beach and a string of small campsites set among shady olive groves.

Mattinata - Mattinatella

Around 2 km from the town the road reaches the sea at Porto di Mattinata, a little fishing harbour where you can eat excellent fish at one of the several *trattorie* on the rocks.

From here on, the *corniche* road has the most spectacular views that

Northern Puglia

you will find on the whole of Italy's Adriatic coastline – dazzlingly white limestone cliffs plunging down to the aquamarine sea bathed in hazy brilliance. This must be one of the few remaining tracts of the Mediterranean that has not been desecrated by tourism.

Bellavista
(snack-bar, Mattinata)

This little road-side hut on the right some 3 km after the harbour has a terrace perched over the sea with travel brochure views. Pull in and have a *bruschetta ai pomodori* – a toasted slice of bread, rubbed with garlic and topped with the sweetest tomatoes and the best olive oil – and a generous beaker of local light red wine. It is ludicrously cheap.

Mattinatella

After another 6 km, the road passes the bay of Mattinatella where there are two or three tiny campsites with their own beaches. Do not be put off by the rough signposting and bumpy tracks; these simple places are idyllic spots to camp. The Villaggio Azzurro is the first you arrive at. There is also a rustic *trattoria* with its own beach access – spend the morning lazing on the sand, then try the *fritto misto di pesce* at this friendly place.

Baia delle Zagare
(hotel, Baia delle Zagare)

A large group of bungalows set amidst olive trees, this hotel is good if you want more than the basic comforts of the small *alberghi* and campsites dotted about the Gargano. It has both a swimming-pool and a lift down to the beach and you could happily pass a week here. It is, however, only open from June to September and best avoided in August. It is well signposted off to the right a couple of kilometres after Mattinatella; *tel 0884-4155*.

Vignanotica

Around 3 km on from Baia delle Zagare there is a chance to visit the small, hideaway beach of Vignanotica, nestling in a wooded inlet – you will have to walk about 2 km, though, to get there. Park at the *area di sosta: Mergoli*, well-marked on the right and take the footpath signed *sentiero pedonale Mergoli – Vignanotica* that starts some 50 m further on. The trek, mainly through shady woods, is delightful and the reward, a quiet shingle beach.

Pugnochiuso

The road now climbs inland through woods of umbrella pine with good high views out to sea. ② *Around 7 km on take the clearly signposted turning to the right for Pugnochiuso.* The road winds back to the sea through dense aromatic Mediterranean scrub. *Bear left after 5 km for Pugnochiuso.* The bay at Pugnochiuso until a few years ago must have been one of the most heart-warming corners of the Gargano coast. Sadly, it is now being submerged under a rash of ugly tourist 'villages'. Still, the coast along this stretch is breathtakingly beautiful. Stop to admire the view at the lay-by 4 km on from Pugnochiuso – the abandoned square tower dominating the next bay is one of the many medieval watchtowers built to guard against Saracen raiders.

Northern Puglia: The Gargano Peninsula

Returning to the main coast road turn right for Vieste.

Vieste

The distant view of this old fishing port perched on its headland is the highspot of a visit to Vieste – from then on it is downhill all the way. The long promenade crammed with campsites and hotels as you arrive will soon convince you that this is a town well on the way to becoming one of Italy's major Adriatic resorts. Its medieval centre whose scruffy streets are packed with restaurants aimed at an international clientele is disappointing. Still, it is not irredeemable and is certainly lively in high summer. *To visit the town, turn right on arriving. Otherwise keep on the road following signs for Peschici.*

Vieste - Foresta Umbra

About 5 km on from Vieste stay on the road bearing right for Peschici.

③ *After a further 3 km, turn off left onto the clearly signposted road for Monte S Angelo and Foresta Umbra.* Driving across this fertile coastal plain through olive groves, *turn right at the junction signed for Rodi Garganico and Foresta Umbra and, after 300 metres, left for Monte S Angelo and Foresta Umbra.* As the road gently rises the broom soon gives way to forest.

Foresta Umbra

The heart of the Gargano is still mantled by an ancient forest that once extended across Puglia. After the hazy brilliance of the coast the gloom of the Foresta Umbra comes as a refreshing change. Run as a national park, the forest is threaded with carefully signposted footpaths and neat picnic sites. Stop at the *posto di ristoro* off to your right, near the crossroads in the centre of the forest, and pick up the useful guide showing these *sentieri* (paths). Then head off on foot into the silence, among the beeches, oaks and pines.

④ *In the middle of the forest, just after the information centre, take the left turn signed for Monte Sant'Angelo.* You soon leave the trees as the road passes out into open limestone country. There are plenty of picnic spots hereabouts if you found the forest too sombre.

Some 10 km after leaving the forest, keep straight ahead on the main road for Monte Sant'Angelo. As the road rises there are plenty of grandstand views over the peninsula. Ahead you will soon see Monte Sant'Angelo dominating the beetling ridge. Though it looks so near, you have quite a haul ahead before arriving back home. Along the road there are characteristic Gargano peasant farmhouses whose distinctive chimneys look like chapel belfries.

⑤ *Arriving at the main road to the west of the town turn left and snake back up to Monte Sant'Angelo.*

• Devout decorations on steps at San Marco in Lamis.

ROUTE TWO: 92 KM

Leave Monte Sant'Angelo following signs for San Giovanni Rotondo to descend through the hairpin bends you traversed at the end of the last route. ⑤ *Arriving on the plain, bear left for San Giovanni.*

This sparsely-populated, fertile upland valley echoes to the sound of cowbells. In early summer the red earth comes to life with wild flowers. ⑥ *At the first major junction bear right, following signs for San Giovanni, and drive through almond groves to the town.*

San Giovanni Rotondo

Astride the ancient pilgrim route to Monte Sant'Angelo, this is the 20thC version of holy ground. Faithful from around the world journey here to pay their respects at the tomb of Padre Pio da Pietrelcina, a humble local priest who died in 1968. Blessed with the stigmata, the five

Northern Puglia: The Gargano Peninsula

bleeding wounds of Christ, he was also reputed to be able to appear in two places at the same time. The pilgrim centre is the modern sanctuary of Santa Maria delle Grazie to the west of the town where his remains lie. Here, too, is the large hospital complex built through his efforts. Those not susceptible to the cult of Padre Pio will find the place rather dreary. *Leave the town heading for San Marco in Lamis.*

Sanctuario di San Matteo

After a short drive through classic open limestone country ⑦ follow the sign bearing right for San Marco. About 1 km further on is a turning to the right for the monastery of San Matteo. An early Benedictine abbey on the pilgrim trail, it boasts a molar tooth of St Matthew. Its austere aspect and impressive setting are of more interest than its interior. It is now a Franciscan friary used for religious retreats.

Leaving the sanctuary return to the main road and turn sharp right for San Marco.

San Marco in Lamis

The modern fringes are not promising but it is well worth hunting out the old quarter of San Marco. Head for the centre of town and park by

• *Cloister of monastery of San Matteo.*

Northern Puglia

• *The 12thC basilica of Santa Maria di Siponto near Manfredonia.*

the main municipal gardens; the *centro storico* lies on the slopes to the right. Wander along one of the several long parallel streets intersected by numerous white-painted steps and look out for the architectural details above the doorways. Festooned with washing and alive with people, these lanes are unknown to tourists.

San Marco in Lamis - Manfredonia

Leaving on the road you came in on, follow the signs for Foggia.

⑦ *Just under 3 km from the centre turn right at the junction where you arrived from San Giovanni, following signs for Foggia.* Notice the characteristic Pugliese walled dewponds along this stretch and admire the distant views of the Tavoliere, the immense wheat plains of Puglia.

⑧ *Just over 8 km from the junction the twisting road straightens out to shoot across the plain. At the start of this stretch turn off sharp left back on yourself on to the unsignposted single-track tarmac road. Only the first couple of km of this road are marked on the map. After 1.5 km, driving between drystone walls and olive groves, keep on the narrow road, bearing right – not into the 'strada senza uscita'. At the small crossroads 400 metres on by a little group of farmbuildings turn left on to a poorer track.* Driving now through more open country, the road runs along the foot of the Gargano hills.

Northern Puglia: The Gargano Peninsula

• *Gargano coastline.*

⑨ *After 5 km you meet the main road. At the staggered junction turn right then immediately left, following signs for Manfredonia.*

Heading for Manfredonia, the plains are covered in olive groves right to the far horizon. Italy produces a third of the world's olive oil and Puglia's almond-scented oil is one of the best.

Manfredonia *Arriving at the Manfredonia bypass, either turn left following signs for Gargano or carry straight on to visit the town.* This busy port and commercial centre is named after its founder, Manfred, the bastard son of the maverick Holy Roman Emperor Frederick II. The castle he built in 1256 still stands amidst palm trees on the seafront in the centre of the city and now houses the interesting collection of the Gargano Archeological Museum (*closed Mon*). The town itself has no great charm other than miles of sandy beaches to the west. Worth a visit, however, is the 12thC basilica of Santa Maria di Siponto, a unique blend of Romanesque and oriental style in a splendid position. It is all that remains of the ancient city of Sipontum that lay 3 km west of Manfredonia. *Follow signs to Lido di Siponto to reach there.*

Leaving Manfredonia return to the main road heading east following signs for Vieste. As you leave there are less-than-attractive views of the large petrochemical works and industrial port.

Manfredonia - Monte Sant'Angelo

⑩ *Some 2 km from the port turn left at signs for Monte Sant'Angelo, then after a further 2 km turn right, again for Monte Sant'Angelo. On the map this is a left turn but there is a little under-pass on the road.*

As you drive up through a series of hairpin bends there are commanding views out to sea and glimpses of the eyrie of Monte Sant'Angelo way above you. You arrive at the town after about 10 km to be greeted by the stacked-up houses of the Junno quarter spread out before you.

Southern Puglia:
VALLE D'ITRIA

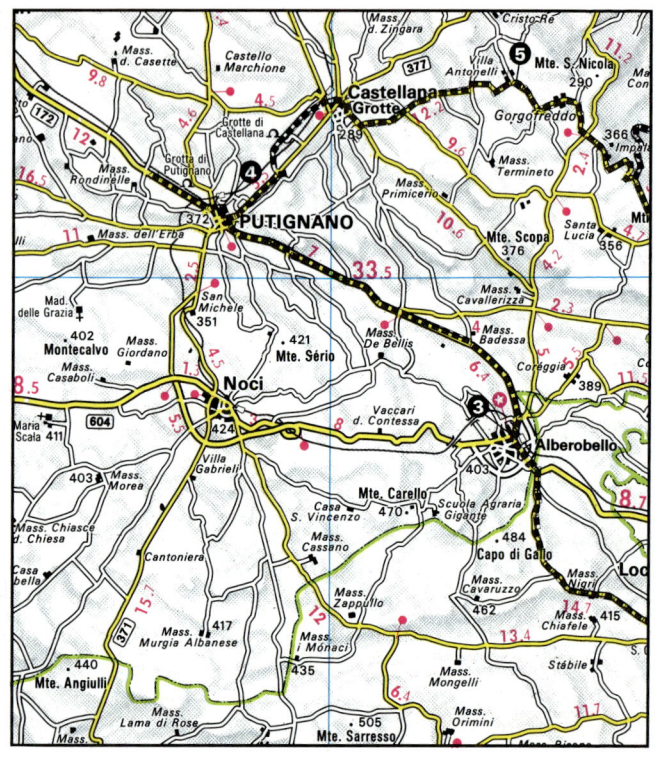

Lying in the heart of the limestone pastrycrust plateaux of Le Murge in Southern Puglia, the Valle d'Itria is home to one of the more singular landscapes in Italy. This smiling valley of family-sized plots of olive and vine is crowded with thousands of *trulli*, tiny primitive dry-stone houses crowned with conical beehive roofs. These pixie-hat cottages topped with cabalistic symbols peep out at you at every turn and at the *trulli* capital of Alberobello the whole town is awash with them.

Even if the cuteness of the buildings gets too much, the area has plenty of other winning charms, including a set of caves reckoned to be the most outstanding in Italy, and a succession of architecturally distinguished towns with not a *trullo* in sight. The first loop of the tour offers the highest *trulli* count but with the baroque splendours of Martina Franca as an antidote. The second includes the dazzling white city of Ostuni – one of the

180

Southern Puglia

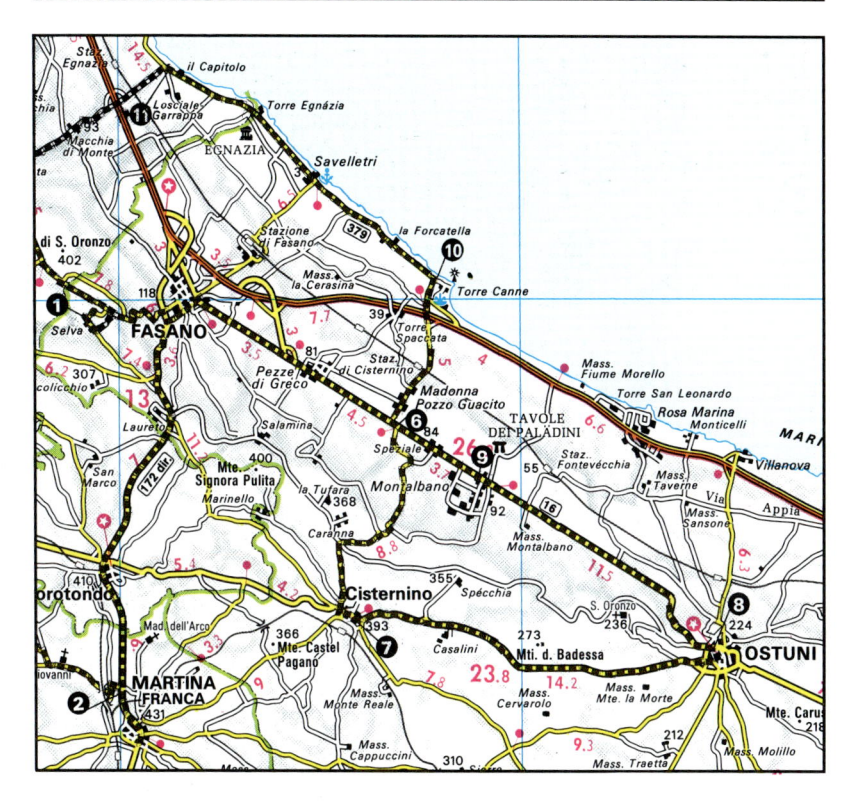

most beautiful towns in Puglia – and a jaunt to the seaside, taking in the moody ruins of the ancient Greek Egnazia.

Bonus points for the bon viveur are the simple but full-flavoured vegetable pasta dishes and the superb fresh fish on the coast. The area also produces a number of outstanding DOC wines, little known beyond the Valle d'Itria.

ROUTE ONE: 87 KM

Selva di Fasano Perched on a spur of the limestone plateau, Selva is a rural retreat set amidst Mediterranean greenery. Any one of the handful of attractive country hotels here would make a peaceful centre for this busy tour – as long as you are happy to forgo the pleasures of a lively town.

La Silvana La Silvana (not to be confused with the more expensive Sierra Silvana)

Southern Puglia: Valle d' Itria

• A piazza, ***Martina Franca.***

(hotel, Selva) is a welcoming and modestly-priced small *albergo* with beautiful views from its large terrace – just the place to unwind with an *aperitivo* after a hard day's driving. Service is friendly and the food above average in the restaurant. *87 Viale dei Pini; tel 080-9331161.*

① *Leave Selva following signs for Fasano* and spot the first of the thousands of *trulli* that will keep you company for most of the journey. Dropping down to the far-stretching olive groves of the coastal plain *turn right 4 km after Selva at the junction with the major road* to head for Locorotondo. Keep on the main road and *bear right after 1 km on to the road signposted for Locorotondo.*

Locorotondo *After arriving at the edge of town, bear left following signs for* centro

182

Southern Puglia

storico, *park and walk to the top of the hill*. The old quarter lies through the ceremonial archway to your left. One of the few towns in the world that actually resembles the drawing on its wine label, Locorotondo is made up of a series of lime-washed streets in concentric circles – hence its name 'round place'. Its refined urban architecture and a more than usually strong civic pride give the centre the quality of being almost one sculptured whole. The neat gardens at the top of the town provide a dress-circle view of the *trulli*-dotted Valle d'Itria.

Osteria di Rosato
(restaurant, Locorotondo)

If you think that good food only comes with starched linen and glasses with stems, this authentic old *osteria* with the wine served in lemonade bottles is not for you. Outside it is a bit scruffy and easily missed – a fly-curtain with *osteria* written on it is about the only sign that you can eat here. Inside, cool and dark as a cave, the owner Agostino Rosato and his wife will give you a friendly welcome and simple but superb local food. Once common across Italy, this kind of place is now hard to find anywhere – as are the low prices. *5 Via A Bruno, near gate to old town at top; closed Tues; price band A.*

Leave, following signs for Martina Franca. A short straight road lined with olive groves and market gardens takes you to the next stop. Look back for some picture-postcard views of Locorotondo.

Martina Franca

Entering the town, carry straight on to the centre to park and walk through the monumental arch into the 17thC quarter. Though larger and scruffier than Locorotondo, this is a noble town with some fine examples of theatrical baroque architecture. Look out for the grandiose Palazzo Ducale and the broken-fronted church of San Martino. The many aristocratic palaces strung with extravagant wrought-iron balconies vie with each other. Best to see the town in the early evening when it comes to life with a crowded and noisy *passeggiata*. The *gelateria* by the main arch has excellent ice creams – stroll about with a cone; everyone else does.

Leave the town on the road you came in on, signposted for Locorotondo. **②** *Just over 1 km from the centre, at the bottom of the hill, cross the level crossing and, 200 metres later, take the first unsignposted turning left. Bear left at the next junction in under 1 km, then turn right at the T-junction signposted at last for Alberobello. Bear right at the next fork in the road and keep following signs for Alberobello. Arriving at the town, take the ring road, following the signs for the 'zona dei trulli'.*

Alberobello

"Alberobello is without doubt the most distinctive village in the world", says the Puglia Tourist Board booklet with equally distinctive modesty. It is, indeed, a strange place, quite unlike anywhere else in Italy. As you arrive in the centre you are greeted by a forest of grey pinnacles,

183

Southern Puglia: Valle d' Itria

• *Massed* trulli *of the Rione Monte quarter, Alberobello.*

decorated with enigmatic symbols. Over 1,500 *trulli* are packed together along with as many tourists. The largest concentration of both is in the Rione Monte – over 1,000 *trulli* stacked up the hillside and awash with souvenir shops and trippers. See it from a distance and explore, instead, the smaller, much more authentic *trulli* district, the Rione Aia Piccola, on the other side of the main road. Alberobello has cashed in on its unique architecture and you may well feel put off by the vulgarity of it all – if you collect kitsch, the souvenirs are hard to beat. However, the town centre is worth exploring with an attractive Corso, mercifully free of *trulli*. There are also plenty of respectable, if expensive, restaurants and an agreeable hotel.

La Cantina *(restaurant, Alberobello)*

This delightful, small, modern cellar restaurant offers a good antidote to *trulli* fatigue. In a tiny kitchen, in full view of the diners, Angela Pepoli produces a loving and imaginative rendering of Pugliese *cucina tipica*. Leave the choice of dishes to her husband Antonio and you will not be disappointed. Like any good restaurant, the menu is seasonal except for the excellent home-bottled vegetables under oil that make a good antipasto. You will find it on the corner of the main Corso Vittorio Emanuele under the elegant neo-Classical building half-way up the

Southern Puglia

street. *Tel 080-9323473; closed Tues; price band B.*

Lanzillotta Avoiding the temptation to stay in the expensive *trulli* hotel featured
(hotel, in all the brochures, try this fine small hotel right on the town's main
Alberobello) square. The comfortable rooms are quiet and not expensive and the
service is friendly. If you arrive after midday, you should have no
problem parking outside the door but, although well signposted, finding
it may tax your patience. *Piazza Ferdinando IV; tel 080-721511.*

③ *Leave town, following signs for Putignano;* all roads lead to the ring
road, so you should not get lost despite Alberobello's exasperating
one-way system.

The smooth, straight road runs through olive groves and vineyards
with *trulli* poking up around every corner. The whole of the Valle d'Itria
is unusual in that its population is spread out across the agricultural land
– nearly everywhere else in Italy peasants tended to group together in
easily defended hamlets and towns. This is testimony, perhaps, to the
area's relatively peaceful history.

Putignano Most visitors pass the town by, heading on to the nearby pink caves. It
is a shame, however, not to stop in the centre of this elegant place. The
old quarter has more modest ambitions than Locorotondo or Martina
Franca but, nevertheless, has a maze of unspoilt traffic-free streets and
alleys with several grand buildings. Look out for the church of San Pietro
with an extravagant baroque interior that looks more like a fairground
than a church.

Grotta di A short detour to see this fairytale cave is much recommended. ④
Putignano *Leave the town following signs for Turi and, about 2 km from the centre,*
(detour) *turn right immediately after crossing the level crossing onto the small track*
marked 'grotta'. You enter the grotto through the *trullo* ahead of you.
Once inside, an old cast-iron spiral staircase winds down through a
cavern of pink icing-sugar stalactites and stalagmites looking like the work
of a mad confectioner. It is an intimate experience with few visitors.

Leave Putignano on the road signposted for Castellana Grotte. Well before
the actual town of Castellana clear signposts direct you to the '*Grotte*'
that have made the place famous across Italy. Claustrophobics might
prefer to head straight to the town of Castellana Grotte.

Grotte di This is the most extensive series of caves open to the public in Italy –
Castellana don't expect anything as discreetly charming as the pink grotto at
Putignano – coach parties swarm here. To see the Grotta Bianca,
reckoned to be one of the most beautiful caverns in the world, you will
have to take the 3-km, two-hour tour; if you just want a taste of these

Southern Puglia: Valle d' Itria

magnificent caves try the shorter, one-hour trip. Dress warmly as it is cold inside. If speleology leaves you mentally cold, you may resent the rather steep entrance fee.

Leave the caves following signs for Castellana Grotte.

The town of Castellana has an attractive enough *centro storico* but nothing to detain you long. But if you happen to be around for the first weekend in September there is, according to the tourist brochure, the "Festival of rabbit and chicken. For two days chicken and rabbit for everybody".

Passing through the town, follow the signs for Selva di Fasano heading east. The road winds through groves of almond and olive growing in rich red earth. ⑤ Arriving at the small hamlet of Antonelli bear right, staying on the main road for Selva and the same again at Gorgofreddo 4 km on. At the crossroads after 1 km carry straight ahead. You now pass through archetypical *trulli* country, almost suburban in its neatness. Shortly before arriving back at Selva stop to admire the views across the coastal plains to the sea.

ROUTE TWO: 78 KM

Follow signs from Selva for Fasano and drop down towards the coastal plain. At the main road junction, turn left.

Fasano Zoosafari Park *(detour)*

A short detour takes you to the first and largest safari park in Italy – an attraction that might appeal if you are driving with children. Along with the lions, tigers, elephants and so on, there are half a million visitors per year. You have been warned. The Zoosafari di Fasano, some 2 km off the main road, is well signposted.

Avoiding the safari park bear right off the main road following signs for Fasano.

Fasano

The slight charms of this working market town are not enhanced by a maddening one-way system and inadequate signposting. *Shortly after arriving at the edge of town turn right then immediately left, following signposts for Pezze di Greco and Ostuni. After about 1.5 km follow the* tutte direzione *sign bearing left, then 500 metres on turn right for Pezze di Greco and Ostuni.* You are now on a quintessentially Italian stretch of road – straight as an arrow, lined with umbrella pines and flanked by ancient twisted olive groves.

Pass through the village of Pezzo di Greco. ⑥ After 4 km take the clearly

Southern Puglia

marked turning off to the right for Cisternino and wind back up to the hills through wheat fields and olives. After another 4 km bear left and left again 2 km on signposted for Cisternino.

Cisternino Arriving at the outskirts follow the signs for *centro storico* to explore this modest but engaging town. A fine example of 'spontaneous architecture', the ancient centre is a jumble of everyday buildings that make a harmonious whole. Few tourists bother to come here – all the more reason for you to stop.

⑦ *Leave the town taking signs for Ostuni.* The patchwork of intensely cultivated fields gradually gives way to wilder open country with broom and pine. *After 12 km you arrive at the fringes of Ostuni.*

• *Limewashed Cisternino.*

Southern Puglia: Valle d' Itria

- *Ostuni dazzling in the morning sun.*

Ostuni

As you arrive follow the signs for the *centro storico* and park in the main

Piazza della Libertà. Nothing in the unprepossessing approaches to Ostuni prepares you for the surprise of coming across the old city itself, proudly facing the sea on its separate hill and crowned with its Byzantine cathedral. Every angle of the town is painted a dazzling white and its beauty lies not in any one particular building but in the glorious whole. Pick up a town plan at the helpful tourist information office in the *piazza* and take time to explore. There are a number of reasonably-priced restaurants in the old quarter – Vecchia Ostuni and Spessite are both excellent places to try robust local cooking.

⑧ *Leave Ostuni following signs for Fasano. Stop to look back at the fine views of the town.*

Tavole dei Paladini
(detour)

The prominence of the romantically named 'Table of the Knights' on the map might lead you to expect much from this megalithic dolmen. Although one of Puglia's oldest monuments, it is, however, a very small experience and very hard to find. Still, it is in a charming spot and the detour is short. ⑨ *As soon as you enter the village of Montalbano take the easily missed turning to the right marked 'dolmen' on to a narrow potholed road. After 1 km you arrive at an unsignposted junction where you turn left.* About 100 metres on park and walk down the dirt track to your right – there, hidden amidst olive and fig tress in front of a little cottage, is the dolmen, one large stone propped up on two others.

Southern Puglia

Regain the main road turning right to rejoin the route.

Torre Canne
⑥ *After passing through the hamlet of Speziale and by the road you took earlier for Cisternino, take the clearly marked right turn for Torre Canne and drive down to the sea following the signs.* Torre Canne is an elegant, small seaside resort with one of the few sandy beaches on this stretch.

⑩ *Leave the town heading along the seafront to follow the barren, rocky coastline.*

La Forcatella
This rude collection of houses huddled on the seashore hides the epicurean highspot of the tour – sea urchins. Here, at rickety tables you can eat *ricci di mare* – plucked minutes before from the rocks – washed down with beakers of cold white wine. This is pure ambrosia for those who like the iodine-and-salt taste of the sea. They are eaten raw, so the squeamish might prefer to carry on to the next village for a proper fish lunch.

Savelletri
This tiny fishing port with its brightly painted boats and the smell of the catch everywhere is the ideal of what such a place should be. You would be missing a treat if you failed to stop to eat fish here.

Da Maddalena
(restaurant, Savelletri)
One of the smarter restaurants here – the air conditioning is a boon in high summer – Da Maddalena has superb fish. Start with seafood *antipasti*, leave out the *primo* unless you want to fill up on pasta, and choose your fish to be simply grilled from the display cabinet. *Spigola* (sea bass) is one of the finest. It is not cheap – fish never is – but it is worth every penny. *Tel 080-729073; closed Tues; price band C.*

Leave Savelletri on the coast road signed for Egnazia.

Egnazia
The ruins of the ancient city of Egnazia are one of Puglia's most important archeological sites. Set beside the sea amidst hayfields and olive trees, it is an evocative place to explore. Little now remains of the city visited in 38 AD by the Latin poet Horace, but there are some beautiful mosaics in the adjoining museum and an intriguing necropolis with burial chambers dating back to the 4thC BC. *Open am Mon-Fri until 1; site open daily until 7.*

Carry on along the coast road and, ⑪ *3 km on from Egnazia, turn left onto the well marked road for Brindisi-Bari. Do not take the further left turn for Fasano but carry straight on. Heading away from the sea towards the hills, cross the main Bari-Brindisi highway, following signs for Castellana Grotte and Selva. At the village of Macchia di Monte carry straight on. The road gently mounts through Mediterranean brush to the plateau. At the top follow the signs for Selva turning left and return on the same road that took you home on the first route.*

Calabria:
LA SILA GRANDE

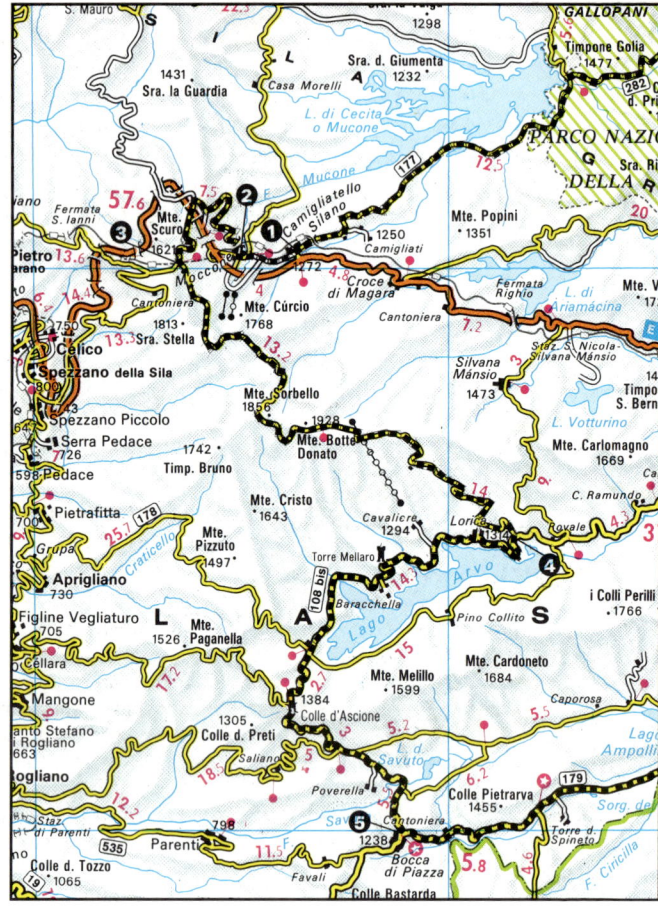

The massive granite tablelands of the Calabrian Sila are an unexpected delight in the deep south of Italy. Looking much like the Scottish Highlands, the area is a haven for botanists and ramblers, and a restful place to pass a few days if you are travelling down the motorway on your way to Sicily. From ancient times, when the timber was used to build the Roman fleet, the immense virgin forest that covered the Sila has been relentlessly felled. There are still, however, ample tracts of woodland that have changed little through the centuries and when the moon is full you might just hear the howling of the last

Calabria

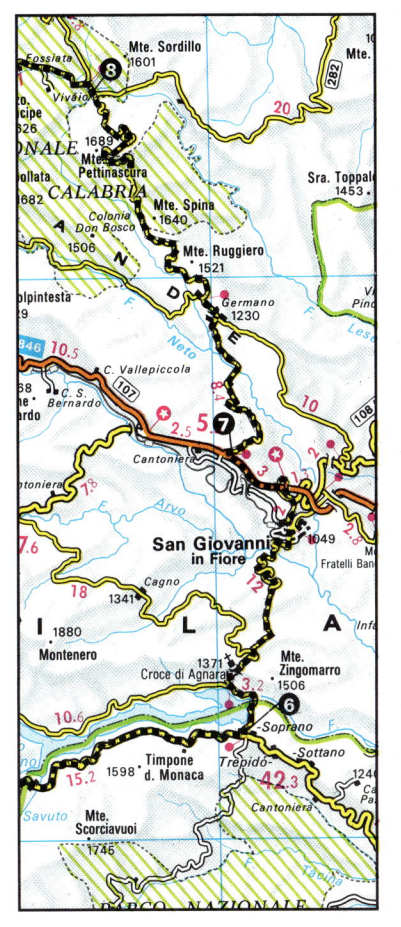

of the Silan wolves.

This circular tour uses the little ski resort of Camigliatello as a base and explores the central area of the Sila, the Sila Grande, the highest and most dramatic part of these Calabrian highlands. Providing variety, it also skirts the Sila's trio of artificial hydro-electric lakes.

Although Baedecker's injunction of 1896 that "letters of introduction to influential inhabitants should be procured" may no longer be strictly necessary, this tour takes you through wild and unpopulated country. Fill up with petrol and put together a good picnic in Camigliatello before setting out. Remember that until early spring the Sila is deep in snow.

ROUTE: 145 KM

Camigliatello Silano

A Calabrian variation on the international ski resort theme has given Camigliatello an uncanny resemblance to the fictional television town of Twin Peaks. Outside the winter skiing season and August, when the Calabrese escape here from the heat of the plains, it is a ghost town. There is, however, a wide choice of hotels and restaurants open throughout the year and, apart from the similar mountain resort of Lorica further along the route, it provides the tour's only overnight stop. It is also a good place to stock up on excellent picnic fare for this restaurant-free journey. The handful of shops on the main street offers knobbly salami (ask for them *piccante* if you want them laced with chillies), rustic cheeses including *buttirri* (an ancient way of preserving butter by putting it in the middle of a form of cheese), a tempting range of *antipasti* preserved under oil, and great wheels of crusty bread to go with it all. A bottle of Ciro, a Calabrian wine of ancient pedigree, is its just complement.

Best buys to take back home are the wild mushrooms. Calabria is second only to Tuscany for its crop of *funghi* and most of it comes from

Calabria: La Sila Grande

• *Marsh marigolds carpet the Silan woods.*

the Sila. Dried or preserved under oil, they are hard to beat both for quality and price, particularly the king of them all, the *funghi porcini*. If you are here in the late autumn you can have the unforgettable treat of eating them fresh.

Lo Sciatore
(hotel, Camigliatello)

There is not much to choose between the modern, Swiss-chalet style hotels here. Lo Sciatore, *tel 0984-578105*, on the main street has large, airy, well-equipped rooms, friendly owners and a passable restaurant at modest prices.

① *Leave Camigliatello on the central street heading west on the road signposted for Moccone which you enter after a couple of kilometres.* The

Calabria

village is nothing more than a small collection of winter chalets with a ski lift. ② *Bear left, following sign for Fago del Soldato and Cosenza, but leave the road 100 metres further on, turning right at the sign for Monte Scuro.*

La Strada delle Vette

The road begins to climb steeply, winding up through pine and beech woods. *After about 5 km keep straight on, following signs for Monte Scuro and Botte Donato. Another 3 km on you arrive at the Valico di Monte Scuro* at an altitude of 1,630 metres, the first of the highspots on this magnificent road. ③ *Turn left here at the first of the two alternative left turns signed for Botte Donato and Lorica.* From here to the little resort of Lorica you are driving the spectacular Strada delle Vette ('the road of the peaks'), a ridgeway through the heart of the Sila Grande that passes the highest summits on the tableland. In the keen air, snow can lie in shady pockets well into May and the countryside is an enthralling alternation of woodland and open meadows with breathtaking views of the Sila around every corner. A small road at a high altitude, it does suffer from potholes and the odd fallen boulder – do not take it too fast. In early summer the drifts of wild flowers, including a profusion of orchids, brighten up every bank.

Monte Botte Donato

After another 14 km you arrive at the peak of Monte Botte Donato, the highest point in the Sila at an altitude of nearly 2,000 metres. As the road begins to descend there are glorious views over Lake Arvo far below. The little road to your left signed for Botte Donato takes you to the ski lift terminus a few hundred metres from the road and a spectacular *belvedere*.

Lorica

④ *About 10 km further on, just before arriving at Lake Arvo, turn right following signs for Catanzaro and Lorica. As you arrive at Lorica take the little detour to the left, signed 'litoranea' (lakeside), and drive down to the lake.* There is a small restaurant and plenty of spots for a picnic – you might even catch site of one of the unusual black squirrels that live here. The village itself is a smaller version of Camigliatello; a spread-out collection of hotels, restaurants and the odd bar. Though hardly a real town, it is one of the few places on the tour where you can buy a coffee or a meal. None of the rather worn modern hotels is very attractive, but the Belvedere Lucanto in faded 1960s style is passable and cheap.

Lago Arvo - Lago Ampollino

Leave Lorica, continuing on the main road, keeping the lake to the left. Lake Arvo is perhaps the prettiest of the Sila's three artificial lakes, formed before World War II to provide hydroelectric energy. *Keep following signs for Lago Ampollino.*

About 13 km on from Lorica you arrive at the Colle d'Ascione. This celebrated pass, some 1,400 metres high, has extensive views westwards to the distant Tyrrhenian sea. Following the signs for Lago

Calabria: La Sila Grande

Ampollino, drive down through this pleasant country of small hills, mixed woodland and open heath. ⑤ *At the hamlet of Bocca di Piazza, take the left turn signposted for Crotone and Lago Ampollino.* The road now curves gently down a wide valley. In this lonely countryside your only company will be the buzzards wheeling overhead.

Lago Ampollino

After about 12 km you catch your first glimpse of Lago Ampollino, the oldest of the Sila's artificial lakes. Back in 1915, Norman Douglas, one of the few foreign travellers to write about the Sila, was deeply sceptical of claims that the proposed lake would "convert these wildernesses into a fashionable watering-place... a Calabrian Lucerne". Time has amply borne him out.

The road now skirts the southern shores of the lake. Look out for the clouds of wild daffodils if you are driving in spring. *After about 5 km, follow signs for Cotronei, bearing left then straight on.* ⑥ *Just over 1 km further on leave the road for Cotronei turning left for San Giovanni in Fiore.* Passing the dam which forms the lake, bear right for San Giovanni and your first glimpse of the town as you drive through tall pinewoods.

San Giovanni in Fiore

"An entire book would not suffice to talk about San Giovanni in Fiore", claims the Calabrian tourist board booklet. You might be more inclined to take Norman Douglas's view that the town has "solved the problem how to be ineffably squalid without becoming in the least picturesque". Either way, it is a most unspoilt Calabrian town – unspoilt meaning that you must expect all the outward signs of poverty and neglect – uncared-for roads, dark dirty streets, unpainted houses.

As when Douglas visited here, a major number of the town's menfolk are forced to work abroad or in northern Italy; today, one third of the total population of 21,000 are emigrants. The ugly half-built houses around the town are their 'savings', a new storey being added with each instalment of cash from afar.

For all this, it is worth getting to the centre, parking and walking around. You will not see many other towns like it in Western Europe. Look out for the hardy old women with leathery skin, whose everyday dress with its nun-like wimple is still their traditional costume. They do not dress up for the tourists – there are none – so ask before you take photographs of them. San Giovanni is noted for its hand weaving – there is a good workshop by the abbey in the heart of the town.

Leaving San Giovanni, the signposting is hopelessly inadequate but you will not get too lost if you follow the main road heading to the top of the town. From here follow signs for Cosenza bearing left which will take you on to the main SS107 Cosenza–Crotone highway. Head for Cosenza for about 3 km.

⑦ *Turn right at the signs for Germano and Bocchigliero on to a quiet country road.* You now wind northwards through mixed forests,

Lago Cecita, artificial lake.

orchards and moorland with splendid distant prospects ahead. *After around 10 km turn right on to the road marked for Bocchigliero then, 3 km on, bear right keeping to the old road.*

Parco Nazionale della Calabria

After a short while you pass signposts marking the start of a wildlife reserve, a section of the Parco Nazionale della Calabria. This is the haunt of the last hundred or so famous wolves of the Sila that still survive. Do not be alarmed, though, as these shy beasts are unlikely to disturb your picnic. The road now descends rapidly through venerable pine woods affording glimpses of the valley of Lake Cecita below. ⑧ *Reaching the flowery meadows of the valley bottom, turn left following signs for Camigliatello and Cosenza.* Off the road here there is some idyllic walking country and plenty of picnic spots. At Fossiata you can see the 'Giants of the Sila' – some 50 towering pines reckoned to be over 400 years old and rising to a height of 40 metres.

Lago Cecita

This is the last of the three artificial lakes on this tour and, although the bleakest of the trio, is a popular haunt for day-trippers from Cosenza. *Reaching the lakeside, turn left marked for Camigliatello.* The road skirts the lake to the south passing through rather blasted and open countryside before entering a more benign fertile plain as you approach Camigliatello and a well earned plate of *tagliatelle con funghi porcini*.

Sicily:
VAL DI NOTO

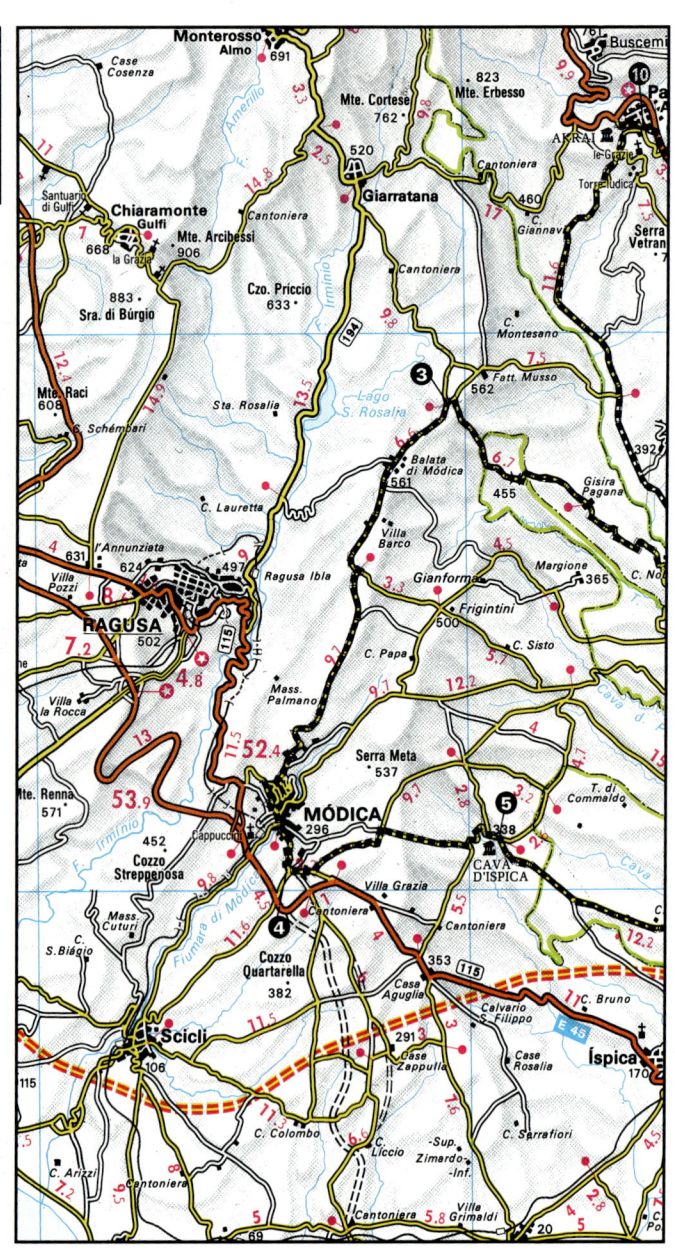

Sicily

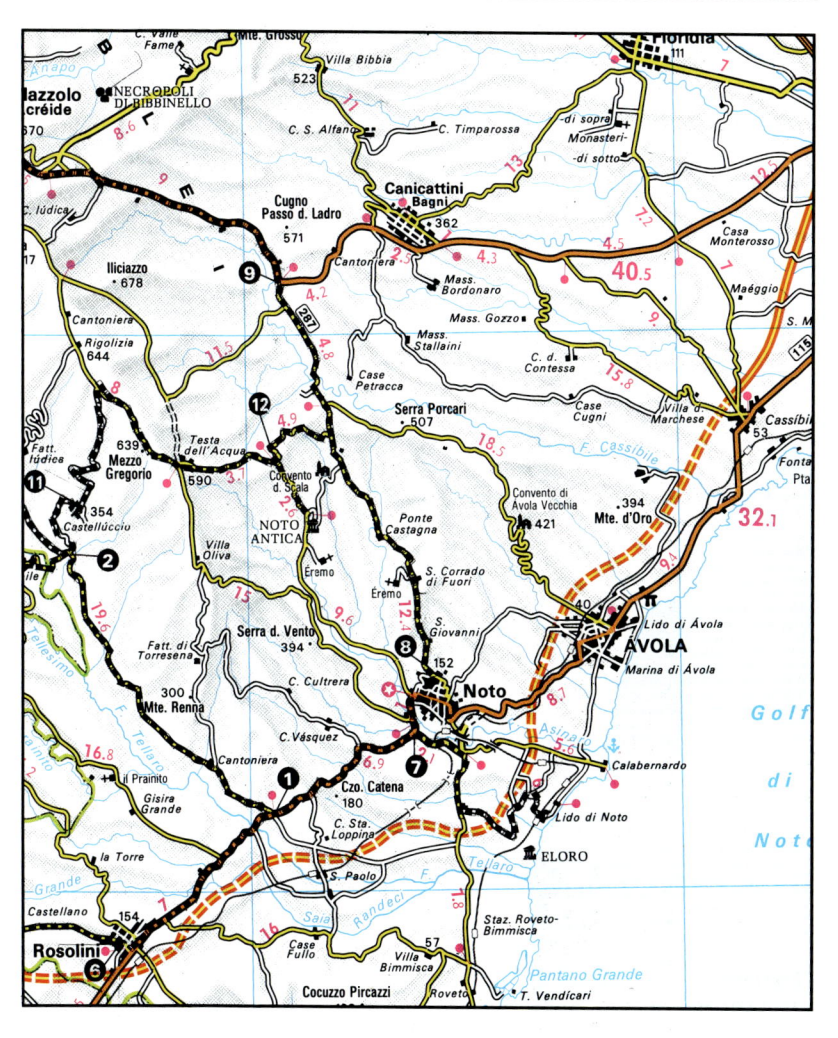

At the crossroads of the Mediterranean, Sicily owes more to the mêlée of cultures and peoples that have figured in its long history than to mainland Italy. Here you are only just in Europe and if you are to enjoy it warts and all – Sicily has plenty of warts – leave any northern prejudices at home. That said, this tour of the southeastern bulge explores some of the most beguiling countryside on the island, relatively unscarred by the

Sicily: Valdi Noto

modern infatuation for concrete that disfigures so much of Sicily and still untouched by mass tourism. The other delight is the flamboyant baroque architecture, which reaches its heights in the town of Noto, the tour's centre. This flowering of 18thC style is all the more remarkable for having grown out of the ruins of the terrible earthquake of 1693 that claimed the lives of 60,000 people.

The best season to drive the two routes is late spring when the roads are lined with an extravagant profusion of wild flowers. However, the midday sun is strong even in May – always carry some water with you in the car and enjoy a Sicilian siesta after lunch. Another word of warning signposting in Sicily is appalling and roads appearing on the map sometimes turn out to be closed off. Directions for the routes are as exhaustive as possible but a degree of stoicism will help with the navigation.

ROUTE ONE: 93 KM

Noto

Noto is an unashamedly theatrical city with the Corso Vittorio Emanuele taking centre stage – a single long street formed by a succession of baroque set pieces – churches, palaces and piazzas. The place appears designed for a spectacle, the very windows of the *palazzi* seeming to be no more than boxes at the opera. The remarkable unity of Noto's architecture rests on its citizens' decision, within a week of the tragic earthquake of 1693, to abandon the old city of Noto and start from scratch some 16 km away. The best time to watch the show is early evening. Join in the stylish *passeggiata*, stop at Costanzo Corrado's for a *granita di limone* (lemon ice), the pure taste of Sicilian lemons, or at the Caffe Sicilia for a glass of Marsala or luscious Malvasia delle Lipari.

Noto's one drawback is accommodation. The town has only one mediocre hotel. The Albergo Stella is admittedly cheap but is run more like a seamens' hostel than a hotel. *44 Via F Maiore; tel 0931-835695.*

Trattoria del Carmine
(restaurant, Noto)

This unassuming little *trattoria* behind the theatre offers some of the most genuine local cookery in Noto. Try *tagliatelle capriccioso* and *coniglio a stimpirata* (rabbit in a sour-sweet sauce). *Tel 0931-838705; price band A.* For a grander meal at a much grander price and with rather fawning service there is the Il Barocco restaurant, well signposted off the Corso.

Leave Noto to the southwest, following signs for Ragusa. The road passes through vineyards and groves of citrus, almond, apricot and olive. It is hard to believe that this amiable road remains part of Sicily's main coastal circuit until the long-projected motorway gets built. Note the

• *Modica: elegant town, precarious location.*

giant agave plants that rear up by the roadside. Their flower stalks like spears of giant asparagus reach up to 10 metres high; each plant flowers only once in its 10-year life.

① *After 9 km turn right off the main road signposted for Giarratana.* In spring the flowery verges on this small road rival the finest English herbaceous border. Come summer little is left but parched grass.

② *After 13 km of this delightful country lane stay on it bearing left, still following signs for Giarratana (the two routes touch here).* You now start climbing away from the intensively-cultivated lower valleys into arid limestone country with drystone walling parcelling up the landscape.

③ *After another 10 km bear right keeping on the main road, and 100 metres later, turn left at staggered cross-roads by small group of ruined houses. There are no signs here. A few metres further on, stay on the road bearing left, and after 3 km turn left at the junction.* The road now heads for Modica across a moody, high limestone plateau. *Arriving at the outskirts of Modica, marked by prosperous modern villas, turn left at the signposts for Modica Alta.*

Modica An elegant large town in an impossible position, Modica is built on the precipitous slopes of two intersecting river valleys. Finding your way

Sicily: Val di Noto

about by car and parking is not easy. Above all avoid the Thursday morning market — best to abandon your car as soon as possible and explore on foot. There are two excellent reasons for stopping. One is the church of San Giorgio, perhaps the finest baroque church in Sicily, with a tremendously theatrical flight of 250 steps to reach it. The other is an excellent restaurant (see below). There are several other delightful baroque churches but Modica's charm lies in its extraordinary location, best seen from the many vantage points at the top end of the town. The two valleys had flowing rivers until the end of the 19thC; they have now been covered over to form the most fashionable streets of the town. Stroll along the Corso Umberto for the smartest shops and try the sweetmeats at the Caffe Bonaiuto.

You might like to stay the night here — it is a town that takes time to explore. The Motel Agip on the Corso Umberto offers inexpensive rooms in an ugly modern block by a filling station — at least they have a car park. *Tel 0932-941396.*

Fattoria delle Torri
(restaurant, Modica)

Giuseppe Barone is a charming young host who is passionate about the food of his native Modica. After a meal in his smart restaurant you might well feel the same. The cooking is based entirely on the seasons, no ubiquitous all-year-round specialities here. Leave the choice to him and you will not be disappointed. In spring you might have delicate ravioli filled with broad beans and dressed with whipped ricotta, followed by rabbit marinaded in tomato, then crumbed and fried. The desserts are a special treat in Italy — liquid chocolate on ricotta and a sharp blancmange of lemon and almond milk for example. All this at very modest prices for such quality. Well signposted in *Via Nativo in Modica Alta; tel 0932-751286; closed Mon; price band B/C.*

Leave Modica from the lower part of town taking the main road signposted for Siracusa. Do not try any short cuts to the next destination — it is a sure recipe for getting lost.

④ About 3 km from the lower town centre you will arrive at a well signposted (a rare treat this) turning off to the left for Cava d'Ispica. After 2.5 km continue straight ahead signed for Noto and Rosolini, then turn right and continue to follow signs for Cava d'Ispica.

Cava d'Ispica

A large sign announces your arrival at this dramatic limestone gorge. The friendly guide lives in the first house on the left after you pass over the bridge and there is a car park on the right. For 13 km the beetling rock faces of this atmospheric site are carved with hundreds of caves. From prehistoric times they served in turn as necropoli, troglodyte dwellings, Christian catacombs, hermits' chapels and animal stalls. The atavistic spirit of the place is in strong contrast to the baroque artifice of Noto and Modica. Ask to see the Grotta di San Nicola with its traces of

• *Caves in the limestone gorge of Cava d'Ispica.*

early Byzantine frescoes and the Larderia Christian catacombs with over 460 tombs carved in the rock and arranged in three long tunnels. The guide is on duty – in theory – every morning and in the afternoon on Tuesday and Friday, but you can take an atmospheric walk through the first 500 metres of the gorge at any time. If you have time, ask the guide to show you his collection of *carri Siciliani* – remarkable examples of 19thC painted Sicilian carts.

Cava d'Ispica - Noto Leave Cava d'Ispica continuing on the main road, signed for Rosolini. ⑤ *After about 1 km, bear right at unmarked fork.* There are good views of the gorge to your right. *After another 3 km turn left at the fork. As you approach the dreary small town of Rosolini bear right, taking signs for the SS115 to avoid the centre.* Admire the wide and distant views ahead down to the sea.

⑥ *Reaching the main road, turn left and follow signs for Siracusa to reach Noto.* As you approach. the dress-circle view of Noto, hanging looking like a theatrical backdrop, brightens up the otherwise uneventful return.

Eloro (detour) A visit to the atmospheric remains of the Greek city of Eloro, some 8 km from Noto, makes an interesting detour on your way back. ⑦ *Shortly before arriving at Noto take the signs to the right for Lido di Noto then follow the yellow signs for Eloro.* The ruins stand by the sea in a

Sicily: Val di Noto

pleasant cliff-top setting, ideal for a breezy walk. The site is open only in the morning but the area is just as alluring when closed. On a hillock about 1 km away stands the Pizzuta, a 10-metre high tower built as a monument to the battle between Siracusa and Athens in 413 BC. Nearby are the small sandy beaches of Lido di Noto, a simple resort mainly catering for Italian tourists – a relaxing place to laze away an afternoon in the sun.

Return to Noto as you arrived.

• ***The road to Castelluccio.***

ROUTE TWO: 95 KM

⑧ *Leave Noto from the top end of the town trying to follow the poor signposting for Palazzolo (you pass the main hospital as you leave so signs for Ospedale will also get you on the right road). As the road leaves the town it rises onto the limestone plateau past extensive terraces of olives.*

Eremo di San Corrado (detour)
About 1 km after the small village of S Corrado di Fuori, a yellow sign for Eremo di S Corrado directs you to a turning on the left. This leads, after about 1 km, to the dramatically-sited sanctuary dedicated to Noto's patron saint. A place of local pilgrimage with a sacred if litter-strewn stream, it is not regularly open.

The road now passes through classic limestone country – weathered outcrops intercut with gorges, a bare and arid landscape that soaks up every drop of water that falls.

Sanctuario Madonna della Scala
Some 3 km after passing over the handsome obelisk-flanked bridge over the Santa Chiara torrent take another short detour to see the Sanctuary of the Madonna della Scala. The turning on the left is well signposted and you arrive at the four-square building after less than 2 km. Lightened by baroque ornamentation, this peaceful haven stands in a magnificent position on a cliff overlooking a gorge. In the elegant 18thC chapel look out for the early Norman-Arabic arch hidden away behind the font.

Return to the main road and turn left, following signposts for the next destination – Palazzolo Acreide. For the next 15 km or so keep on the road following the signs for Palazzolo.

⑨ *Turn left on to the main SS124 for the last stretch of the journey. You will see the town ahead of you long before you arrive.*

Palazzolo Acreide
Arriving at the edge of the town, follow the yellow signs for the Teatro Greco. The signs direct you through the heart of the town. The few tourists that pass here mostly come to see the ruins of the ancient Greek city of Akrai that lie to the west. However, it would be a shame not to make a brief stop in the modern city. A medium-sized, working market town, it was completely rebuilt in the 18thC in the wake of the 1693 earthquake. Dwarfing the main *piazza* is the spectacular church of San Sebastiano with its extraordinarily ornamented façade that looks more like silverwork than stone. Inside you can see bits of the legendary Roman martyr neatly laid out on a velvet cushion and a clutch of paintings of the arrow-struck youth. Explore the streets off the *piazza* before getting back in the car to follow the signs to the Teatro Greco.

Sicily: Valdi Noto

• *The church of San Sebastiano, Palazzolo Acreide.*

Akrai

Founded by Greeks from Siracusa in 664 BC, the ancient town was built on a strategic hilltop with broad views of the surrounding countryside. Today, apart from the magnificent site, the main attraction is the well preserved, intimate Greek theatre. Look out also for the intriguing funerary carving in the solid rock of the *latomie* (stone quarries) to the left of the theatre. *Open daily 9 until an hour before dusk; closed Mon.*

Akrai - Castelluccio

⑩ *Return towards Palazzolo on the road you came up on and after 500 metres take signs to the right for Noto. After another 500 metres take another right turn signposted to Falabia, then after a few metres go straight on, again for Falabia* (a place which seemingly exists only in the minds of local sign writers). Stop to admire the outstanding views westwards. The road now gently descends through an idyllic pastoral landscape of small hills, fields and scattered cottages. *After about 10 km keep straight on, following signs for Castelluccio then again carry straight on at crossroads after 2 km.*

Sicily

② You arrive at a small collection of houses and shops after about 7 km where you turn left, then immediately left again. You may recognize this spot from the first route. 300 metres on turn sharp left into a tiny lane with a small, easily missed sign for Castelluccio. The road now winds up, flanked by drystone walls, verges rich in Mediterranean wild flowers and almond orchards.

⑪ After about 3 km you arrive at the derelict hamlet of Castelluccio where you turn left and then, after 400 metres, carry straight on. Do not be put off by the small potholed road, it improves shortly.

Castelluccio After less than 2 km you will spot on your left a cave with a modern arch built in its entrance. Now used as a sheep pen, this is the first of the numerous prehistoric carved rock tombs that litter the surrounding area. The rocky outcrop above you is the site of one of Sicily's earliest Bronze Age settlements, and although all the significant finds are now in the Siracusa museum, it is an evocative place. For those whose interest in archaeology is slender, the attractions are the splendid views and the extravagant Mediterranean flora. As the road continues to twist upwards many other caves, cut in the limestone, are visible and from the top of the plateau there is a view right back down to the primitive site.

Castelluccio - Noto Antica *After passing the site, bear left and at the stop sign turn right for Noto.* Ahead of you stands Noto's radio-astronomy station. *Arriving at the small hamlet of Testa dell'Acqua keep straight on now following signs for Burlo.* In early summer the road ahead now resembles a drive through a rock garden.

⑫ After about 4 km take the right-hand turn signposted for Noto Antica. From here on tall, sombre cypresses line the road to your right, making one of the few spots on the tour that provides enough shade for a picnic.

Noto Antica The ceremonial arch and the adjacent ruins of a castle mark the entrance to the mournful remains of the old city of Noto. Passing through the arch you can either drive or walk through what little is left of Noto Antica and there are many shady paths to explore amidst the plant-smothered ruins. At the extreme southern end of the site is the lonely church built to commemorate the destruction of the city.

Noto Antica - Noto *Leave Noto Antica bearing left after passing through the arch, climbing up the road you arrived on. Bear left continuing on the main road. ⑫ At the junction now take the right turn signposted for Noto. The road descends through a series of sharp bends. Then turn right again for Noto to return by the road on which you started the tour.* The map shows an alternative, more direct route to return to Noto, but do not be tempted to try and find it – it is now closed.

INDEX

Includes: towns, villages and hamlets given a substantial mention; places of worship or with a religious association; villas, parks and notable natural features.

A
abbeys:
  Praglia 38
  S Martino al Cimino 130
Acciaroli 158
Acqualagna 110
Acqua Rossa 130
Acquaviva 114
Acuto 151
Affile 147
Agliano 59
Agropoli 161
Aia del Diavolo 102
Akrai 204
Alatri 152
Alba 52, 54
Albenga 70, 71, 72, 79
Alberobello 183
Altipiano di Arcinazzo 147
Alto 70, 77-8
Amalfi 157
Anagni 155
Aosta 63, 67
Aquileia 31-2
Arqua Petrarca 37
Arabba 19
Arnad 64
Arvier 68
Assisi 116, 123
Asti 60

B
Bagnaia 127
Bagni di Lucca 88, 95
Bagnoregio 131
Balze, Le 98
Barbarano Vicentino 41
Barbaresco 58-9
Bard 64
Bardineto 75
Barolo 56
basilicas:
  Aquileia 31-2
  Monte Berico 40

Benabbio 95
Biella 50
Bolsena 131, 132
Bolzano 15-16, 23
Bomarzo 127
Bominaco 143
Borghetto d'Arroscia 79
Borghetto Santo Spirito 73
Borgosesia 44, 47, 51
Bozen see *Bolzano*
Bra 58
Brendola 40
Busseto 83

C
Cagli 114
Calascio 139
Calizzano 75
Camigliatello Silano 191-2, 195
Campiglia Dei Berici 41
Campitello 19
Campo Imperatore 138-9
Canazei 19
Canneto 104
Capodimonte 133
Capo Palinuro 167
Caprauna 78
Capriva del Friuli 30
Castagnole delle Lanze 59
Castel del Monte 139
Castellana 186
Castelluccio 205
Castelmonte 27
Castelnuovo Fogliani 85
Castelrotto 22
Castel San Pietro Romano 149
castles:
  Arquato 85
  Aymavilles 67
  Ca'Marcello 37
  Fenis 67
  Frontone 113
  d'Ocre 140
  San Vitale 82
  Sarre 68
  Sarriod de la Tour 68
cathedrals:
  Anagni 155
  Ferentino 154

Catinaccio 17-18
Cava d'Ispica 200
Cave 149
caves:
  Bambocci 152
  Castellana 185
  Putignano 185
  Stiffe 142
  Toirano 74
Ceriale 72
Certaldo 100
Certosa di Trisulti 152
Châtillon 66
Cherasco 58
Chiesa Arcipretale, Noventa Vicentina 34
Cisano sul Neva 77
Cisternino 187
Civiasco 45
Cividale del Friuli 26, 27-8
Civita Castellana 118
Coggiola 48
cols:
  Col del Cuc 19
  Col Rodella 19
  Colle Caprauna 78
  Colle di Joux 65
  Colle San Bernardo 76 151
Collodi see *Villa Garzoni*
Convento di Sant'Angelo 140
Corinaldo 112
Cormons 26, 30, 33
Corvara in Badia 20, 21
Corvera see *Corvara in Badia*
Costigliole d'Asti 59
Courmayeur 63, 69

D
duomi:
  Biella 50
  Este 36
  Monselice 37

E
Eggental see *Val d'Ega*
Egnazia 189
Eloro 201
Este 36

Index

F
Falerii Novi 118
Fasano 186
Fasano Zoosafari Park 186
Ferentino 154
Ferento 130
Fermignano 108
Fidenza 80, 82
Fie' allo Sciliar 22
Fiuggi 145
Fiuggi Città 147
Fiuggi Fonte 147, 151, 155
Foligno 121
Fontanellato 82
Fonte Cerreto 137-8
Fonti del Clitunno 120
Forcatella, La 189
Fossa 141
Fossombrone 108, 111, 115
Furlo (and gorge) 108, 111, 115

G
Gambassi Terme 100
Garessio 76
Genazzano 149
Goraiolo 94
Gorizia 30, 33
Govone 61
Gradoli 132
Grinzane Cavour 54
Grödner Joch see Gardena pass
Grödner Tal see Val Gardena

I
islands:
  Bisentina 133
  San Giulio 47
Issogne 64-5

K
Karerpass see Costalunga pass
Karersee see Lake Carezza
Kastelruth see Castelrotto

L
lakes:
  Ampollino 193, 194
  Arvo 193
  Bolsena 124, 125, 131
  Carezza 17
  Cecita 195
  Fimon 41
  Orta 42
  Vico 124, 130
Lardarello 97, 102
L'Aquila 134, 135-6, 140
Locorotondo 182
Lorica 193
Lucca 88, 93
Lugagnano 87
Lustignano 104
Luvigliano 38

M
Manfredonia 178
Marina di Ascea 158, 164
Marta 133
Martina Franca 180, 183
Mattinata 171
Mattinatella 173
Modica 199
Monastero di San Benedetto 147
Mondavio 112
Monforte 55
Monselice 37
Monte Botte Donato 193
Montecatini 104
Monte Catria 114
Monte Cimino 129
Montefalco 121
Montefiascone 133
Monte Sant'Angelo 170-1, 175, 179
Monte Stella
Morra, La 57
Mossa 30

N
Naples 158
Marni 118
Nasino 77
national parks:
  Calabria 195
  Foresta Umbra 174
  Gran Paradiso 68
Noto 198, 202, 205
Noto Antica 205
Nova Levante 15, 17
Noventa Vicentina 34, 39
Novi Velia 167

O
Ogliastro Cilento 163
Omegna 46
Orgiano 39
Orta San Giulio 47
Ortisei 22
Ostuni 180-1, 188
Otricoli 118

P
Paestum 157, 162
Palazzolo Acreide 203
Palestrina 144, 149
Palmanova 32
Pancole 101
Panider Sattel see Pinei pass
Parma 84
passes:
  Campolongo 20
  Costalunga 18
  Gardena 21
  Pinei 22
  Pordoi 19
Pavia di Udine 29
Peltuinum 143
Pergola 113
Pescia 88-9, 93, 95
Pieve di Teco 79
Piglio 151
Pioppi 158
Pisciotta 167
Pizzome 90
Poiana Maggiore 39
Pollenzo 57
Pomarance 102
Ponte Coccia 95
Ponte Nova 16
Pont-Saint-Martin 63, 64
Ponzone 51
Popiglio 94
Portula 49
Pozzo d'Antullo 151
Pré-Saint-Didier 69
Pugnochiuso 173

Index

Putignano 185

Q
Querceto 104

R
Ranzo 79
Roccabianca 83
Rocca d'Arazzo 60
Rome 116, 118
Ronciglione 129
Roncole Verdi 84
Rosazza 49
Rosengarten see *Catinaccio*

S
Sacro Monte 44
Saint-Pierre 68
Saint-Vincent 66
Salle, La 69
Salsomaggiore Terme 87
sanctuaries:
  Eremo di San Corrado 203
  Madonna della Scala 203
  Madonna di Novi Velia 165
  San Matteo 176
  San Michele, Brendola 40
  Valsorda 75
San Gimignano 97, 101-2
San Giovanni in Fiore 194
San Giovanni Rotondo 170, 175
San Lorenzo in Campa 113
San Marcello Pistoiese 94
San Martino Cilento 163
San Martino del Carso 31
San Marco di Castellabate 159
San Marco in Lamis 176
San Pier d'Isonzo 31
San Secondo 82
Santa Cristina Valgardena 22
Santa Maria della Quercia 126
Santa Maria di Castellabate 159
Sant'-Ippolito 111
Santo Stefano di Sessanio 139
San Vivaldo 100
St Christina in Gröden see *Santa Cristina Valgardena*
St Ulrich see *Ortisei*
Sasso Pisano 103
Savelletri 189
Sella Group, The 19
Sella gruppe see *Sella Group*
Selva di Fasano 181, 186, 189
Serralunga d'Alba 55
Soragna 84
Sorbolongo 112
Soriano nel Cimino 128
Spello 122
Spoleto 119
Strada delle Vette, La 193
Strada Panoramica Zegna 49
Subiaco 144, 148

T
Tavole dei Paladini 188
Teolo 39
Terni 119
Testa Grigia 65
Toirano 74
Tramonte 38
Torre Canne 189
Trevi 121
Trivero 49

U
Udine 28-9
Urbania 109
Urbino 106, 108-9

V
Valduggia 47
Valentano 133
Valgrisenche 68
valleys:
  Ayas 65
  Cogne 68
  Ega 16
  Fassa 15, 18
  Gardener 21
  Gressoney 64
  Mosso 51
  Tanaro 78
Vallo della Lucania 164
Valtournenche 67
Varallo 42, 44-5
Velia 164
Vellano 94
Velleia 86
Venice 26, 29
Verduno 57
Verres 65
Vicenza 40
Vico nel Lazio 151
Vieste 168, 174
Vignanotica 173
Vigo di Fassa 18, 19
Vigoleno 87
Vigolo Marchese 86
villas:
  Barbarigo 37
  Basilica 90
  Farnese 129
  Garzoni 89
  Lante 127
  Mansi 92
  Nero's Villa 148
  Poiana 39
  Reale 92
  Sceriman 39
  Torrigiani 93
Villeneuve 68
Viterbo 124, 126, 133
Volterra 97, 98, 102, 105

W
Welschnofen see *Nova Levante*

Z
Zibello 83
Zuccarello 76